DON'T LOOK BACK

Philippa Tyndale is a former personal finance journalist with Fairfax publications in Sydney. While on holiday in Bali in 1996, she met a few of Opportunity International's small business clients. Since that time she has work as a volunteer for the organisation, in the areas of communications, fundraising and documentary making. She has also travelled with David Bussau to a number of the locations where Opportunity International has programs.

Philippa believes passionately in the small loans provided by the organisation to its clients, as she has seen first-hand the positive effects they have on the quality of people's lives. She lives in Sydney with her husband Andrew, a banker, and their three children Tim, Liam and Imogen.

DON'T LOOK BACK
THE DAVID BUSSAU STORY

PHILIPPA TYNDALE

ALLEN&UNWIN

All author royalties from this book have been donated to:
Opportunity International Australia
Level 6, 163 Clarence St, Sydney NSW 2000
Ph: (02) 8259 0404
email: opinfo@opportunity.org.au
website: http://www.opportunity.org.au

First published in Australia in 2004 by Allen & Unwin

Allen & Unwin
83 Alexander Street
Crows Nest NSW 2065
Australia
Phone: (61 2) 8425 0100
Fax: (61 2) 9906 2218
Email: info@allenandunwin.com
Web: www.allenandunwin.com

National Library of Australia
Cataloguing-in-Publication entry:

Tyndale, Philippa, 1960– .
  Don't look back: the David Bussau story: how an abandoned
  child became a champion of the poor.

ISBN 1 74114 395 0.

  1. Bussau, David. 2. Opportunity International (Australia).
  3. Philanthropists – Australia – Biography.
  4. Non-governmental organizations – Australia – Biography.
  I. Opportunity International (Australia). II. Title.

361.740-92

Set in Sabon 11.5/14 by Midland Typesetters
Printed by Griffin Press, South Australia

10 9 8 7 6 5 4 3 2 1

For the unsung heroes: the thousands of committed field workers, fundraisers, boards, supporters and volunteers who make up Opportunity International.

Acknowledgements

In working through David Bussau's passports since 1967 my list of customs' stamps—far from complete—reached 900. Each of these entries represents a plane trip, a project, a series of meetings and a bunch of close friends. The cast of players in David's life story is overwhelming. I would like to acknowledge the contribution of those who count David as a dear friend yet could not be included in this book due to the limitation of its size.

I extend my heartfelt thanks to the Bussau family—David and Carol, Tasha and Rachel—for sharing with me the joyful and painful, even embarrassing, moments that add so much humanity to the story of their lives. In particular, I'd like to thank David for his generous and open contribution. He made time for interviews when he clearly had none to spare. As a forward-looking individual, retrieving parts of a lost childhood from his memory came with a personal cost.

Thanks to my whole family for enduring a distracted or absent wife, mother, daughter and sister throughout this process. Special thanks to Andrew, Tim, Liam and Imogen, whose support in terms of encouragement, love and patience is immeasurable.

I appreciate those who stood by me with advice, research and support as I struggled to rein in a story that sprawled to every continent. This includes the Opportunity International Australia team—Emma Dale, Julie Taylor, Renee Christiansen and Belinda Sullivan—and my friends Peter Downey and Merilyn Buckley. Gareth Winter from the Wairarapa Archives and Wendy Page from

'Australian Story' at the ABC also provided helpful background material. Thanks to Bob and Heather Neilson for the initial means to travel, to Susy Cheston for lending her wisdom and experience, and to Leigh Coleman for his humorous storytelling and memory for detail. My gratitude goes to Nyoman IriantoWibawa (Alit) at Dinari in Bali, James Solomon from India, Alexis Beggs and Larry Reed in the US, Roweena Mendoza and the CTRC team in Manila, Ruth Callanta from Manila, Denis Perry in Australia and to the scores of other people around the world who agreed to be interviewed or helped with research material.

My thanks also to Jo Paul and Joanne Holliman and the talented editorial and creative team at Allen and Unwin for easing me through the publishing process.

Most of all, I'd like to applaud the true heroes of this book: the poor entrepreneurs of the developing world, who work hard each day to build a hopeful future for their children. David Bussau agreed to tell his tale so readers could hear the stories of Opportunity clients and be inspired. His successes are their successes.

Contents

Speak up for those who cannot speak for themselves,
for the rights of all who are destitute.
Speak up and judge fairly;
defend the rights of the poor and needy.

Proverbs 31:8–9

Prologue

The call came early one evening, late in 1974.

A routine call: 'The latch on that new gun cabinet isn't working', said the voice down the phone. 'We're hosting a cocktail party tonight and the guests are arriving in an hour.'

There was a pause.

'We need you here, right now,' it bellowed.

The young builder exhaled. He could hear his wife putting their two young daughters, Tasha and Rachel, into the bath. After a busy day, he dreaded having to go out again. But he reached for his car keys and faced the heavy evening traffic.

The call had hit a raw nerve. 'My life is no longer my own', he thought. 'Here I am working at night, when I should be home with Carol and the girls'. Yet, he couldn't say no. He prided himself on his detailed work and contented clients.

As he drove, something gnawed at him. He was agitated, annoyed at being summoned, and frustrated at being at the whim of the rich. Distant memories swelled of another time and place, a childhood controlled by other people. He had put all that behind him long ago. As he approached the Bellevue Hill home his thoughts drifted to his French joiner, Ari Neves. When Ari had first started building this gun cabinet, he wanted it to be his best work. He smiled as he remembered Ari pounding his first attempt into kindling with a mallet, annoyed with a flaw in his work.

David Bussau pulled his car into the driveway of the mansion of Kerry Packer, media tycoon and Australia's richest man. His thoughts had softened and his equanimity was restored. He had nothing against the Packers. They had given him interesting work. He dealt mostly with Mrs Packer, whom he found to be pleasant and polite. David had previously worked on the Woollahra home of Kerry Packer's mother and was then contracted to make some expensive cocktail cabinets and the gun cabinet in the magnate's home. David was a skilled craftsman. He fixed the latch quickly and before long he was back in his car, heading home to his family.

Given his tough start in life, David had every reason to be proud. He was thirty-three years old and his construction business employed almost one hundred people. As a teenage boy mowing lawns, he had dreamed of the financial comfort he now enjoyed. He adored his family, kept himself fit by playing squash and soccer and helped out at the church in his spare time. Life was good. But cracks were starting to appear.

'What was the point of it all,' he wondered. 'Isn't there more to life than being at the beck and call of wealthy clients?'

Increasingly over the weeks that followed, David pondered these thoughts. Was it all just about making money? The business was fine . . . but where was the challenge? How was it helping anyone else? The idea of making more money and building a bigger company for its own sake seemed devoid of purpose.

In his work on palatial homes around Sydney's harbourside, David had seen how success and money consumed people. There was little he saw that he wanted to emulate. The desire for wealth seemed insatiable for some. Enough, it seemed for them, was always that little bit more, as Rockefeller had said. Some of his wealthiest clients even fought him down to the last cent, or refused to pay for work he'd done. The hypocrisy was crushing. He instinctively knew he wanted more from life, but what? David didn't have to wait long for an answer to this question.

On Christmas morning in 1974, millions of Australians awoke to the news that Cyclone Tracy had battered Darwin. People had died. The city was destroyed. Australians were shocked at what they heard from the northern city. David knew straight away he had to respond.

Gathering a building crew, he flew into Darwin as families streamed out, their homes and lives broken. His team would help with the mop-up and start the long process of rebuilding. He had no way of knowing then how significant his spontaneous response would become, and how radically it would change the course of his life. Over the next three decades, this action led to others that would have a profound effect on millions of lives. David Bussau had heard his calling to a place from which he would never look back.

1

Abandoned

David Thomas Williams, not yet nine years old, stood shivering in his short pants, staring up a long pebbly-gravel drive. It was an icy August afternoon in 1949. The bus he and his younger brother had ridden from the poor end of town was gone, and there was no going back. Behind him cars rolled by on busy High Street on their way to town. The Anglican Boys' Home at Lower Hutt, New Zealand, was the first address David would remember.

In his right hand he clutched a large leather bag. It was light and almost empty—it held just a few pieces of clothing and a note for the matron. Even so, it was too bulky for him to carry with ease. 'C'mon, Bruce. Remember what Wocky said about this place. It's never boring,' he encouraged his brother, who stood beside him.

David took a few steps, dragging his bag, and then took a few more, working his way up the drive to the verandah of a low-slung timber building. His heart was heavy with thoughts of what lay ahead. At least the turmoil at home had been familiar. He'd learned to handle that. His friend Wocky had told him a few things about the Boys' Home, but he was nervous all the same. Why didn't his mother want him? Why was he coming to this place? What had he done wrong?

Beside him, in the middle of the circular driveway, was a finely trimmed lawn dotted with large trees and with a clump of bamboo rising up from its centre like a crown. He could see that the stand of bamboo was criss-crossed with tracks.

Good hiding spots in there, he thought. He felt a little better, took a deep breath and pulled up his chest to stand tall. The thought took root. Yes, it might be good to be away from all the arguments, the yelling, and the menace of violence that hung over home. There would be no more cowering from a brandished knife or roaming the streets, wondering if it was safe to return.

'And who might you young men be?' A stout woman with closely cropped hair looked down at them from the verandah of the old house. She already knew the answer to her question. She was expecting the Williams boys. She now examined them with well-trained eyes. She was used to boys arriving malnourished. These two looked all right, although they were stick thin.

Since the war, it was not unusual to find struggling single mothers in the valley who couldn't feed their kids. Even if the fathers hadn't been away at war, the pressures of wartime ripped families apart.

'I'm David and this is Bruce, ma'am,' David replied, his head bowed. He wouldn't meet her gaze.

'And your last name?' she probed.

'Williams, ma'am.'

'I'm Miss Menzies, the matron. The boys call me "ma". We have some rules around here. I'll explain them to you when you settle in. You'll be in my care now.'

'Yes, ma'am,' David replied, glancing up to take in his new guardian. He expected little from adults. He had found it was always best to look after himself.

'Bring your bags in now and I'll show you your bunks and give you your clothes. Each boy has his own number so you'll know which clothes are yours. We swap to larger sizes at the start of each year. You'll have a locker near the front door for your shoes and socks. Understood?' Miss Menzies was crisp and businesslike and David could tell there would be no arguing with her.

David and Bruce followed her inside the old building, taking in the smells and sounds of their new home: linoleum polish, a stew simmering on the Aga stove and the faint playful yells of boys in another part of the building.

Miss Menzies directed Bruce to a dormitory for younger boys, right beside the matron's room near the front door and then led David further along the hall, past a room filled with hand basins. Beyond that was a second room with rows of big concrete baths. It was his first taste of institutional life. He was awed by the scale and number of everything he saw. At the end of the corridor they came to a cold dormitory lined with ten utilitarian metal beds, each with a kapok mattress and grey blankets.

'This is yours,' Miss Menzies said, nodding towards a bed in the corner. 'Make yourself at home, lad. The dinner bell goes at 6 pm and we expect you to be prompt.'

Miss Menzies left and David sat on his bed, alone. 'No, I won't cry,' he thought, reassuring himself. 'This won't be so bad.'

The Home, 'Hazeldene', had belonged to a wealthy business-man who had left it to the local diocese of the Anglican Church. They'd added bathrooms and bunkrooms for the boys. Even with its rows of lockers and institutional furniture, the Home's high ceilings and carved kauri woodwork hinted at its original grandeur.

Miss Menzies was one of two women looking after almost forty boys at Hazeldene. Her assistant, Miss Adams, was fifteen centimetres taller than Miss Menzies and wore her grey hair pulled back tightly in a bun. She worked at the home as a volunteer. She loved children and didn't need the income. Miss Adams was the daughter of a judge, and came from an important family: the Sefton-Adams. She owned a property in the bush at Silverstream, in the upper reaches of the Hutt Valley.

David Williams was born in the midst of the Second World War, on 10th November 1940, in Wellington, New Zealand. His mother, Marjorie, and his father, Lewis Edward Williams, both came from the South Island. Marjorie was twenty-seven and Lewis thirty-one when David was born, and Bruce came along two years later. Already, there were an older brother and an older sister in the family, but for the younger boys they may as well have been a different generation. Well before David and Bruce were sent to the Boys' Home, their father had left for Auckland—they never saw him again.

Before the Home, David lived with his family in a small prefabricated government cottage on York Street, backing onto Woburn Railway Workshops at Moera, a working-class suburb of Lower Hutt. The cottage matched all the others in the street; it had three bedrooms, a sitting room and a kitchen, an outdoor washhouse, scullery and bathroom. As an adult, David would have no recollection of the Moera house.

David and Bruce played cricket and soccer after school and found adventure on the streets of Moera. One holiday, on their barefoot wanderings around the Randwick Road shops, they came across a bigger boy looking for coins in a phone booth. This was something they liked to do as well, in case someone had overlooked some change. It was their best chance at getting money for sweets. This boy, Robert, had sandy blond hair and a compact, athletic build. He seemed friendly and open, and the Williams boys soon learned he had a grandmother living just down the road, and his mother and aunts lived there as well.

'I come back to Moera for the holidays, and so do my cousins,' he told the boys after they struck up a conversation. 'The rest of the time I live down at the Anglican Boys' Home on High Street. They call me Wocky down there.'

The neighbourhood boys all gathered at the vacant lot beside Wocky's grandmother's place for their cricket games. Occasionally, when he decided to tolerate the younger boys, the eldest Williams brother, John, joined in. But most of the time he was more interested in girls and music, and shooed the younger ones away. He was in his late teenage years, wore long pants and smoked.

Wocky was forbidden from crossing busy Randwick Road and going anywhere near the shunting yards. That didn't stop him crossing it to make his way around to David's place in York Road, but he never dared venture inside. He had heard the yelling that carried out into the street as they played. Whatever was happening in there, it was not a happy place to be. David spent as many hours of the day as he could away from his house. He and Wocky had more than sport in common. Wocky also had two much older siblings and a father who lived elsewhere. Fathers were a taboo topic. Wocky had been born and raised in Australia, but then his mother Myrtle had left her husband and moved to New Zealand.

For the first few months in New Zealand, Wocky was bumped from aunt to aunt so as not to be a burden on one family.

Eventually Wocky's mother saw no way out of her dilemma but to put her son into care. She was thrilled when a place came up at the Boys' Home run by the Anglican Church.

Wocky returned to Randwick Road for the holidays to stay with his cousins, and his mother came by bus to visit him every second week.

Wocky had been at the Home for three years before the Williams boys arrived. He eased their way by introducing them to some of the forty other boys. He had pretty much toed the line and stayed out of trouble. He had even worked out a comfortable truce with the worst bully in the Home, Ross Smith. Smith was a small, dark-haired boy who was freakishly strong and used his years at Lower Hutt to hone his skills of bullying and manipulation. He liked strong opponents who at least made an attempt to stand up to him. He had subtlety and patience, and his attacks were sly and unheralded, often starting with his arm around a boy's neck, held tight almost to strangulation point, or an arm twisted right up and round the back, ready to snap. Smithy soon put David to the test.

'Hey, new boy, Williams, make my bed,' he demanded. David bristled. He wasn't going to be pushed around, not by Ross Smith or anyone else.

'Make your own bed,' David replied, defiantly. It was just what Smithy wanted.

'Make my bed or I'll smash your head in.'

'I don't want to make your bed,' David shot back firmly.

Smithy grabbed David and held him in a quiet corner, like a boxer in the ring, bumping his jaw and asking, 'Still won't co-operate?' with a sinister grin on his face.

'No, I won't.'

'Are you gonna do it?' He eyeballed David, tightening his grip on David's collar to subdue his prey.

'Ah, OK, Smithy, I'll do it,' David choked out. He had maintained his resistance as long as he could without suffering any serious damage.

'Good decision.'

Smithy's bullying skills developed. He obsessively wrote away for books and magazines on jujitsu, self-defence and weight training, and as he gained strength and new skills he liked to test them out on the boys around him.

David was angry at being bullied but didn't know how to resist. 'I'm not going to put up with bullies like Ross Smith when I'm older,' he told himself.

However, some aspects of David's new life were safe and predictable. Each day the cook, Mrs Atkinson, made porridge for breakfast and a concoction of oatmeal, weetbix, raisins and coconut—which she called concrete—for afternoon tea. At night it was wholesome meat and vegetables, but there was never enough. The boys always felt hungry; they were so hungry they would overcome their revulsion to tripe or liver or fish enough to eat it. At mealtime they scrambled to sit around a long cream table, with Miss Menzies, Miss Adams and any visitors presiding at the 'top table'.

Ladies from St James's Anglican Church came each week to darn socks and mend badly treated clothes, and the curate cut the boys' hair once a month. On Mondays Miss Perfect hauled in wood to build up a fire under the big copper, and worked her way through the mountain of washing.

Though life at the Home was impersonal, David felt more settled than he could remember. The 'Homies' travelled to Eastern Hutt school in a pack, in khaki shorts and shirts and bare feet. In the eyes of the public they were a pack of wild lads without parents to pull them into line. At the time this didn't bother David at all. It was only as he approached his teen years and first became aware of admiring glances across the classroom from Corinne Puddle, the sweetheart of his year, that his thoughts changed. For a time he returned her stares with a smile, until he realised the futility of his dreams. Deep down, he felt a shame. 'I won't ever be good enough for her parents,' he thought, and silently laid his feelings to rest.

Some of the boys did have parents who came to visit every week or fortnight, arriving with boxes of Queen Anne chocolates or money for their children. David watched them come and go. He trained himself not to pine for a family, and when the desire for material things got too strong, he simply stole what he wanted.

One day, not long after David and Bruce were sent to the Home, their mother Marjorie came back for them. David didn't know why—perhaps she'd changed her ways, or her financial circumstances had improved.

He and Bruce were called to the front building. Their mother disappeared into Miss Menzies' timber-panelled office, and then David and Bruce were summoned in. Miss Menzies looked directly at the boys. 'It's time to go home with your mother now, so please go and pack your bags.'

'I won't go,' David replied. There was a stunned silence.

'David, I want you to come home with me,' his mother commanded. 'Things will be better.'

'I won't do it, I'm not going with you,' he said, with a rising voice. No amount of pleading would convince David to return to that house of neglect and abuse. 'Leave me alone,' he yelled and ran away.

Miss Menzies said, 'It might be best if you come back for him tomorrow.'

Marjorie Williams turned and left and didn't come back the next day. David never saw or heard from his mother again.

For David, the process of building a new identity, that of David Williams, orphan, had begun when he was left at the Home. He couldn't remember his father, but he liked to picture him as an American serviceman. There were many posted in the South Pacific who came to New Zealand's shores for a break from the fighting. In David's mind he wasn't without a father, anyway. Each Sunday the boys filed into the big recreation room of the Home for Sunday School, led by Miss Saul. The Bonifant family lived next door and their young children, Valerie and John, slotted in with the boys. Their mother, Gladys Bonifant, was an assistant teacher.

Mrs Bonifant greeted the boys each Sunday with: 'This is God's house, He is here today. He hears each song of praise and listens when we pray.' It was a respite from the harshness of Home life. The music was a source of comfort to David and he had a sense of homecoming as he went through this gentle weekly ritual.

One Sunday David heard the words that would begin to lay the foundation for his life's work. 'For my father and my mother have forsaken me, but the Lord will receive me.' They came from Psalm 27. David's spirit stirred deeply as he listened to his Sunday school teacher read the passage. Was there a father who wouldn't abandon him, hurt him or judge him? Was there a father who wouldn't walk away as his own father had?

'Very early in the piece I became aware of God', David was later to reflect. My first image was of a father and me as his child. During that period that image meant everything to me. God meant someone who cared about me and accepted me. Someone who had a purpose for me and gave me a sense that I belonged. You needed someone to turn to.' From that time on, David had a new father to whom he turned when he felt worthless or abandoned. This father became his source of strength.

Bruce Williams was not faring as well as his brother David. Older boys taunted him for small things, like hair that stuck out, and called him names. David was stronger, more athletic and better looking. His days on the streets in Moera had given him a strong instinct for survival. Though he was kind to his younger brother, their lives diverged. They lived in different dormitories, and by the time they made it through the institutional treadmill, they may as well have been from different families. Life became a battle for survival, and any allegiances between the boys, by necessity, came second to self-interest.

Even at the tender age of nine, work was a big part of David's life. Soon after the boys returned to the Home from school each afternoon, the gardener, Gilbert Kimberley, set them to work shovelling dirt, pulling weeds and spreading mulch before streaming inside tired and sweating, with dirty fingernails and knees that would have to be scrubbed before they were allowed to sit down to dinner. There were jobs to do inside as well. Polishing the linoleum floors of the long passages around the Home was David's favourite. Three or four of the boys rode along on old blankets while others pulled them up and down over the floors. The smell of linoleum cleaner would always remind him of the lighter moments of working in the Home.

Miss Menzies and Mr Kimberley supervised homework for those boys who had it. 'Everyone with homework come to the dining room now,' they'd announce. They soon sorted out the scholarly boys to be watched, encouraged or even pressured, from those with no academic aptitude, whom they left alone. Miss Menzies heaped praise on Wocky when he came top of his class in mathematics, but soon undermined his triumph with the warning, 'You'd better do just as well next time—or else.'

David was not among the hardworking scholars. He tolerated his homework, but lived for sport. Mr Kimberley was a gifted sportsman, and he encouraged and taught the boys to play tennis, cricket, football and softball on the wide green lawns to the side of the building.

Sport was a source of both unity and division for the boys. No matter what sport or game they were playing, there were always enough bodies for two teams, with reserves, and Miss Adams often joined in when they played tip or baseball on the front lawn. Through sport they worked out their natural pecking order, jostling to swim faster or swing higher or hit harder than the next boy. In the Home, many of the boys grew stronger and fitter than their classmates at Eastern Hutt who were not as physically active.

In the early 1940s the local doctor, Dr Dudley, had installed a swimming pool at the back of the Home. It was filled from an artesian bore without a hint of chlorine. The water simply got dirtier and dirtier, until the green slime inching across its surface and sides grew too disgusting for swimming. Then it was emptied and the boys were each given a scrubbing brush to clean the pool.

A private pool in New Zealand in that era was unheard of, and in summer the boys were the envy of the neighbourhood. Not so in winter, though, when they were forced to swim two laps of the pool naked as a way of toughening them up. They were always nervous at the prospect of neighbourhood girls spying on them as they quickly performed their morning ritual. Recreational swims through the summer holidays, morning and afternoon, like every other aspect of the boys' lives, were strictly regimented. Each boy kept his swimming costume and towel on the hooks lined up along the wall of the play shed.

'Line up at the gate until the bell goes, boys,' Miss Menzies commanded. When the bell sounded she ceremoniously unlocked the pool gate and the boys streamed in. Miss Adams stood by in her black woollen swimsuit and the boys lined up for a turn to be pulled along by her in a rubber tyre tube.

Although Miss Menzies worked hard for the boys, her concern for her young charges was not always discernible to them. To the boys, she was a strict disciplinarian whose word was law. The threatening tone of her voice mostly pulled the boys up, but she was generous with the strap if bellowing didn't work. One unfortunate boy, Tony, came to know the full force of the matron's anger when he committed the crime of talking in the dormitory. He had toughened himself to routine and discipline, so when the matron gave him six swift whacks of the strap he refused to flinch. He locked his teeth into position and steeled his belly as she whacked him a second time, and when for a third time he stared blankly, she flailed him until he finally broke and cried out in agony. For the next week, he lay in bed on his side and stomach nursing twenty-one welts on his back and legs, with Miss Adams occasionally comforting him. The local minister severely chastised Miss Menzies when word of the abuse made it back to the parish management, via a curate who came to cut the boy's hair and noticed his discomfort. He ordered her not to strap the boys again and issued a list of appropriate punishments, including going to bed without supper and withdrawing privileges like going to movies or on excursions.

However Miss Menzies was soon back on the strap again. In David's time, she saved punishment for any demeanor, which were mostly related to unruliness, until late in the day, before dinner, when she applied the strap to the hands and bare behinds of the line of nervously sweating boys.

If anyone was caught leaving the grounds of the Home to venture across the road to the local shop they could count on time locked in an isolation room reserved for the worst offences. David was smart enough to keep his head down, but even so he received his share of lashings. Over time, the boys, David included, became resistant to physical pain. It was far better to take six good cuts of the strap than to be banned from watching the much anticipated Friday night movies.

Matron also took a hard line with bed-wetters, who all slept together in a bed-wetters' dormitory and each morning were paraded in front of the other boys as they took their wet sheets to the laundry room to be washed.

Miss Adams offered the only affection most of the boys experienced in the home. David would remember her as a gentle person with a genuine concern for her charges. She employed an effective form of crowd control that held out the best reward of all, individual attention, although with forty boys vying for her affections they were thinly spread. Whoever was ready for bed first could choose the story for that night and enjoy the unparalleled pleasure of a goodnight peck on the forehead from Miss Adams.

She was a well-educated woman who knew by heart a wide variety of stories from Greek mythology and the classics so loved by the boys. Their favourites were King Arthur, Robin Hood and any stories by Hans Christian Andersen.

Even better were the occasional excursions in small groups on the train to her home at Silverstream. Here she spoiled the boys with a big afternoon tea and the freedom to run through the orchard, feasting on any of the fruit they could reach. The house at Silverstream was a two-storey building with a croquet green and tennis courts. Inside, it was filled with heavy antique furniture, stern portraits and rich timber panelling. Its floors were scattered with bear and tiger skin rugs so exotic the boys spent hours pondering their origins.

Amid the drab grey of his childhood, a golden moment would stand out in David's memory. One summer, when he was about twelve, a buzz went through the Home. 'There's going to be a huge party and we're all going.' The rumour was soon confirmed by matron. 'Mr Arthur Clouston has invited us all to the opening of his new mill up at Akatarawa. He is sending cars to collect us this Saturday,' she announced at dinner one night. 'I expect you all to be on your very best behaviour. No swearing, no fighting, no unruly behaviour.'

Clouston's mill was twenty kilometres from the Home, near a forest rich in the native timbers of rimu, totara and matai. The family patriarch, Arthur Clouston, was a rough-talking maverick with a soft heart. He had a special interest in helping underprivileged children, and for many years delivered free firewood to the home.

By Saturday morning, the boys were bubbling with anticipation, which reached a high point when a procession of cars curved along the driveway to the front of the Home to ferry them, like princes, up to the party. There were more than two hundred and fifty boys and girls at the mill, including the children of Clouston's employees, forty or more from the Anglican Boys' Home and a large group from another home, St Joseph's, at Upper Hutt.

Once there, it was a child's heaven. In one area, a gaggle of children ran behind a squealing greased piglet, laughing, arms and legs flailing as they switched direction to follow the pig. Others were organised into running races and egg and spoon races where they competed for cash prizes. At one stage the children heard an aeroplane flying low overhead and looked up to see wrapped sweets cascading from the sky onto the grass around them. They scrambled to gather as many as they could, but need not have worried. There was more food than even two hundred and fifty hungry children could possibly eat.

Long tables displayed a feast of sandwiches, chicken, apples, cream-covered sponge cakes and small iced cakes, all colourfully decorated, and as much lemonade as they could drink. It was a feast beyond David's imagination.

At the day's end, when they could no longer gather enough energy for another game or devour another cake, they climbed back into the cars for the ride home, their bellies and souls satisfied, their hair blowing in the cool wind.

David never questioned why Arthur Clouston gave them such a lavish day out. Clouston had also grown up in an orphanage and knew how much they would relish the gesture. It delighted him to see happy children. It became a tradition for the Cloustons to throw a Christmas party for the boys each year but in David's memory, nothing quite matched that first big party.

David's childhood ended abruptly at the age of thirteen. When the boys reached their teenage years they were shipped north to Sedgley Boys' Home at Masterton. They travelled for two hours or more by bus, winding in a nauseating spiral up and over Rimataka Hill into the rich green Wairarapa Valley.

David Williams made the move to Sedgley in September 1953,

two months before his thirteenth birthday, in the company of another boy from the Lower Hutt Home, Robert Mason. Now a master was in charge of them, and they could not expect the luxury of settling-in time. 'Williams and Mason, you'll start at Masterton Central School tomorrow morning at 8.30,' Mr Jonkers ordered in his thick Dutch accent. 'Report to the kitchen at 5.30 am. You'll be on dishes for the next three months.' Chores, school, chores, and then play, in whatever time was left. This was to be David's new life.

2

Sedgley

The morning started at five when the boys on milking duty left
the cossetting warmth of bed to creep, still dozy with lingering
dreams, past a warren of dormitories and out to the side of the
building. Here, in an open-sided shed smelling of sour milk,
musty hay and sloppy dung, the cows shuffled expectantly, their
udders bulging. David enjoyed farm work. It was better than
washing a mountain of dishes and ironing scores of shirts. In
milking there was the certainty of the gentle, rhythmic squeeze on
the teats and the violent squirt of milk into the tin bucket. The
warm, frothy liquid sloshed as he shuffled across the courtyard to
a milk tub that was later skimmed of its cream with a ladle.

Later in the week, when enough cream was collected, it was
sent to be churned until globs of butter could be pulled from the
buttermilk. They were then moulded and presented to the cook
for the boys to spread on their bread. Most weeks there was
butter left to sell outside the Home, or to trade for other fresh
food they needed.

The boys doing other jobs hugged their slumber for as long as
they could, but by 6.30 each morning the dormitory was empty.
Sedgley was a ten-hectare working farm and the three dozen lads
living there were the workforce. Before breakfast they fed the chickens, helped prepare breakfast and lunch, and worked through a

mountain of dirty clothing and linen in the huge laundry. After school they weeded the vegetable and flower gardens, mowed the lawns, finished the washing and ironing, and helped with the dinner. When the evening meal was finished there was cleaning up and the dishes to do. It seemed their lives were reduced to three-monthly cycles of chores that kept them busy from dawn to bedtime, with a break in between for school. In the realm of work, there was no difference between the stronger, sportier lads of Sedgley's and the smaller, weaker boys from the Anglican Boys' Home. They were all expected to pull their weight.

The endless workload may have been monotonous and exhausting but David later saw the Sedgley schedule as beneficial. 'In the bigger picture, I look back on our work regime as good training. We were taught to do all the practical jobs of running a farm and a household and we learned to focus all our energies on the task we were assigned. It became a matter of survival. There was no choice. We had to do all the duties we were rostered to do. You could embrace it without shortcuts, and become tenacious, or fight it and be miserable. We endured the work and the end goal was to get the job done.'

In the holidays, when other boys scattered to grandparents or home to single parents, or found their way into foster families, David eschewed the comfort of a foster home. 'Maybe I just got it in my head to strive, to produce, but even at a young age I pre-ferred to be engaged in some sort of activity,' David said. By his teens he had lost the concept of 'family'. 'In terms of a normal family life, my sensibility didn't experience it. I didn't pray for it or pine for it,' he said. He felt a drive to move on, to work hard, to learn new things. He was learning to look forward, a skill that would be critical in later years. He trained himself not to store painful thoughts, and quickly discounted any negative comments he heard.

David's arm was among the first to shoot up at the end of the school term when Mr Jonkers read out a list of jobs going on local farms: 'We have a position for two weeks picking potatoes down Carterton way.'

'I'll do it,' David said, and when the final school bell rang for holidays he was on his bike, peddling the twenty kilometres or more to a local farm, where he bunked down in a straw-filled barn. He spent his waking hours trailing up and down the rich soil rows pulling up the tubers and throwing them into a sack he dragged along beside him. At the end of the day his hands were raw, with dirt ingrained into a road map of reddish black lines and a black arch lining the inside of his fingernails. His back and leg muscles ached, but he didn't complain.

Schoolwork was a different matter. David spent his intermediate year at Masterton Central School before joining the older Sedgley boys at Wairarapa College, the public high school just a couple of streets from the Home, in February 1955. Most of the faces around Sedgley were familiar to David when he first arrived in Masterton. Wocky and his crowd of friends had come up the year before, and David slotted in with their games readily enough. Ross Smith, short but muscular from exercising with weights, had already staked out his territory with his tough-man tactics. He was butting up against authority figures in the Home and at school, and still delighting in the art of cutting down tall poppies around him.

The boys operated within the boundaries of a working-class, anti-academic sentiment that thwarted any aspirations they had. Apart from the talented few, most accepted that they would always be farm workers or labourers. An early description of Sedgley said, 'It provides a training in farm pursuits for those boys who are not adapted to other callings.' And later, 'Every effort is made to equip the boys for the battle of life and to place them in the way of earning their own living.'

David saw it differently. 'There was a perception that we were delinquents who wouldn't amount to much.' Nothing in his early years had taught him to think otherwise, and at Wairarapa College he was reminded of his lowly position with jarring regularity.

'David Williams?' the teacher read from the roll at the start of each school year.

'Yes, sir,' David would reply, sitting shyly at the back of the classroom.

'What is your phone number?'

'No phone, sir,' he replied quietly.

'Are you at Sedgley Boys' Home?'

'Yes, sir,' he said, sliding lower into his seat as his classmates turned with pitying looks to size him up. Only the poorest children and the 'Homies' were without phones by this time.

Games in the school playground divided along the lines of Homies versus the rest, and the Homies, with their superior strength and careless attitudes, licked the other children every time. They may have bickered at the Home, but at school the Sedgley boys formed a self-contained and formidable mass. They were recognisable by their worn clothing, each boy with his own number penned heavily onto each item; the numbers would be scratched out and replaced by new ones as the clothing was recycled from boy to boy until it finally fell apart.

The sorting of classes according to intelligence, supposedly, at Wairarapa reinforced the notion of the Sedgley boys as an underclass. The middle-class children of accountants and lawyers filled academic streams while working-class children filled the commercial, agricultural or trades classes. Learning a trade was the highest achievement most Sedgley boys could aspire to.

Some of the boys did resort to crime and violence. Ross Smith was expelled from Wairarapa College for beating up his geography teacher, and ensured that boxing was taken off the agenda at another high school when he turned a school boxing match into a blood bath. Later, on the streets of Wellington, Smith and his gang frequently clashed with gangs of 'bodgies' and made a point of crashing islanders' parties. Smith eventually met a gruesome end when a tram ran him down as he was escaping a group of bulky islanders he had just insulted.

In 1957, David showed enough academic ability in school to graduate from the class learning trades to one that included rudimentary accounting skills. However, he failed to meet the aggregate score of two hundred in his four best subjects needed to move to the next grade. He was back at Wairarapa College the next year to try again.

In class, David was invisible. He was the quiet boy sitting distractedly at the back of the room, not wanting to be there. It was only on the sporting field that he gained a profile, a sense of having some significance in the world. On the soccer field or cricket pitch he was fit and confident. In his teens, David had

17

grown to be large and robust, far from the undernourished four-year-old boy who, prior to being sent to the Home, was once considered at risk of malnutrition and bundled off to the Otaki Health Camp by the government for proper food and care. The hours of hard physical work around Sedgley had made him strong and focused. He played cricket with boys several years ahead of him at school and in his final year was captain of both the Wairarapa College First XI cricket team and Firsts Soccer team. He played tennis and swam, and was adept at any sport he attempted.

Sport was one of the few areas where Sedgley boys could shine, and they were often placed in the top sporting teams at school. David's friend Wocky was high school swimming champion, a member of the school's cricket and rugby teams and an excellent gymnast.

The boys erupted into casual games of cricket or soccer in spare moments at the Home. 'Here, throw us the ball,' a call would go out, and the boys would huff and wrestle around the dormitory until the master shut down their game with threats of punishment. At the back of the Home they could spread out in a full-blown cricket game, or fall into French cricket in limited space nearer the building. As he grew older, David naturally took up an organising role. He was often the one to call, 'Time for a game of cricket, guys,' and to assign the boys to fielding or batting positions as they arrived to play.

Sedgley was set up for sport. The Masterton Jaycees, a service club, had sweated through digging a swimming pool in the summer of 1953, and another benefactor had built a well-equipped gymnasium at the rear of the building. Each Thursday evening David eagerly lined up with the other boys for gymnastics lessons from Rex and Stan Tatton, local brothers who had been New Zealand champions in the sport. The Tatton family owned a Masterton car dealership and had a history of helping out at Sedgley.

The strength and precision of the Tatton brothers as they moved deftly on the pummel horse in their crisp white singlets captivated David, and he longed for such skill. He was not the only boy lost in personal dreams of greatness.

Sedgley had a bicycle track and an obstacle course, and the boys could spend hours on weekends riding over bumps and racing each other around the track. David knew his neighbourhood mowing jobs would never pay for a brand new bike, but with ingenuity and a hunt around the local rubbish dump for discarded bike frames he built his own. If the parts were twisted or rusty he soon learned how to straighten them out, and if he was lucky enough to find wheels, he knew how to take out any buckles. David's bike was his most precious possession. It was more than a mode of transport; it was his source of freedom, and he guarded it ferociously. His bike meant he could go further afield and make a faster getaway when he stole mudguards or a headlight from the rows of bicycles lined up outside the local movie theatre. A childhood of petty theft gave him unshakeable realism about things like stealing. Later, he knew not to accuse and judge people quickly in matters of human frailty.

'Lights out, boys. No talking now,' the master called down the hall at bedtime. Darkness descended on the dormitories at nine each night, signalling the start of the boys' nocturnal activities. Most night-time exploits were motivated by hunger. In the early years, David and his friends escaped through the window into the stillness of the night to help themselves to sweet apples from the nearby orchard. The windfall apples they were allowed to gather from under the trees in daylight were never enough.

Later, there were mass breakouts. They'd slide from their beds, making sure to carefully plump up their rugs into boy-size forms with pillows. Sometimes David escaped alone and undetected into the garden and made his way to a fort he had built during the day.

Forts were damp and dirty hideaways the boys dug around the outlying areas of the Sedgley grounds. Their secret entrances, just big enough to crawl into, were disguised by putting timber or iron across them and replacing the grass. At night they became private candle-lit domains into which they could crawl to escape from the pack. Here they would stash their pilfered treasures, carefully wrapped to keep out the earthy dankness and burrowing thieves. Close to the forts was an elaborate system of holes for hiding tins of money that the boys had managed to withhold from the matron, and would later use to buy a sweet bun or a piece of fruit. There was a system of forced savings: the boys relinquished most of their odd jobs earnings to the matron for safe keeping and she distributed it back to them when they needed to pay for movies, haircuts or to watch a visiting soccer team.

David looked forward to entering his fort; there were few places at Sedgley where he could be alone and he made this nightly adventure a ritual. One, two, three, four, five . . . he counted out the steps from the willow tree along the stream, turned to the south towards the private boys' school next door, where the sons of wealthy local farmers received a grammar school education. Six more big steps and he stopped. He gently pulled away the grass on a barely noticeable mound and dug with his hands to uncover a rusty tin box, always looking over his shoulder for other boys who might be spying on his hiding spot. Though the boys lived as brothers, they could never really trust each other. Secrecy was always the safest way. David knew he would survive if he was self-contained. Then he slid into his dirty fort to count out his savings and enjoy some sweet biscuits he'd stolen on a warehouse raid.

He couldn't remember which boy first discovered a gap under the eave of the warehouse, but word quickly spread through the dormitories. That kind of communication was another secret night-time activity. It had to be. A careless boy might let something slip in earshot of the master, and that would be the end of the biscuit supply.

The cold air bit David's ears as he whistled down the Wellington Road on his bike. Within minutes he could fill his rumbling stomach with sugary treats—and have some left over. A reconnoitre of the building for security then a short leg up the drainpipe, hands locked over the ledge and belly pulled in to crawl through the gap. First-timers grabbed for the first packets they saw, but David sought out the best: the chocolate-covered, chocolate-filled, sweetest and tastiest of the biscuits. Then he was out of there, careful not to crush his delicacies. It wasn't long before the owners of the warehouse pegged out the biscuit thieves and ended a great outing for the boys.

Still, the journey into town each Sunday morning to the Anglican church opened up other opportunities. There was just enough time between leaving Sedgley and the start of the church service each Sunday morning to snoop around one or two buildings in town which might be fruitful targets for night-time raids. One enterprising group uncovered a secret stash of beer hidden under the local plumber's shop, which was built over a creek. For a short time, until the plumber discovered that his beer supply was diminishing, the shop was a favourite stopover on the way back to Sedgley for the weekly Sunday baked dinner, although with just one or two beers passed around half a dozen boys, there was little risk of over-indulgence.

Opportunism was an essential part of Sedgley life. David, like most of the boys, took into adulthood an attitude of 'What do I have to lose?' 'Failure wasn't really a big deal. You just took a chance on everything,' David recalled. When the local bakery van arrived each week to deliver the day-old bread and cakes the bakery had generously donated to the Home, David was often among the group of boys peeping around the corner to spy on the driver.

'He's gone. He's in the kitchen now. Quick, go, go,' the lookout called. The boys would make a lightning raid, stuff their pockets and mouths full of today's cakes and bread and vanish before the driver came whistling cheerfully around the corner again. By the time he discovered the theft, later in his rounds, there was no chance of nailing the culprits.

When the annual fair rolled into Masterton, David was among the boys who plotted ways to cycle down to the fairground at night to be part of it. The owners of the amusements welcomed them. They asked few questions of the eager Sedgley boys, which was just how the boys wanted it.

First David found work on a stall, spruiking in front of a row of colourful revolving clown heads as the townsfolk filed by. 'C'mon, who'll give the clowns a go? Everyone wins a prize here,' he smiled at the passing sea of faces. Another year it was the dodgem cars, where he jumped from car to car untangling traffic snarls and rescuing trapped children. Often the boys stole more money from the amusement owners than they were paid. The risk was worth it. The lure of money was stronger than any punishment the fair owners or a Sedgley master could mete out.

21

A hard-working, well-meaning board administered Sedgley, mostly from St Matthew's Anglican church in the centre of town. The board worked busily at raising donations and bequests and gathering food and clothes for the boys. And even though David stole when he could and took more from the offering plate at church than he put in, the years of teaching drilled the values of service and generosity into his core.

Others noticed his helping nature. David approached his neighbourhood mowing jobs with fervour, knowing he would be assured of more work along the street behind the home if he did the jobs well. 'Lad, you're doing a good job. You'll go far,' one of his employers once told him.

David had never had high expectations of himself. He had never heard encouragement like this before. The words rang in his ears. The masters and matrons may have provided for his physical needs, but encouragement and direction in life were both sadly lacking. After that day, he dared to dream about 'going far'.

Like the other Sedgley boys, David rarely expressed his inner thoughts to others. The closest times were those spent hanging out at the Sedgley bike shed, the workshop where they repaired or built their bikes.

'When I leave this place I'm going to get a job in the city,' one boy started.

'I'm going to buy a farm around here and marry a beautiful girl,' another pledged.

David's plans were a little bigger. 'I'm going to be a millionaire and be self-supporting by the time I'm forty.' From the small amounts of pocket money he had earned he knew money meant freedom. No one could tell him what to do any more. He could make his own decisions.

At the age of fourteen his quest for extra money led David to work at Donald's, a local Masterton company manufacturing wool presses. This holiday job held promise. It paid more than labouring on a farm or mowing lawns, and he looked forward to using some of the trade skills he was learning at school. Wocky, now called Rob, had also been offered a job at Donald's and each morning the pair pedalled their bikes down High Street into the town to join the older men in the factory.

The Donald family were large landowners in the Wairarapa even before the town of Masterton itself was founded in 1854. When David and Rob started work there the factory was run by Haddon Donald, the great grandson of the founder, Donald Donald.

'David, you'll be upstairs in carpentry and Robert, come with me to the engineering area,' the foreman directed on their first morning. To the boys these were serious jobs, even if they earned less than the men working there.

By midway through the summer he had already spent long hours feeding pieces of timber into the jaws of the bench saw. He loved to watch the staggered blade cut a perfect dissection. He challenged himself to make it finer, straighter, smoother, each time. One sticky summer day he gently guided the timber onto the whirring blade, expecting it to slice through as it always did but this time his perfect cut was upset by a twisted knot in the timber, which jerked David's hand forward as the blade and knot met. The unguarded saw had jumped off its course and David's fingers were now where the timber had been. Just as neatly as it had cut through the timber, it now sawed off four of the fingers on his left hand and ploughed into his thumb. He looked down in disbelief to see three gushing stumps where his fingers should have been. 'Help me,' he gasped weakly to his co-worker nearby. One finger flapped helplessly and his thumb was nowhere in sight. The blood spurted without aim, streaking the sawdust on the floor red. Then came a rush of sickening pain, a thousand sharpened needles driven into his fingers, weaving up his arm in overwhelming waves until he swayed and fell to the floor, unconscious.

David was bundled into an ambulance, a cloth tightly wrapped around his one tenuously remaining finger. In the panic a workmate thought to sort through the bloodied sawdust for his other fingers. Desperately, he sifted and found one fingertip, then another.

'Quick, put it on ice and follow the ambulance,' the foreman commanded, still looking for the other two fingertips. 'Your friend cut his fingers off,' the foreman told Rob after the ambulance had left. 'We found a finger and his thumb but couldn't find the other two.'

23

At the hospital doctors sewed David's two fingers back on. It would be months before he had full use of them again, but he had survived a dangerous loss of blood and it appeared the remaining digits would still work. He awoke from his operation to a kind face smiling down at him.

'What have you done to yourself, young man?' the nurse asked. 'That's some way to get out of work.'

He tried to smile back but could barely move his lips before falling into a dreamy unconsciousness. There was no pain now, no feeling at all. Everywhere he looked was light and whiteness. The following days were a haze of caring faces, needles and stinging pain each time the nurses came to change his dressings. There was no clarity to think about even his immediate future. Then it crept into his consciousness. No sport. How can I play sport without fingers?

'Nurse, will I be able to play cricket again?' David asked.

'Lad, you'll be fine. You won't be a pianist, that's all,' she replied, setting his mind at rest. 'And they won't look all that beautiful either, but they'll work.'

At thirteen David had survived a close call with a .22 calibre bullet he and his friends found beside the road on the way to church one Sunday morning. This was a fascinating discovery for a group of teenage boys, but what were they going to do with such a find? They devised a game of Russian roulette, where they stood in a circle throwing rocks at the bullet to elicit some kind of reaction. The bullet soon responded, shooting up in David's direction and grazing his calf as it passed. He and the other boys scampered on to church, where David sat in pain through the service with a handkerchief wrapped around his leg.

David used the Donald's incident to master the art of pain management. His memory could dull and excise the distressing pictures. His mind could steel itself to endure and cover the pain. Nothing would ever hurt like that again. Later in life he could bring a hammer down hard on his hand and still finish the job before attending to the injury, or slice his foot and be on a plane within hours with dozens of stitches in the wound. He could also witness other people's pain and destruction and be driven to act rather than being overcome.

The three weeks he spent in Masterton hospital were among David's happiest memories of youth, a time of rare peace. For the first time he could remember, he was away from all the other boys for an extended time. There were other patients in David's ward, but they did not compete for the nurses' attention. He enjoyed the gentleness of human touch on his skin as the nurses bathed and dressed his wounds.

'Nurse, what do you think of New Zealand's chances against the Australians in the cricket?' he asked and then tied up the nurse in conversation for as long as he could about her favourite sport or sporting team. Growing up in the Boys' Home had taught David just about every childhood prank going, and he found the nurses willing and good-natured targets. With all the nurses' attention, he barely spared a thought for the boys back at Sedgley. They were not allowed to visit and, knowing their timetables, he had not expected them to come.

As David anticipated, there was little fuss made over him when he returned to the Boys' Home. School and daily chores continued and he was expected to start back where he left off, with some concessions for his handicap. It was now impossible for him to milk a cow, and dishwater posed an infection risk, but he could still dry dishes or feed the chickens with his good hand.

The nurse was right about his injuries. He could still kick a soccer ball, and when time healed his wounds, he could catch a cricket ball. He knew he would have to work on these sports, as he could no longer be a gymnast. He could join in the horses or mat work or vaulting, but could no longer grip the horizontal bars or rings.

The Donald's accident also gave David his first capital. Some months after he returned to the routine of Sedgley, the master called David to his office.

'David, I'm holding in my hand a letter from the government. It says you're entitled to £2000 in compensation for your fingers,' Mr Hills told him. 'I will arrange for the money to be deposited into a trust fund until you are eighteen years old so you can't spend it before then.'

David could hardly believe his good fortune. The habits of work and saving had been instilled in him from the beginning of his time at Sedgley. All his earnings from mowing lawns were saved for him. He had learned to be careful with money. Now, in the form of one letter, and at only fourteen years of age, he had more money than he had ever dreamed of, more than he could earn in five years of mowing lawns, and he had four years to plan how he would use it. He expected this process to be like every other facet of his life. He would figure it out for himself, without parents to work with him through the possible consequences.

In David's time at Sedgley, the boys' carers came and went. It seemed there was barely time to get to know one couple in charge before they were replaced by the next. Mr and Mrs Jonkers, master and mistress in 1953 when David arrived, had a short tenure. Their predecessors, Mr and Mrs Hibbs, had run Sedgley for sixteen years and earned the respect of the boys for their fairness and their genuine interest in the boys' lives. It was hard to follow in the Hibbs' footsteps. A popular local family, the Hills, whose children mixed freely with the Sedgley boys, took on the role while the trustees sought a permanent replacement. When they appointed someone, it was an Australian couple, the Bakers, who drank to excess and were moved on quickly. Then came the couple who were to have the greatest influence on David.

Lyndsay and Vera Bussau were not as popular as the Hills, and they did not command the respect of the Hibbs, but they came with a more relaxed approach, which gave newfound freedom to the boys. In his final year at Sedgley, Rob caught the eye of Diane, one of the most attractive girls in his year at Wairarapa College. Their romance at school was blossoming, though it had an uncertain future. Relationships with girls were forbidden, even as the Sedgley boys got older, so if they wanted to see a girl it had to be an illicit meeting.

In the early stages of his relationship, Rob crept out at night or found an excuse to do an errand and meet Diane around the corner. Now, under the Bussaus, he could visit Diane's home each Sunday for lunch with their blessing. For David, relationships were not an issue. His time was consumed by sport and work and he already knew that from a parent's point of view he would not measure up for any girl he fancied at school.

26

The Bussaus and their five-year-old daughter, Rochelle, arrived at Sedgley at the beginning of 1956. Lyndsay was an Australian who had moved to New Zealand straight out of teachers' college, met and married Vera, then joined her family's haberdashery business in Auckland. He was a tall, thin man with dark silver hair, glasses and a moustache. His wife was small and round. She had a volatile temper and dominated her husband. Her father had been mayor of the town she grew up in and life was proving to be a disappointment for her. She made it clear that she felt the role of mistress at a boys' home was beneath her.

'Mrs Bussau appeared to call the shots, and she was not consistent in her judgments or punishments, and they never seemed to be working to a "big picture" which included the future of the boys under their care as the prime focus,' was Rob's opinion.

As an only child, Rochelle, or Rocky as she was soon known, had led a lonely life; now she found it intimidating to be living among this crowd of noisy boys and young men. The boys saw her as shy and protected. One day David approached her as she sat playing quietly with her building blocks in the corridor outside the Bussaus' quarters at the front of the building. 'What are you making, Rocky?' he asked.

'A house,' she replied. David sat down beside her and helped her make a more elaborate house than she could ever have made herself. He was quiet and gentle, not like some of the boys, who were boisterous and frightening. David also fixed her bike, and soon Rocky sought him out after school and followed him if his chores were indoors. Rocky become the first person in David's life to steal his affection.

Lyn and Vera warily observed this growing friendship as David stepped into the role of big brother to their little girl. They soon realised that his influence was a positive one, that Rocky was happier with David around.

The Bussaus lived in separate quarters at the front of the Sedgley building. Their sitting room had shelves of china knick-knacks and delicate tea sets that could never be considered hardy enough for the rough Sedgley boys to use. Yet the Bussaus started to single David out for attention, and with growing frequency he sat in the Bussaus' sitting room sipping tea from fine bone china and savouring home-baked biscuits with all the refinement he could muster. The warmth of a home was new to David. He enjoyed it, and Rocky frequently hounded her parents to invite David to play with her.

'I think they really wanted Rocky to have a big brother. We got along well, and I liked having a younger sister too,' David said. He was approaching the age when he was expected to go out into the wider world on his own, and the idea of belonging to a family, with some stability and security, appealed to him.

By now he was one of the older boys at Sedgley, and had gained a reputation as a helpful lad, one who didn't bully the younger boys or grumble as he worked. In 1956, his name appeared on the Sedgley Honour Board, right under that of his friend Rob, who had won the award the previous year.

In other ways David was starting to take advantage of new freedoms under the Bussaus. He still attended Wairarapa College—in body rather than spirit—and continued to play cricket and soccer. At sixteen he knew he should be thinking of how he would support himself in the years ahead. Odd jobs would never take him where he wanted to go. One day, on his way to watch a visiting team play his local heroes in soccer, he chanced upon a business that satisfied both his need for an income and his love of sport. People were lining up for hot dogs on their way to the game. 'That's a busy business,' he thought, before approaching the man on the stall with questions about the price and turnover of hot dogs in a night.

'Would you rent me a stall?' David asked. The owner agreed to rent a stall for a day at a time, and soon David was selling hot dogs on commission down at the football ground whenever there was a game. The business thrived under his enthusiastic management, and soon he saw an opening for another stall. He picked up a younger Sedgley boy to work with him. He discovered the thrill of building a business, and his confidence blossomed as he added more stands, using his natural ability in leadership to bring on more boys. 'I must have been reasonably aggressive, because within a few weeks I had two stands, with someone else running one. I ended up with three or four, not working but just organising, within two or three months.' It came naturally and easily to him. He quickly learned to get other people to work with him.

By the next year the Bussaus were ready to move on. Sedgley had only ever been a stopgap position for them, and when a teaching job for Lyn came up in Timaru, on New Zealand's South Island, he took it. Soon after, they pulled David aside. 'We're moving to Timaru. Would you like to come with us?' Lyn asked. David had already isolated himself from the other boys of Sedgley by accepting the Bussaus' favouritism, and even though they resented him for it—'They're not doing you any favours by adopting you,' someone told him—he was ready to make a complete break. He needed to start a new life, and the Bussaus offered him a safety net for the transition from institution to adulthood. David was not concerned about burning his bridges to the past.

David then changed his name by deed poll. It was the first step he had taken to fit in with the Bussaus. He knew he could never truly be part of a family with a different name, but part of him longed to fit in. Besides, the name 'Williams' held no happy family memories; there were no relatives to consider or heritage to preserve. With a new name and family, in a new town, at a new school, he could start afresh. From that point on, David Thomas Williams became David Thomas Bussau.

3

Conquering Hills

Before living with the Bussaus, privacy was something David rarely experienced. Without the clang of a bell for breakfast, the crows of roosters on the farm and the mirthful chatter of a crowd of boys, waking was eerily quiet. Instead of scrambling from his bed to milk the cows or prepare the breakfast or wash the clothes of forty boys, David now rose for breakfast with Lyndsay, Vera and Rocky, the three people he called his family, in an uneasy intimacy.

The move to Timaru, a small coastal town an hour's drive south of Christchurch, was a pleasant change of atmosphere for the Bussaus. As a holiday haven for inland-dwelling South Islanders, Timaru was more relaxed than Masterton. In summer, crowds milled along the boardwalks of Caroline Bay in the twilight hours, licking ice creams and eating greasy fish and chips. Timaru gave Lyn Bussau the chance to work in his chosen vocation, in a private girls' school. The family moved into a rented timber house close to the centre of the town. It had a long drive, a small garden at the back and a paved area at the front where, in the little spare time he had, David amused Rocky with hopscotch and skipping or helping her with her bike.

It should have been ideal. Lyn and Vera were free of the responsibility of forty boys and Rocky still had her favourite big friend to play with. Lyn Bussau had little interest in being a handyman around the house and he welcomed an energetic and capable worker. With their new son so willing to pick up most of the responsibility for mowing the lawn, caring for the gardens and general fix-it jobs, life was easier for the Bussaus.

Yet the domestic ideal soon unravelled. For David, the reality of family life after a decade of self-reliance was much harder than he'd imagined. He was dedicated to Rocky, but found it difficult to form an emotional attachment to his new parents. The relationship felt forced and awkward. He was stumbling towards manhood, and the demands of parents now placed an unwelcome net around him. On reflection, he admitted that he'd seen the Bussaus as a secure route out of the Boys' Home and into the wider world. 'Even though I changed my name to Bussau, it didn't mean there was a good relationship with the Bussaus. I now see it as clutching at straws, being seventeen years old and wanting to be included in a family. It was a very strange relationship.'

In the end, the emotional strain of a fabricated family life was more than he could cope with. Now he was living with Vera and Lyn, the Bussaus' family tensions felt more pronounced to David. The arguments and loose tempers took him back to an earlier time of disharmony in his birth family, to memories he had locked out many years ago. He withdrew into his work and sport. He began to tire of all the Bussaus' demands.

Rocky, though only seven years old, was starting to notice the tenseness of the relationships around her. One bitingly cold Sunday the Bussau family set out in the family car, rugged up against a wind blowing in off the Southern Alps. Sunday drives around the town of Timaru were a delight, a short trip to the nearby escarpment gave clear views of the jagged mountains lining the horizon to the west. On the infrequent clear days, sightseers were rewarded with the pointed tip of Mount Cook rising up above the lesser peaks.

As they motored out of town, Lyn Bussau had a bright idea for an experiment. 'Let's see how far we can go on a gallon of petrol,' he said lightly, knowing there was a container of fuel in the back when the sniff of petrol in the tank ran out. They drove up and down the gravel roads behind Timaru, weaving along the gentle foothills, circling the town for some time before the car let out its last gasp and coasted down a rolling incline. The four sat in the car contemplating the next move.

'David, get out and fill the tank, would you, please?' Lyn asked.

'Sure.' David climbed out and walked around to the boot to collect the spare petrol, his jacket flapping in the cold wind.

'David shouldn't have to do everything, Daddy,' Rocky blurted out when he had gone. 'Why does he do all the jobs?'

'He likes being helpful,' her father replied. At times, he too felt a little guilty.

'But it's not fair,' Rocky said.

'We've given him a home and family. This is his way of repaying us,' Vera cut in. Rocky fumed in the back. She gave David an apologetic smile as he jumped into the back seat beside her, shaking with cold. He smiled back warmly.

Soon after arriving from Masterton, in May 1959, David enrolled at Timaru Boys' High School. At the time, joining school teams seemed the best way to pursue his obsession with soccer and cricket, but as he had no academic aspirations, school soon lost its appeal. Within six months he dropped out, without making a single lasting school friend. He signed his name at the top of his leaving certificate exam paper and left without answering any of the exam questions. At the same time he let go of his childhood dream of becoming a professional soccer player. He had shown some talent in this area. The school paper, the *Timaruvian*, reported at the time, 'Bussau, until he left, was a very keen and skilful player, especially in hard defensive play.' He made it as far as South Canterbury senior regional team, but no further.

With school behind him he busied himself with work, quickly passing through jobs at a hardware firm called England McRae Ltd, the local telephone exchange and a sports store called Hendersons. His only friend was a young Canadian skier he worked with named Don, who was visiting New Zealand during the northern summer. Here he found a kindred spirit, someone who shared his love of sport and his energetic approach to life. During the day he learned to string tennis racquets and fix golf clubs and fishing rods, and on weekends David and Don took off for the Southern Alps, just an hour away, for cross-country skiing.

'I'm going to find something of my own again,' he told Don, explaining how well the quick turnover of the hot dog vending vans had worked for him. 'I'll stick to fast food, something I know.' He started looking in Caroline Bay, the centre of Timaru's summer action. Within days, he approached the Greek owners of a hamburger shop set up in a caravan down by the water. At first he worked for them on weekends.

'Would you sell me your business?' he asked one day. They agreed on a price of £1000, to be paid off in instalments. It was the ideal business for David, giving him a healthy profit in return for long punishing hours. In a few months he sold the hamburger bar and bought a fish and chip caravan along the same board-walk, making a tidy profit from the goodwill he had built. It was a lifestyle that left no time for reflection or loneliness. Every day was filled with work, often eighteen hours each day. Yet once again he lost interest in the business as soon as he was running it smoothly and profitably.

When an opportunity arose for the Bussaus on the North Island, David decided to go his own way. His time with the Bussaus had brought little joy other than his relationship with Rocky, and he decided there was no future in family life. Rocky was devastated when she learned that David was leaving. Losing her brother became a lifelong source of sadness for her.

'Don't worry, Rocky, I'll visit you as soon as I can,' David told her.

'But you won't be living with us any more,' she cried. She would never understand what had happened, and no one ever fully explained it to her. She just knew her parents were upset and didn't want to see David any more.

'That's no way to repay all we've done for you,' she heard her mother Vera tell David angrily as he packed up to move. But David knew he had paid his dues. He wondered whether his com-pensation money had been the reason for Vera and Lyn taking him on, rather than caring for him or wanting a big brother for Rocky.

He sold the fish and chip caravan and walked away with £5000 and a wiser head for business. Early in 1960, when he was nineteen, David moved to Auckland, on New Zealand's North Island, to bigger challenges, and the Bussaus moved to Raglan, a town three hours' drive from Auckland.

Now, fending for himself, for a while he did not even notice his lack of friends or family. Daily survival was his first challenge. He had no thought for the future.

He went through the papers until he found an advertisement about a house in Sandringham, a lower middle-class suburb near the centre of Auckland. 'Lodgers wanted: Family home, all meals provided and washing done. Three pounds per week.' This sounded just about perfect. Betty Jamieson answered the door of the Sandringham house to see David smiling on the other side of the screen door. He was a good-looking man, and not much younger than her.

'Hello, I'm David Bussau. I've come to see the room you've got to let,' he said.

Ron and Betty Jamieson lived quietly with their three young children in a modest three-bedroom house. Ron was an ambitious young man who wanted to own his home by the time he turned twenty five. He and Betty had just started their own business, called Action Uniforms, making uniforms for work and school. They knew taking in boarders would put a strain on the family and their small home, but the extra income would help.

'We'll have three boarders here and only two spare rooms, so I hope two of you won't mind sharing,' Betty told David as he followed her on an inspection of the house. 'The children will be sleeping in the lounge room until we build our extension under the house,' she explained.

'I really don't mind communal living, I've had it most of my life,' he replied, without further explanation. 'I'd like to take the room, please.'

He stayed for a cup of tea, soaking up the welcoming atmosphere of the Jamiesons' kitchen, and as he left gave Betty a warm hug, without a hint of self-consciousness.

David could now turn his mind to his other immediate need, an income. He quickly found a position at a fertiliser factory while he hunted around for another small business to buy. His limited experience told him that the best businesses were those where the vendor loaned him the money to buy them. In this case it was a home cookery or bakery, called 'Busy Bee', in the light industrial Auckland suburb of Newmarket, not far from the Jamiesons.

'I wouldn't say I was strategic about it, lining the businesses up to work out which had the most potential. First of all, it was how much could I afford and whether someone could finance me into it or not. In the first bakehouse I was able to put down a £5000 deposit because the owner wanted to get out quickly. That shaped the decision more than if it was profitable,' David said.

There was only one problem with the Busy Bee bakery. David had no experience of baking. However, he could flip hamburgers and deep-fry fish and chips, and was game to learn anything. His upbringing taught him that he had nothing to lose by taking a risk, and he had worked since the age of nine: farm work at Sedgley, summer jobs at Donald's and the fertiliser factory, in a freezing works, on the wharf as a labourer, and picking fruit and potatoes. At least now that he was working for himself he would reap the rewards.

Still, cooking at the Busy Bee bakery proved a greater challenge than any job David had tried before. The shelves inside the window of the bakehouse were crowded with tempting trays of cakes and pastries. The baking smell inside the shop wrapped a veil of comfort around customers as they made their choices. There were light-as-air sponges weighed down with cream and strawberries, boxy lamingtons with coconut crumbs falling off them, and tarts filled with lemon curd or fruit. There were pies— apple and custard and savoury mince—apricot slices, pavlovas and sausage rolls. David made every product he sold each day, single-handed, with just a shop girl to help with sales.

For the first month the previous owner was on hand to teach him about the business and the indelicate art of cooking in bulk. 'Just throw in a bag of flour and a handful of salt,' his teacher told him. There were shortcuts and tricks to learn, like recycling the stale apple pies into apple crumble. Then he was on his own, filling in his gaps of knowledge. Once, after hours of unsuccessfully trying to perfect lamingtons, he slumped down in the middle of the coconut crumbs and sponge slabs, and cried. Mastering the baking of pavlovas proved just as agonising. He groaned in frustration each time he slid out yet another tray of deflated meringue. Once more the oven temperature was not quite right, even after the heat had come off the oven at the end of the day, and he thought it cool enough to slide in his trays of egg white whipped with castor sugar. For now he was defeated, but under his breath he vowed, 'Tomorrow, I'll nail this one.'

David worked from four in the morning until six in the evening. When the bakery finally closed its doors, he was often exhausted to collapsing point. Yet there was always another plan. This was one of David's talents: an eye for spotting opportunities. One day in conversation over dinner with the Jamiesons, he told them, 'I'm going to expand into the catering business. There are offices and shops around Newmarket and no one to cater to them.' It wasn't long before he was out delivering quiches and platters of freshly made sandwiches to boardrooms and functions in the area and beyond. He pushed himself hard, and never stopped to consider whether or not he actually enjoyed the work.

The Jamiesons were equally busy raising three children, looking after their lodgers and overseeing a now thriving business. Betty wore herself down to the bone, often rocking her baby with one foot as she ironed, with tears of exhaustion running down her cheeks. Their hard work paid off—they were later to own a large factory and a rural retreat outside the city.

The Jamiesons were more of a family to David than anyone he had known, and they were the only camaraderie he had at the time. David and Ron spent hours watching and discussing soccer. At the end of the work day, David relaxed by playing with the Jamieson boys or picking up a saw and hammer to help Ron with chores.

Being a loner hadn't bothered David at all until now, but despite the frantic pace of his business, he became aware of a void where there should have been friends. Besides that, there was a strong spiritual pull. He had never lost that sense of having a spiritual father, of the spiritual relationship which had sustained him in his childhood loneliness. He now missed that dimension of his life. 'I always had that sense of a God as my father, that I had a destiny, that there was someone looking after me, although I probably didn't verbalise or intellectualise it.'

He looked for friends and soon found them. In 1962, at the age of twenty two, he went back to his Anglican roots, to St Chad's at Sandringham. St Chad's had a lively youth group of thirty people whose social lives revolved around Friday night gatherings, dances and weekends away at Simkin House on Waiheke Island, a retreat an hour and a half away by boat on Auckland Harbour. David appeared one Sunday at St Chad's and plunged straight into a planning meeting for the group.

One young girl in particular was in the meeting that day, and took an immediate interest in the newcomer. She thought he was strikingly handsome with his intense blue eyes, crooked teeth, and a swathe of straight brown hair swept to one side. His looks and athletic physique combined to give him a quiet presence. Though he came across as reserved, he was brimming with confidence and ideas, a natural leader who was not afraid to speak his mind in a room full of strangers. Carol Crowder's first feelings about David were confused. She was indignant that he was dominating their group, miffed that he appeared to be taking over their planning.

'Who does he think he is, coming and telling us what to do?' Carol leaned over and whispered into the ear of her best friend, Sherryl Riggs. But secretly she was impressed by his boldness.

Carol did not escape David's attention either. She stood out to him as sweet and feminine. She was tall and slender, with soft grey eyes and wavy brown hair cut short.

'I saw a degree of sincerity and integrity in her. I don't know if we were compatible at that time, but on reflection we were both very accepting of other people,' David remembered.

Carol and Sherryl were like sisters. They were both tall, they lived in the same neighbourhood, and attended the same school, and each summer Sherryl spent holidays with Carol's family at the beach near Mount Manganui. For several years they'd both taught Sunday School and been part of the choir at St Chad's. After school on Friday the girls dolled themselves up in their best dresses and starched petticoats to work as junior shopgirls at the flagship Farmer's Department Store downtown on Queen Street. Carol's father, Norm, had put in a good word for them. He was general manager of a division of the company that produced heavy-duty footwear for soldiers and factory workers.

Carol's interests and upbringing were the opposite of David's. As an only child Carol had enjoyed a lifetime of individual attention, something David had known little of, and she put enormous effort into her friendships. Her good friends allowed her to unlock her imagination in a way she could not do on her own, through concerts and tap dancing and making costumes. Music filled the Crowder house, mostly the Dixieland and cabaret her father played on the piano in dance halls around Auckland.

Carol was not well when she first met David, at the age of eighteen. At fourteen, as she and her parents stood waiting for a taxi alongside other weary families after a busy day at the Auckland Easter Show, Carol had blacked out. Her legs folded to the side and she slumped to the ground before she had time to call out or grab an arm to break her fall.

Phyllis Crowder screamed when she saw her daughter's body lying crumpled on the gravel verge with blood flowing from a gash over her eyebrow. She and Norm rushed to Carol's side, leaning over her to feel for a pulse and signs of consciousness. When Carol came around she was dazed and confused, and Norm scooped her up and into a taxi to their home, where the family doctor treated her. In the following days, doctors in the hospital carried out a series of tests and diagnosed epilepsy.

Despite medication, Carol's seizures continued, and by the age of eighteen had escalated in frequency and seriousness. Increasingly, her illness was affecting her ability to do the things she loved, like singing in the choir or going dancing with her friends. Carol was embarrassed and bewildered by her epilepsy, and did everything she could to hide it. The close friends who knew about Carol's seizures often covered for her. 'She had to go home; she's not feeling well,' Sherryl would explain after Carol had left a party or youth group meeting.

When David met Carol it was just before the height of her epileptic fits. She was in her second year at Epsom Teachers' College in Auckland. David was twenty two and fully occupied in his bakery business. At first glance the pair appeared to have little in common. Carol had no interest in sport and was not athletic herself; nor did she understand business. Yet over the months of group gatherings the two were increasingly drawn to each other.

38

They found they shared a love of children. Carol later met Rocky on one her visits to Auckland to see David, and on several occasions went with David down to Raglan, bringing gifts of the latest magazines.

One day David gathered the courage to take Carol out alone, arriving at the Crowders' door and barely slowing down to greet her parents before they went out driving in his blue Bedford bakery van. David saw something special in this girl. For a start, she was accepting of him and didn't seem to want to change him. She knew the art of making deep and loyal friendships, and the value of these relationships. He noticed the care and love she poured into those around her, and how that warmth and affection extended so naturally to him. It brought a new and intriguing dimension to his life, lived for all these years with few close bonds. David was not put off by Carol's illness for a moment. He learned to ignore it, perhaps because he didn't really understand it.

David wasn't the only one setting his mind on a match. Carol's mother, Phyllis, had David pegged from the first day she met him.

'Keep an eye on him, Norm. That's the man Carol's going to marry,' she confided to her husband after the couple left that night. She watched them grow closer over the following months: she saw David's warmth as he stood watching Carol play the piano, the glow in his eyes when he arrived to see her. Phyl felt happy and peaceful about this man who was winning the heart of her only child.

Once the courting process started, David was out the door and around the corner to Carol's house the moment dinner finished at the Jamiesons'. Soon after, David moved from the Jamiesons' to the 'Boys' Flat', a two-bedroom apartment nearby with a reputation as the place to hang out for parties and meals, no invitation needed. Three lads shared the flat, and David shared a room with Bruce Fuller, who was slightly older than him. The men talked as brothers about girls, jobs, life. David had talked about a family outside Auckland and Bruce assumed it was his own family. David never mentioned the Boys' Home in their long talks.

David and Carol met with their circle of friends at dance halls buzzing with crowds of fresh-faced young people from across

Auckland. They danced the evenings away to big band swing music and the early rock and roll of Bill Haley and the Comets. The women were decked out in full dresses with barely concealed stiff petticoats, and the men wore tight pants and pointy shoes, their hair slicked with oil and flicked back for full effect. Later, the Beatles captured their imaginations and they bopped to *A Hard Day's Night* and *She Loves Me*.

The following year Carol's health deteriorated further. She had always set herself high standards. She was musically and academically talented, and worked hard in college (and at school before that), often fretting over the quality of her work, even when it was well beyond her teachers' expectations. She was sensitive to tension between people and had a level of perception well beyond the physical.

It seemed, through this intense time, that business was David's first love and Carol his second, although she never complained. Things came to a head one night when David and Carol were joining a group of friends at a ball downtown. Carol dressed in her long silk gown, styled her hair and slid into her satin shoes. By seven in the evening she was ready and waiting, looking forward to the night ahead.

The phone rang. 'I'll be a bit late, I'm just getting ready. Shouldn't be long,' David told Carol.

'See you soon,' she replied. She sat on the sofa in the lounge room of the Crowder home, sure that David would knock on the door at any minute. She was still waiting at 7.30, and growing increasingly anxious.

'It's fine, darling, I'm sure he'll be here soon,' her mother reassured her but Carol's heart steadily sank.

Then the phone rang again.

'Sorry, Carol. I couldn't stay awake. I'll be there in a minute,' David promised. She perked up and sat waiting. When he had not arrived an hour later she peeled off her gloves, sad and resigned.

'Give it a few more minutes,' Phyl said, trying hard to keep Carol's hopes alive.

'He's not coming, Mum. He's fallen asleep again,' Carol replied. She was disappointed and hurt, though she would never reveal this to David.

Finally, after three calls to Carol and two hours late, David summoned the energy for his night out and arrived at the door with a bunch of pink roses. He felt bad about being unreliable. He needed to do something about it.

In long conversations with his roommate, Bruce Fuller sensed David's nervousness about making a commitment to one girl. In recent weeks, David had backed off a little in his relationship with Carol and had even escorted other girls to the movies. Bruce took it upon himself to hurry the process along. One Saturday he phoned Carol and asked her to see a movie with him.

'Bruce, I like you very much, but I don't think so,' she replied politely.

'Carol, I know that David will be going to the Civic with someone else this evening so why don't you come with me and show him you don't care? Let's see what his reaction is,' Bruce suggested.

That night, Bruce and Carol sat in clear view of David and his date, and Bruce later made a point of telling David how much he enjoyed the evening. The plan worked to perfection.

On 22 February 1964, David took Carol for a hike up the volcanic outcrop of Mount Manganui, the place of her fondest childhood memories, several hours' drive from the city. Part of the way up to the conical peak they stopped to survey the foamy waves of the surf beach in one direction and boats lined up in the harbour in another.

The time was right. David took a deep breath. 'I suppose we should get married or something, he blurted out.' Clearly, he had not given much thought to his words, but he was now sure of this step. Their love had grown slowly and naturally. This moment was merely an extension of the journey. Still, the question surprised Carol. It took a few moments before she replied, 'I'd love to.'

The rest of the day was filled with talk of their marriage. They agreed that out of respect David should approach Norm for Carol's hand in marriage, and as soon as possible.

The following week David came to the Crowder home and found Norm in the kitchen, sitting at the kitchen table with a glass of whisky in his hand. 'Norm, I'd like to marry your daughter.'

David was polite but firm. There was not a hint of nerves. For him, it was just protocol.

Norm stood, glared at David, and said flatly: 'Like bloody hell!' Then he stormed out of the kitchen, across the back lawn and up the path towards his vegetable garden, leaving David stunned. David may have inspired love in Carol's mum over the months of courtship but, as he now discovered, it would take her father longer to come to terms with the idea of marriage for his little girl.

Phyl followed Norm out the back door and reassured him, 'He's the one for her.' She knew Carol could thrive with David. Within minutes Norm was back in the kitchen and asked David, 'Do you really mean it? Well, let us think about it.' It was Norm's way of dealing with change: a short panic before settling on a course of action.

This should have been the happiest and most carefree time in Carol's life. At nineteen, she had everything in her favour: a man who adored her and whom she would marry within months, a close circle of friends, parents who doted on her, a promising career. With medication, her seizures were now under control. In her rational mind, there was not one thing to be worried about but it was all about to come crashing down.

One Friday evening, while working at Farmers, Carol stood at the top of the ten-storey airwell which plunged through the centre of the building. Inexplicably she was drawn to the cavern below her and overcome with desire to throw herself down and fly to the bottom. It was a momentary fancy, but powerful enough to rock her to her core. She pulled back, shaken, frightened by the seductive force of her thoughts.

The next week she snapped. She fell into a deep sleep that lasted for two days, and when she finally awoke she was unable to function. Her parents could only sit by, panic-stricken and helpless, awaiting the outcome of their daughter's emotional freefall. It was the end of her life as she had known it. She was suddenly frail and incapacitated. For months, even the routine activities of shopping or going down to St Chad's with her friends or singing in the choir became an ordeal beyond her capability. It would be several years before she could return to teaching.

The reasons for this illness were never clear. Though later she would learn it was an episode of serious depression, at the time doctors could not explain what was happening to her. It could have been her acutely sensitive nature, or that her high expectations of herself to succeed became more than she could bear. She had certainly found it hard work trying to conceal her seizures from those around her and lead a normal life as a teacher.

Other phobias soon crept into her psyche. At train stations she was mesmerised, drawn to the trains as they screamed into the station, and she fought the sensation of wanting to throw herself at them. The fear that she would do it left her paralysed as a train sped by. Sleep became her escape from reality, the place where she retreated when she could no longer reach out or face her fears.

Phyl was vigilant for any sign that Carol might harm herself. She had no idea what to expect and it was hard to pin the doctors down to answers. Each time Carol stepped out the door with her friends Phyl was on edge with the fear that her daughter would not return. She was only at ease when Carol was with David.

Carol's sickness brought out qualities Phyl had not yet seen in her future son-in-law. He was patient and attentive to her needs, calling at the Crowder household most days after work. When he took her out, he helped her over any difficulties or embarrassment. Instinctively, he knew how to ease Carol's suffering.

There were few outward signs of Carol's illness. On one visit to her psychiatrist, an associate of the specialist asked Carol and her mother 'Now, which one of you is sick?' She looked the picture of good health. Few around her understood or knew the extent of her illness. There was an undercurrent of 'Pull yourself together, girl', although no one ever said that to her face. A minister told her mother, 'She just needs a jolly good spanking.' Those around her gradually found out that she was ill, and while most were empathetic and supportive, she still felt embarrassed.

After two years in the bakery business, and with a growing richness in his personal life, David was ready to conquer the next hill. He sold the Busy Bee bakery for £30,000, six times what he'd bought it for three years before, and used the proceeds to buy his fifth small business, Betta pancakes and pikelets.

Trading up was now familiar territory to David. Once again, he asked himself, 'Here's a business—how do I make money?' He was steadily increasing his wealth by picking up the margins on the goodwill that he built into each business. 'It was never going to be a life's work, I just wanted to make a few thousand pounds on the way. I always put money into upgrading equipment, and made money on goodwill when I sold it.'

David was forever looking at ways to increase production, improve efficiency and find new markets. It didn't take him long to work out a strategy for the new business. If he could automate the production process he could make enough pancakes and pikelets to sell his product under other brand names.

Carol's uncle, Dud Crowder, was an engineer and David asked him to design a pikelet-making machine. He came up with a big hopper that travelled over a three metre long hotplate and squirted out either pancakes or pikelets. Once David perfected this process he took out the global rights to the pancake maker. He now had to find new ways of selling his product. He approached the two largest bakers in New Zealand, Tip Top and Fielders, and contracted with them to make and package his products under their names. He then built up a distribution network with the supermarkets, placing his products across the country under many different names. He was able to spin the distribution off into a separate company, which he sold so that he could concentrate on manufacturing.

He found a market in the South Sea Islands and before long he was up cooking at 2 am so his baked goods could be on a 5 am flight to the island of Noumea in the Pacific Ocean and fresh on the shelves before breakfast. He worked so hard he couldn't function, at times collapsing on sacks of flour during the day to catch a short sleep. Again, David was doing most of the work himself, only employing help to turn the pancakes over on the griddle, and to package and label them.

He visited up to fifty bakery businesses in a day to make deliveries. On one early morning delivery run his insane hours caught up with him as he was driving down a hill in his van. Failing to see a pothole in the road, he veered to miss it and came to a sudden stop when he ploughed into a lamp post. Not all his food was packaged, and hundreds of fresh pancakes and pikelets rained down on him from behind his seat.

It took two years for the challenge to go out of that business and by then David had divided Betta into three separate companies, one of which included the worldwide patent rights to his pancake-making machine, which he sold to three buyers at a substantial profit. He had established a career pattern of entering into a business or project with no experience, learning it (by making mistakes), mastering and then improving it, and moving on. There would never be any dwelling on failures or clinging to triumphs. Life was a continual march forward.

David and Carol's engagement was a time of joy and anguish. Phyl and Norm were not sure Carol was well enough to go through with the wedding. Carol was able to function but not at her peak. She still had good and bad days. She alternated between crying and sleeping, and wondered how David could go along so steadily, never losing his temper or making her feel guilty.

Carol's psychiatrist was clear about the best cure for her illness. Heavy medication had tamed her seizures and depression but left her subdued. At one point he feared she would be dosed with the sedative Mogadon for the rest of her life. He knew that, somehow, this fellow David was a positive influence on her. It crossed his mind that David's care could hold the key to Carol's future health.

'She should get married. It's the best thing for her now,' he told the Crowders.

Carol had her own fears about making it through a day in which all eyes would be on her. She had always shied away from that sort of attention. When she voiced her concerns to her psychiatrist, he was firm. 'You'll get married if I have to drag you down the aisle.'

So that was it. The date was set for 8 May 1965. She and David would marry at St Chad's, among close friends and family. There was no question of who would be alongside her that day as chief bridesmaid. Carol knew she couldn't get through the wedding without Sherryl.

Love was in the air. Even before David arrived in Carol's life, Sherryl had met the man she would marry, Alex Wilson, and her wedding was to follow David and Carol's within weeks. Carol would be there as chief bridesmaid. There was much to look forward to, if only she could rise above her illness. David had no doubts. 'I didn't even factor her illness in or think about it. I loved her and that was it.'

Building Foundations

The days and weeks before the wedding put everyone to the test. When Carol tired of making choices about which lace would suit her dress or if she should have lilies or roses in her bouquet, she just lay down and slept. Some days she couldn't raise any interest at all in the arrangements, so strong were the sedatives the psychiatrist had given her.

The wedding dress proved problematic. Carol's fear of trains and their mesmerising effect on her was so powerful that she became immobilised whenever she heard the clatter of steel on tracks. The trains' vibrations brought a dread so deep that she stood petrified, glued to the floor until the train passed and she could breathe again. The dressmaker's home was across town and couldn't be reached without passing through a long tunnel over which the trains clack-clacked every few minutes, so each fitting was a nightmare for both Carol and her mother—it seemed they could never make the journey without encountering a train.

To make matters worse, the psychiatrist ordered Phyl to expose Carol to her worst fears, to stand and watch as train after train passed by until she was no longer afraid. So they set out for Kingsland station, where Phyl led Carol, who was sick with anticipation, down the stairs to the concrete platform. Its spare wooden benches and tin awnings for shelter were benign enough until Carol heard the rumble of a distant train. Then she panicked.

'Mum, don't make me do this,' she pleaded. Phyl would have relented had she not been desperate to help Carol overcome her phobia. The doctor's plan was unsuccessful. He had now run out of ways to help her.

David was unshakeable through Carol's trauma. He approached marriage in the same way as business: he was going to jump in and work it out as he went along. He knew there would be mistakes—there always were—but he would learn from them.

Phyl was becoming a mother to David. She made him the sweets he loved and fussed over him. It was a degree of attention he had never experienced. Phyl could see that he loved her daughter in a complete way, through the hardships and good times, so how could she not love him? But secretly, she feared he would not be able to cope with the dark early years. She told Norm, 'If David left I wouldn't blame him.'

The invitations went out the obligatory six weeks before the wedding. David was not surprised when the Bussaus declined the invitation. There had been only sporadic visits, mainly to see Rocky, and David once took Carol down to meet them. Still, David and Carol had both hoped Rocky would come as part of the wedding party. She was fifteen years old, almost a woman, and she loved the idea of dressing up and being on centre stage for such a big occasion, but it was not to be. The Bussaus not only forbade Rocky from coming to the wedding; they demanded she cut off all contact with David. It was a painful break. David respected the Bussaus' decision not to be there but found it much harder to understand why they would not allow Rocky to come.

By the time the wedding day came around, Carol was beyond panic. Her psychiatrist had given her a high enough dose of sedative to allay any seizures, and even offered to come along himself. The drugs took the emotional edge off the day. She looked serene and radiant. Her wide grey eyes were peaceful, and joy shone through the dullness. Her smile was broad and frequent. David stood at the end of the aisle looking proud. No one could have guessed at the torment and effort that had gone into getting Carol to the altar.

At the end of the day, Phyl was more relieved than elated. She had prodded, pulled and almost carried her daughter into her wedding and when Carol and David were on their honeymoon, she slumped into her own exhaustion.

Within a few days David and Carol had made their way down to the South Island of New Zealand in David's bakery van, meandering from Nelson to Christchurch and through the peaks of the Southern Alps to Queenstown, then up the rugged west coast by the glacial lakes of Milford Sound. They were ecstatic to be finally married, but it was far from a carefree start to their lives together. The illness hung like a dark cloud over Carol's days and she seemed powerless against it. 'Depression can be so terrible it's almost impossible to climb out. There is a self-centred element to the illness, where you're not capable of thinking how people around you are affected. It's like you're stuck at the bottom of a grey pit, and you have to be pulled out because you can't get out yourself,' she later reflected. There were times when Carol quietly wept as they drove.

'I'm sorry,' she would apologise, as she struggled to pull herself from the abyss. She felt guilty that her new husband had to endure her ups and downs.

There was no chance of Carol teaching; her illness would not allow it. Yet she knew she would never regain her health sitting at home alone while David worked long hours. She decided to find a job that would not tax her mentally or emotionally but would give her social stimulation and occupy her time. She found work in a hairspray factory, screwing the lids onto canisters. It was mindless and undemanding work, and just what she needed. Though her parents were not wealthy, she had led a comfortable middle-class life. The experience of factory work opened her mind and heart to working-class reality. She found the girls she worked with kind and accepting.

In the first months of marriage Carol steadily withdrew from social functions for fear that she would collapse or make a fool of herself when confronted with one of her phobias. As Carol became lonelier, David worked harder. In response, Carol's doctors recommended a complete break from their environment, time away from friends and family and routine. David had also reached this conclusion. He did not understand the psychology behind Carol's illness, but he instinctively knew that she could learn to be more independent and function again. He was concerned that she would believe the doctors who told her she would be drug dependent for life.

David decided that they should go to Sydney—the first stop for many young New Zealanders in their journeys abroad—and booked two berths on the *Oriental Queen* for January 1966. He believed that in Australia Carol would be free of the nagging anxiety that friends would discover how sick she was. Carol was too doped-up to fight the decision. She would go along with whatever David thought was best.

Sherryl had been beside Carol through the most terrifying moments of her illness. 'A change of scenery will be good for you,' she told Carol, but deep down it was a painful wrench to let go of her dearest friend; it was almost as hard for her as it was for Norm and Phyl. 'We'll be back soon,' Carol told them, thinking of this trip as a short holiday. The newly married Bussaus had bought a strikingly beautiful few acres of native bushland at Titirangi, outside Auckland. They planned to return to New Zealand to build their dream home when Carol's health improved.

To Carol, leaning against the timber rail of the boat as it sailed out of Auckland Harbour, their departure had a sense of unreality. She was detached from it all, an observer of the tears, the sad waves. Beside her, his arm protectively around her shoulder, David found it hard to feel any sadness. In his mind he had already moved on—he was already out to sea and staring past the horizon. He had left nothing behind.

Within hours the break from New Zealand appeared to be working—the three-day voyage was filled with new people, games and laughter.

David had sold his businesses before leaving New Zealand. The new owner of the pancake business agreed to pay in instalments, so David was accumulating a nest egg at home. He and Carol invested some of the proceeds in the Titirangi land and kept a modest amount for their arrival in Sydney. For the first two weeks they stayed in a hotel in Kings Cross, then found a flat to settle into at Rose Bay, not far from the water. Within days David had swung into his characteristic industriousness. He rose before dawn to deliver papers then grabbed a quick breakfast at home before leaving again for labouring jobs around the city. He spent evenings in the living room stringing tennis racquets he collected from sports stores, sometimes as many as fifty at a time.

One day as David perused the employment section of the paper an advertisement caught his eye. A building company was looking for a foreman. 'I could do that,' he thought, without considering his lack of experience. He knew nothing about construction, other than the bits and pieces he had learned along the way at Sedgley, but he knew he could learn just about anything by watching people.

The next day he arrived on a building site to meet the boss, a small, nuggety man named Jack Ginnery, who bore the nickname 'Skeeta', from 'mosquito'. Skeeta was a rough and ready plasterer who had moved into general building. In his younger days he had played rugby league for Eastern Suburbs, but he wasn't a typical hard, football-playing man. He was kind and generous and spent his spare hours helping the elderly in his community through the local church. Skeeta and David clicked, and David found himself working in construction, an entirely new field.

Within months of moving to Sydney, David had a chance encounter with one of the few people in the world he could call an old friend. He and Carol were out shopping at Bondi Junction, in Sydney's Eastern Suburbs, when Rob, David's childhood friend from Sedgley, appeared in front of him. Beside him was an attractive blonde woman David recognised as Diane, the girl Rob had been dating at Wairarapa College when the boys were at Sedgley.

'Dave? What a surprise! What are you doing here?' Rob asked.

'I moved over this year. I'm working in construction,' David responded.

Rob and Di had arrived in Sydney not long before the Bussaus. Rob had worked his way through an engineering degree in Christchurch, with some help from a Masterton businessman, and at times bluffing his way into good jobs in his holidays. David was not surprised to hear how well Rob had done.

In the course of their conversation Carol and Di discovered they shared a birthday, 11 October, and they soon bonded in friendship. Over the next few years they met frequently, and when they had their first children, each couple chose the other as god-parents.

Rob was surprised to hear how David had stepped into his first building job as foreman on an expensive Eastern Suburbs house renovation. Confused, he asked, 'How did you get the job? Did you work in building in Auckland?' As an engineer, Rob was meticulous about the experience of the person he chose as foreman on any site.

'No, the bloke just gave it to me. He asked me, "You reckon you can do the job?" and I said, "Yes",' David replied. 'Then I shot down to the library and read all these books on building.'

Rob laughed, 'But didn't he guess you weren't trained?'

'No, not at all. Really, it isn't that hard. It's just organising a few guys,' David said in his understated manner.

This was true. To David it didn't seem like a job that needed qualifications. These were skills that could easily be absorbed by watching how others went about it, or through trial and error. It was like rallying the boys at Sedgley: just a matter of pulling everyone together and working out who would take on each job. He was starting to view his orphanage years as the best training in life he could have had. Later, he would joke, 'I was born with a silver spoon in my mouth. No parents to worry me and no relatives to be on my case all the time.'

Jack Ginnery soon discovered that his new foreman was an exceedingly useful fellow. He would give anything a go. If there was simple electrical work, like disconnecting cables, or straightforward plumbing to be done, David would dive in and do it, working it out as he went. Not only that, David was also in a position to help Jack out of a sticky situation. Some time earlier, Jack's accountant had duped him out of money and left him battling bankruptcy. Now Jack could only work on small jobs because he was forced to pay cash for all materials. David was able to set up a line of credit through which to buy supplies so the pair could take on larger jobs. This led to an early partnership and an expanded business. Later, David took over the company.

When they arrived in Sydney, one of Carol and David's first tasks was to find a spiritual home, a place where they could worship each Sunday. They tried a church near their flat in the Eastern Suburbs but found it cold and unwelcoming. At work, David discovered that Jack Ginnery was involved in an active church, the Waverley Methodist Mission on Oxford Street in Bondi Junction.

The next Sunday the Bussaus were welcomed warmly at Waverley. Before long, this group became their Australian family, the people who would see them through thick and thin in the years ahead. This church would become the launching pad for both David and Carol's lifetime work, and the place where they would grapple with finding their place in the world and in ministry.

The Waverley church was one of the most active in the area. Its clubs and programs for each age group satisfied David and Carol's shared desire to help out in their community and, before they knew it, most weekends and weeknights were consumed by community activities. Jack Ginnery soon enlisted the Bussaus on Saturday nights to help with a group for older members of the community—the Evergreens. David became the bus driver and collected elderly people from their homes around the Bondi area for what was often their only outing of the week. Once at the hall they were offered dinner and entertained with amateur music and theatre. Jack Ginnery's training as a plasterer was put to good use as he laughed and joked with his older friends and served out generous ladles of jelly as indelicately as he applied plaster. 'Here you go, dear,' he would say cheerfully as he slapped the bowl down in front of an older lady. Little did she know that the same buckets were washed and back on the building site on Monday.

On Friday nights they gathered young people for 'The Junction Club', a night of billiards, games and supper. On weekends they hired buses to collect young boys from a local home to go for hikes and picnics outside the city, or took up to thirty elderly people from the aged care home for tea and coffee in the bushlands of a local national park.

The activities proved to be just what Carol needed to help her climb outside her own despair. She felt a little better each day and when a sister church in Paddington set up a small kindergarten, she could finally put her teacher training to use. Yet a great sadness hung over her: she was still far from well enough to have her own children, and there was no telling when, or if, she would ever be free of her dependence on medication.

By now David was twenty six years old and had already put in more than a decade of hard work. He was itching to explore the world, spurred on by the tales of Dale and Eric Nyback, a Canadian couple he and Carol had become friends with in Sydney. Carol, in contrast, had much less inclination to leave Sydney; for her it was already a big step away from Auckland. She was still finding her feet under the veil of medication. Reluctantly she agreed to travel, and midway through 1967 the two couples set out for Naples by boat, in the Lloyd Triestino Line's *Marconi*. They crammed into a four-berth cabin at the bow of the ship to save money. A two-week voyage to Naples via Hong Kong and Singapore became a six-week journey when the boat was turned around at the Suez Canal, and had to backtrack down the east coast of the African continent and around the Cape of Good Hope.

It was an excruciating setback for David. Two weeks of mindless leisure would test him but six weeks on a boat, with its limited activities and lack of opportunities to build something, anything, was almost unbearable. He simply could not join Carol in quietly reading, day in and day out. Each morning he rose to jog around the boat; he repeated the ritual in the evening. In the long hours between jogs he swam up and down the pool, went skeet shooting, or found another passenger to compete with at table tennis in the games room. He had to stay busy. To keep his sanity, he threw himself into every activity on offer over the six weeks they were at sea. If there was to be a fancy hat parade in the evening, David would spend the entire day fashioning the most elaborate of hats. At least that way he was employing some of the creativity that paced inside him.

Each morning David and Carol sat down in the common room for Italian lessons. In six weeks they could learn enough Italian to arrive with a workable knowledge of the language. Later, when David's work took him on frequent visits to Latin America, the basics of Italian he learned on this trip helped him quickly adjust to Spanish.

In Naples the two couples bought an old car and set off around Europe in the manner of countless young colonials, stopping in hostels housed in broken-down castles set high in the Alps, living and eating as cheaply as they could to eke out their limited finances. By his own admission David was the worst of travellers, always wanting to be on the move to the next activity. 'We've seen the leaning tower of Pisa, let's move on. What's the next city?' He had a fine eye for detail when it came to building but his excess energy and need to keep moving would not allow him to slow down and soak up the finer points of European culture.

In Paris the Bussaus and Nybacks parted company and the Nybacks flew home to Canada. The Bussaus gave their car to the owner of the small hotel they had stayed in and flew to London, where as New Zealanders they could both work. By now their savings were running low, and they knew they had to earn some money if they were to make it to Canada, which was what they had planned to do. In England David worked in a joinery as a carpenter, then in a boring job in a bread factory, standing at the end of a machine watching the dough come out.

Carol found employment in a sweets factory, hand-wrapping Easter eggs and other treats, and for the first time came face to face with bigotry. 'There were a lot of Indian girls and the way the management treated those girls was disgusting. They were so racist and horrible to them. They didn't speak to me like that but they didn't like me much because I liked the Indian girls.'

They had planned to emigrate to Canada—Carol would teach at a school in the town of Prince Rupert in northern British Columbia and David would work in construction—but their resolve soon faded when they realised how isolated it would be tucked up under the cold panhandle of Alaska. It seemed smarter to keep travelling and find their way back to the familiarity of Australia. They returned via Japan just as winter reached its coldest point, and then travelled through the Philippines—this was in the early years of the Marcos regime. The poverty of Manila distressed Carol but she found a warmth in Asia that she hadn't experienced in Europe, and she was touched by the friendliness of the people she met in the hostels. She had no idea at the time how closely she and David would be tied to this country.

By the time they arrived back in Sydney, David and Carol had exhausted their finances and needed to start work immediately. Within days David resumed his building business and they found a flat within a short walk of the water at Rose Bay. Carol set off to town in search of work, not knowing what she wanted or would have the confidence to do. She wandered past the clothes shops and jewellery stores of Pitt Street, then turned the corner into Market Street. Retail was daunting. She was not suited to hard sales. She hit George Street and saw Dymocks, one of the largest bookstores in the city. She immediately felt comfortable among the crisp paper smells and the rows of interesting-looking titles. She thought it would be wonderful to work among them. Then, as if she had said the words out loud, the store manager told her an employee had just left and she could have a job that day if she wanted it. She was thrilled to be easing back into the working world and stayed at Dymocks for 18 months, until she felt ready to return to her chosen career of teaching. Her first job back, teaching a primary school class at Rose Bay Public School, was a nightmare, with an unruly class of spoiled children. 'I found out the teacher I replaced had left with a breakdown and here I was recovering from one.'

With each step in David and Carol's lives together their roots were growing deeper into Australian soil and their ties to New Zealand were loosening, though Carol still spoke to Sherryl and her parents at least once a week. David's business prospects were far brighter in Sydney than they would have been in Auckland, and they had let go of the dream to settle in Titirangi. By early 1969, when the joyful news came through that Carol was pregnant, they had decided that their future was in Australia.

They had many close friends in Sydney. While David built a warm mateship with Jack Ginnery, Carol grew closer to Jack's sister Ruth Moss, her teenage daughter Elizabeth and their boarder, Di Buckley. The Moss family—Ruth, her husband Alf and Elizabeth—had for many years lived in a big old home across the road from Centennial Park, a vast parkland with duck ponds and bicycle tracks, horse tracks and wide green spaces. Close to what are now some of Sydney's most populated and expensive suburbs, each weekend it sucked up crowds of Sydneysiders looking for relaxation and open air. The Moss' boarder, Di Buckley, became one of Carol's dearest friends.

The Randwick side of Centennial Park was decidedly unfashionable in the 1960s, with its rows of homes built in the Federation style, so named because it marked the birth of the Australian nation in 1901. At that point in Australia's history the new and modern was valued more than the old. Victorian cottages, Federation homes and mansions were going under the bulldozer all over Sydney to make way for boxy apartment buildings made of bricks in the bright reds of the Australian desert, with small windows and balconies.

Alf Moss ran a corner store at Edgecliff called 'the friendly store', a neighbourhood gathering place. He was a strong, hardworking man who had been stationed in Darwin during World War II, and was one of the Australian soldiers sent into Japan for the clean-up after the nuclear bombs destroyed Hiroshima and Nagasaki in 1945.

One Sunday the Moss family invited David and Carol over for a party at their home. After lunch Alf pulled David aside. 'Dave, why don't we check out the old house two doors along? It's up for sale.' That was the last any of the guests saw of David for the afternoon.

When he reappeared, he and Carol were the proud owners of a garish maroon and mustard-painted Federation home on a large block of land right opposite the park, for $26,000. David soon divided the rambling house into three small apartments. 'I always had a sense of getting rid of debt pretty quickly. When I bought the house I had three mortgages and was paying thirty per cent interest. I'd paid it off within a couple of years. I didn't like the idea of owing people money. Even in business I'd pay people's bills pretty quickly.'

Over the following weeks and months, David and a fast-expanding Carol worked their way through each room, repairing walls and floorboards, painting, and finally adding their own decorative touches. The Darley Road home would become a hub in years to come: a place of work, a haven for foreign visitors, a refuge for the disenfranchised, and an early home to the Australian end of a global aid organisation.

The Moss and Bussau families now lived two doors apart and enjoyed a relationship that was more kin than friend. Sadly, Alf Moss had been sick for many years. Like most of those exposed to the rays of the atomic bomb, the invisible killer—radiation— seeped into Alf's body and ever so slowly, over thirty years, sapped the life from him through insidious diseases. Still, he managed to keep his little store going for twenty three years before it became too much for him to handle.

As Alf's sickness progressed, David became the handyman who would help with anything from renovating the house to changing a lightbulb. In later years, when David travelled most of the year, Ruth waited patiently for David's return, sometimes for weeks, to have her lightbulbs fixed. It was a kindness that was readily reciprocated. Ruth stood by Carol through her loneliest times and barely a day passed without contact between the two women.

When Di Buckley married Garry Cairncross, the family extended again, and the Bussau and Cairncross children grew up as cousins. Over the years, no one ever asked David about his background. 'It never came into the picture. You didn't delve,' said Garry Cairncross.

Natasha, David and Carol's first-born, arrived on 29 October 1969. David was almost twenty nine and Carol twenty five.

'What if the medication has affected the baby?' Carol asked David in the last weeks of the pregnancy. This concern had worried her for weeks.

'It'll be all right,' he reassured her. Yet she still worried as the labour pains grew stronger and stronger. When she arrived at the Crown Street Hospital the contractions suddenly stopped.

The threat of induction was enough to bring back the contractions and the pain of childbirth soon engulfed her fears. The hospital had only just started allowing fathers into the delivery suite, and David was not going to miss out. He fussed over Carol as she laboured, badgering the nursing staff for updates on her progress. As Natasha appeared, complete and healthy, the couple shed tears of relief.

David never doubted his ability to be a good father. He always knew he would be a good provider, and a family seemed the most natural extension of his relationship with Carol. 'I was looking forward to it because it was a family I didn't have. I never dwelled on my background being different. It didn't occur to me to analyse my past, and I never thought parenthood would be different for me because I didn't grow up in a family.'

That Christmas, Carol's parents came over from New Zealand. Her father Norm was entranced with his three-month-old granddaughter, rising early each morning to feed her, catching her smiles every chance he could. He seemed happier than Carol could remember. For both parents there was as much joy in seeing Carol as a mother as there was in meeting Natasha.

At the airport, as Norm and Phyl prepared to board their plane home, Norm turned to wave and smile at his daughter. At that moment Carol was overwhelmed with a feeling that this was the last time she would see her father. It was her sixth sense, something she had experienced only a few times before. Six months later Norm died of a massive heart attack. Just days before, he had told Bruce Fuller, David's former flatmate, 'I've been to Australia to see my granddaughter and if I go now I will die a happy man.'

Phyl was a strong and independent woman. After Norm died, she stayed on in the Housing Commission home they had shared for their entire marriage, until she finally bought her own home. In Auckland, Sherryl and the Riggs family adopted her into their fold, and Carol took comfort in the knowledge that she was in good hands. She made the journey to Sydney at least once each year.

David and Carol's second daughter, Rachel, came along on 24 December 1971. Carol now had the family she had thought she could never have. As the babies grew into toddlers David related to them as he had learned to relate to Rocky. He played. He wrestled and crawled on the floor with them and built tents under the table with a blanket and broom. When they were older he initiated pillow fights, often to Carol's mock dismay.

The house grew along with the children. David had set up a joinery workshop in the large shed at the back and brought in a French joiner, Ari Neves, to work with him in his growing construction business. He then built two flats on the rear of the building for additional income, although they became rent-free retreats as much as a source of rental income.

David was now the boss, the owner of the business, though he never drew a line between friend and employee, and rarely expected his team to do anything he would not join in himself. If there were bricks to be moved, David donned his work clothes, pulled on his terry-towelling hat and set a cracking pace that the other men struggled to keep up with.

By the early 1970s Carol's mental health was growing steadily stronger, although at times she struggled with the physical exhaustion of raising two little girls. She was prescribed five different medications, each of which she took three times a day. The build-up of drugs in her body robbed her of energy, and she wondered if they weren't making her feel worse. 'I'm just going to lie down,' she'd explain to the girls, who were too young to understand, as she spread out toys on the rug at her feet and lay down on the couch for a nap. She could only hope that she would wake if the children needed her. The responsibility weighed on her. 'These babies are depending on me. I need to pull myself together, to get out of myself,' Carol told Ruth, who was usually on hand to help. Finally, she was so fed up with the dragging tiredness that she went off all her medication. In one rash moment she threw out the Mogadon that stabilised her, the Nortriptyline for depression, the Dilantin for her seizures.

Her body responded immediately to her withdrawal from drugs. Numbness spread from her face right down her arms. She had no idea what was happening to her but she was determined to make the break. After struggling for two weeks she felt noticeably better and was far more alert. She finally decided to tell her doctor what she had done.

'I've decided to go off all my tablets, and so far I'm feeling fine,' she told him.

'Well, I'm taking no responsibility for you doing that. That is a very dangerous thing to do,' he responded, upset—naturally—that he had not been consulted first.

But Carol felt better. 'I could feel a great malaise or oppression lifting off me, and my mind started to feel clearer than it had for years. One day, I just suddenly had this impression that a scar on my mind had disappeared. I felt my mind was healed.' She discarded the last of her medication and the seizures and phobias stopped. She emerged from the oppression of her illness a stronger person. Through the hardship of illness, her faith in God had blossomed. She learned not to worry about small things. She now knew what mattered in her life.

Out from under the haze, she had a renewed respect for the role David had played. 'I think David is probably the reason why I got better. He was a wonderful support and mainstay and really loyal to me. He just sailed on, never thinking I'd be sick forever. I think it was probably a blessing that he didn't understand much about mental illness, because it can be such a long term thing and he just thought it would pass.' For the first time in many years, Carol could join David in looking optimistically to the future.

5

The Economics of Enough

By 1973 David was operating a string of businesses. The building industry in Sydney was booming and he could afford to be selective in the work his company took on. David's clients in the Eastern Suburbs, who had sizeable budgets, valued his high-quality workmanship. His eye for detail led him into the finicky area of restoration, and he was soon working exclusively for a stable of architects who catered to Sydney's elite. Already he had expanded the small building company he had bought from Jack Ginnery, forming two new companies, Crowder Constructions and Bussau Constructions. He would always have half a dozen jobs on the go at once. At the age of thirty three he ran a company with around one hundred employees.

Yet he was concerned about becoming a victim of his own success. A larger company meant more responsibility and less relaxation with his family. As the demands on his time and money grew, the satisfaction he had always found in meeting ever-larger challenges was dissipating. Instead of working alongside the men, on the tools or with a hammer in his hand, he now spent his days tied to a desk, negotiating with suppliers, getting materials on-site, or meeting architects and clients.

'I was in a management role when I prefer to be active. You get to the point where you realise you are in business for the people who work for you, not for yourself. It becomes business for the sake of business.'

The construction industry had more than its share of issues for David to deal with. Meeting the needs of a large workforce was a full-time job in itself, with workers' compensation claims, both real and faked, and a high turnover of tradesmen and labourers. 'There was a building boom, so tradesmen could just walk onto a job anytime and get work,' David recalled. Then there was the question of how large he should go. To grow he would need to borrow large amounts of money and invest in heavy construction equipment such as trucks and cranes.

David brought in a business consultant to advise him, and a report soon came back outlining a new structure to consolidate and streamline his construction businesses into one corporation. There was no doubt in his mind that the advice made sense, and that following it could take him into the major league of construction. The potential was there, waiting to be taken up. The only problem was that it did not sound like fun. Would he be trapped? Locked in? It was one thing to build a business, but could he survive within those boundaries?

The answer soon became clear when he thought about his personal life. He was finding less time for the relationships and activities that mattered. First to go were the simple pleasures of the working week—the Wednesday afternoons when he and some of his team skipped off work to play squash at Dover Heights. Then it became harder to find time for long jogs around the tree-lined tracks of Centennial Park after work. Fitness had been a lifelong discipline, and now he could only cram in occasional exercise. 'If anything hacks into that time, that creates frustration, so it reflects physiologically. My body was not functioning at full capacity. I could feel that I was not in good condition.'

Finally he began asking himself, 'What's the point?' He came home and complained to Carol, 'These bricklayers are making more than I am. People phone me from six in the morning until ten at night, usually to grizzle about something. Why am I doing it?' It was a topic that bubbled to the surface with growing frequency. 'From a business perspective, I just didn't feel it was worth it. I was working long hours, the children were three and five, and a bigger business would have taken me away from the family more and required some huge investment.'

He was feeling trapped—it was time to fight his way out. 'Being boxed in is about the worst thing that can happen to me, and it probably accounts for why I don't like to hang onto things. Things tend to capture you. Subconsciously, I need my liberty. It is probably a reaction to the time in the Boys' Home.'

Behind his growing dissatisfaction David had other, more significant questions. How much wealth was enough? At what point should he stop pursuing his own interests and direct his talents towards others? Where was God in all the activity of his business life? He had rumbled along from one small-scale success to another and now, as he stood at the edge of large-scale success, he baulked. He was discovering that his quest was not for success in itself, but for significance. He wanted to make his mark on the world but he was beginning to think it would not be in the building business.

David was now finding more satisfaction in his community work through the church than in the business world. Despite the hardship, David's time at Sedgley had left him with a positive view of the church as a vehicle responding to the needs of the community. 'All the people who used to come to make sure we were kept busy were all people from the church. The swimming teachers, soccer coaches and gymnastics teachers were all from the church. They all made a positive contribution to our development.'

Early in their marriage David and Carol had wrapped themselves in church activity at every level, though David had realised long before that his personality, with its intense independence and entrepreneurial streak, excluded him from any conventional role. At times over the years he had struggled to operate within the confines of the church hierarchy. He was now searching for an expression of his faith. What was the role for someone like himself, a lay person with a simple willingness to help? David loved working with young people and went back to his Sedgley roots to set up a weekly gymnastics program for young boys in the Waverley neighbourhood.

By his early 30s David was one of the older and more aggressive players on the church soccer team. He was a formidable and at times rough player who would sooner run down the opposition than let a goal past. In his last soccer-playing days he twice broke a leg and once broke his jaw. He also had a capacity for drawing younger people to his team. He knew from his own experience how positive an impact sport could have. Leigh Coleman, the son of the local minister, Reverend Ron Coleman, was among his younger team-mates. Leigh was a rabble-rouser, full of spirit and good fun. He would later find his life intertwined with David's in a remarkable way.

One day, Jacques Embrechts, a Dutch fitter and turner who had migrated to Australia in 1969, and his wife Janette came to the Waverley church. The Bussaus soon befriended the couple, and within weeks David enlisted Jacques for the Waverley soccer team and offered him extra work as Ari's assistant in the joinery. Not long after, the Embrechts' marriage failed and Janette left. Jacques, unable to manage the rent of their comfortable flat near Centennial Park, was bewildered and unsure of where to go next.

One Saturday he heard a knock at the door. 'Jacques, it's David,' a voice called from the other side.

'Dave, what are you doing here?' Jacques asked as he opened the door.

'I can't leave you here like this. I have a truck outside and I'm going to move your things. We have a flat at the back of our house that you can rent for $25 a week,' David offered. Jacques could not argue. He soon settled into the one-bedroom flat and came under the nurturing care of Carol, who invited him to join the family for dinner each evening when he came home from work. They never asked him for rent and he often had to push it onto them.

It seemed to Jacques that everything he had had been ripped away from him, starting with his marriage and home, and followed by the theft of three cars in one year. He reached his lowest point when, on the same day his third car was stolen, his cat, a source of comfort in his loneliness, also died. 'David picked me up all the time. He seemed to know just the right moment to be there. I was in a very bad situation for quite a while,' Jacques said. 'I was on the verge of saying "Let me die", but every time I felt that way David kept me going. He already knew how strong and forceful I could be and he saw me falling in a hole,' Jacques recalls. When he lost his third car David suggested he use Carol's car, and for weeks Jacques commuted to work—he was a store manager in Bankstown—in Carol's Mini Minor.

After five weeks Jacques said, 'Carol, this can't go on—you need your car.' She insisted he keep her car, but soon afterwards Jacques came home from work to be greeted by David in the front garden. Parked in the driveway beside him was a 1500 Volkswagen he had brought for five hundred dollars. 'Jacques, what about this?' David asked. 'It's yours.' Jacques was flabbergasted.

'I can't take that,' Jacques told him at first. And then, after accepting it, insisted, 'I'll pay you back as soon as I can.'

'I don't want the money, but if you feel a strong need to repay it, that's fine,' David told Jacques.

When Jacques later tried to pay David back, he was always rebuffed with, 'Just go and help other people with it', or, 'Help me out by doing a bit of work' or 'Playing soccer with me is repayment enough.'

'David was not interested in the money—he made money so easily. He was more interested in people caring for each other,' Jacques said.

Jacques became a surrogate uncle to Natasha and Rachel. As a small girl Rachel was often waiting on the doorstep of his flat when he arrived home. She would greet him, looking up with her wide eyes and blonde curls, with 'I'm coming to say hello' or 'I came to clean your flat', closely followed by 'Where's the cookies, Jacques?' once she made her way into his domain.

The Bussau girls grew up with an extended family of friends and acquaintances who came to stay in one of the flats at the back of the house. As far as they knew, it was quite normal to lead open lives, with a flow of dozens of people in and out of their home each week, and to never know who might join them for a meal or come to stay.

While David was growing restless in his business in the early 1970s, he was also looking for larger-scale community programs. He still had a notion that his upbringing had prepared him for a particular role that he was yet to find. In the church he was the first person the leadership turned to when there was something to fix or a building to renovate, and he gladly gave his time and building skills to help. But the role of helpful handyman seemed too easy. He already knew he could build. Surely he could be stretched and use his organisational skills? Jacques, who spent many nights out with David collecting and distributing food for the needy or helping with young boys on bus trips, came to admire David's effortless ability to organise people and events. 'He was so gentle and so strong, and the more gentle he was, the stronger he was. This man only needed to use few words—just a tap on the shoulder and something was organised.'

The Waverley congregation at this time had moved from Bondi Junction and joined with Paddington while a new church was under construction. The Paddington group was chronically poor and could barely pay the salary of its minister. Each Saturday parishioners ran a small market stall that brought in a little extra income. One Sunday after church, David and Carol went back to the home of Reverend Russell Davies, the minister, for a cup of tea. This week Jacques came too, and they all sat down to discuss the difficulties the church was facing, and what they could do to help. They came up with the idea of extending the market, agreeing that it would help with the church's financial position and build a sense of community around the church. It might even bring people in to worship.

David and Jacques set about building a pergola around the outside of the building, a cover for the first half-dozen stalls. They bought some steel and Jacques welded two large trolleys, each 150×120 centimetres, to stack the tables on. The market was an instant success. Within weeks the number of stalls grew to twenty five and Jacques welded more trolleys for stacking more tables.

Family and friends were all drawn into the new project. At six o'clock each Saturday morning the Bussaus, Jacques and a group of friends were down at the church pulling out the tables for the stall holders, taking the rents and setting up their own stalls.

They gathered up all the old clothes they could find to set up secondhand clothing stalls, side by side.

The market soon swelled across the church property, growing until it spilled over onto neighbouring land, attracting hundreds of stalls crowded with handicrafts, clothes and food, drawing thousands of shoppers. Today the Paddington market is a Sydney landmark.

The markets attracted a range of practitioners of alternative methods of health care and spirituality. Among them was a friendly couple teaching transcendental meditation (TM), a form of meditation in which participants clear their minds and focus on a mantra as a means of reaching spiritual purity. David was intrigued by the couple's claims that they could improve his spiritual state. They told him his quality of life could be improved by TM's concept of peace and harmony, stability and spiritual awareness.

He decided to put the claims to the test. 'What can TM give me that my own faith in Jesus can't?' It was a genuine question. Over the years his own personal growth through studying the teachings of Jesus Christ had brought him all of the qualities they talked about. He had a real desire to exchange ideas about faith and spirituality. For several months he attended TM classes in the church hall, each week sitting diligently with crossed legs, stilling his body and relaxing inwardly into the mantra. Each time he tried to focus on the mantra he found his mind dimming, and he would quietly slip into a light sleep. Two hours of meditation proved a physiological impossibility for David but in his prayer life and daily actions he was already able to reach a point of tranquillity.

Though his teachers found it hard to accept that their pupil could be tranquil and deeply spiritual without practising TM, David parted from the group amicably. 'They couldn't work out why I didn't get stressed and anxious, explode, confront or be contentious.'

The TM experience reinforced his belief that his own Christian faith could deliver the same and more. Increasingly, he understood that his beliefs were pointless if he was not living and acting by them. He resolved to further align his lifestyle and spiritual life.

The reasons to leave the business world were outnumbering the reasons to stay. David had never yearned for social or political power or influence. When he thought about it, he didn't need a huge amount of money to live on. There was the family to think of, but he was confident that no matter which direction he pursued he could always provide for them. The Bussaus' lifestyle was simple and they intended to keep it that way. David had never craved fast cars and multiple houses. Both he and Carol were happy for Natasha and Rachel to be educated in public schools.

It was at this point, in late 1974, that the evening call from the Packers, Australia's wealthiest family, brought David's confusion about his working life into focus. David may not have acted on his resentment at being answerable to others, had an act of God not come along to literally change the course of his life. Australians awoke on Christmas morning, 1974, to the nation's worst-ever recorded natural disaster. Cyclone Tracy had whirled its nasty way through the Arafura and Timor Seas for seven hundred kilometres, along the barren north coast of Australia. Tracy made its striking point the small, relaxed city of Darwin, a place where Asian and western cultures blended comfortably. Its gardens were abundant splashes of the vibrant oranges and hot pinks of bougainvillea, sweet-smelling frangipani and groves of palms. Its simple timber houses rose on stilts to let the breeze flow and provide extra shelter underneath in the wet season.

Darwin residents heard the cyclone warnings on Christmas Eve, amid the festivities of barbeques and beer. Most were well prepared for cyclones and knew the procedures. They knew they had to stock the house with food, fill the bath with water, tape the windows, remove anything outside that could move, and retreat to the bathroom or under the sturdiest furniture, with mattresses nearby for protection.

But no preparation was adequate for Cyclone Tracy. In a few ferocious hours Cyclone Tracy killed fifty people (another sixteen were missing at sea) and rendered 20,000 residents homeless. Most Darwinians were left with only the clothes they were wearing. They were bruised by flying objects, crushed by collapsing walls, sliced by loose sheets of corrugated iron from roofs and traumatised by the calamity. Boats in the harbour were either sunk or found in small streams many kilometres away and aircraft were picked up and thrown around like toys. Families watched everything they owned destroyed by one fierce wind.

It was days before the rest of Australia could connect by television with Darwin, and when the pictures came out they were graphic and horrifying. David and Carol, like millions of others, watched the images of devastation. 'I could take my guys up there to help,' David commented to Carol. The next Sunday in church a call went out for help. Hostels and other church property had been destroyed. There were thousands of families left homeless and dispossessed.

Soon David had a plan in motion. 'Are you interested in coming to Darwin?' he asked Rod Johnson, one of his team of employees. 'I'll pay your airfare if you'll donate your labour.' David was never wary of putting his own money towards good projects. 'Why not? I'm game,' was Rod's reply. David then rounded up Ari Neves, Ken Needs, a business partner, and others until he had organised a working team of twenty to go with him. A young Welshman, sixteen-year-old Vince Harris, whom David had taken on the year before as an apprentice carpenter, signed up for the adventure. Later, he and Rod Johnston would return to Darwin by road in David's old blue Valiant station wagon. Like Rod, Vince appreciated that in David's team, even as a teenager, he had a voice. 'I never felt that my opinion was less important than anyone else's.'

Within a fortnight of the cyclone, David's building crew, armed with toolboxes, met at Sydney airport, bound for Darwin. They found the city a wasteland, with pockets of homes left strangely unscathed. The townspeople were still in shock and little had been done to help them get back into their homes. Many families had fled the Northern Territory, but others decided to stay, crowding into school and church halls, camping under tarpaulins or sections of their houses if they still stood. Some Aboriginal families returned to their traditional land in the bush.

David had never experienced a disaster scene before. As the team moved across the devastated city, past untapped hydrants spewing water, and tangles of metal—cars, roofing iron and power lines—he discovered within himself a steely pragmatism that allowed him to divorce himself from the emotion of what he saw and look for the most efficient way through. In many ways he was in his element. He had a group of people to organise and it would take all his creativity to make the most of the short time available to the work team.

For three weeks David and his crew rushed from house to house, repairing a roof at one house, setting up a workable bathroom or kitchen at the next so a family could return home. At the end of each day they retired to a hostel opposite the airport that had survived the cyclone. The team planned to work during the week and take a day on the weekend to rest, but the need dictated otherwise. 'What are you doing at the weekend? There's a family out at Parap who could use some help,' David asked a few of the team on the first Saturday. When they arrived at Parap there was not much left of Ron's home and he and his wife were living in a caravan while their children slept under the house. Ron was so thrilled when David and his men arrived to set up a functional bathroom that he invited them all back.

'There's a barbeque on here tonight, you're all welcome,' he offered. In the middle of the disaster zone Ron had somehow rescued a freezer full of barramundi, and now offered a fish barbeque to say thanks.

Before going to Darwin, David had started a rigorous process of sifting through his motives and principles. He knew he was comfortable making his own choices rather than following the crowd. At one point in Darwin a public phone was out of order near the hostel and people could call anywhere across Australia without charge. Long distance calls at that time were prohibitively expensive, and many workers in the Top End felt isolated and lonely. As word passed around the community there was a constant line-up of workers at the phone waiting to talk to their families down south.

Vince Harris was as eager as any of his colleagues to call southern friends and was at the box each night after work. He was curious about David, who stayed back at the hostel and didn't once attempt to contact his family.

'David, why aren't you calling your family? You can talk to them for free,' Vince asked on his return one day.

'I don't want to call Carol just because it's free to call her,' David replied.

Increasingly, David was examining his motives. He found being in Darwin exhilarating; he was doing compassionate work that was both challenging and satisfying, yet he worried that there was an element of selfishness about his good works.

'Is this really about me helping people or is it about me feeling good about myself?' he wondered. It was a question that would come back to him again and again through his life.

When the exhausted team finally fell onto their flight back to Sydney, David was frustrated. They had done as much as they could but he knew how much more they could contribute to the mammoth task of putting Darwin back together. His contact in Darwin was the Reverend Doug McKenzie, a Uniting Church minister who had been living there for many years. 'You should come back here, David. We need someone like you to help us,' Doug McKenzie commented as he left. At the time, the Uniting Church was the second-largest employer in Darwin (after the Northern Territory government). The church had already made the decision to be involved in a rebuilding program and enlisted a man called Ken Nowland to get it underway.

Doug was not making idle conversation when he told David they needed him, and David was not back in Sydney for more than a few weeks when he received another pivotal call. 'David, we're going to bring work teams from all over Australia to help rebuild Darwin. Are you interested in taking over Ken's job of co-ordinating it all when he leaves?' Doug asked. David told Doug he would discuss the plan with Carol. He would need time to wrap up building contracts and attend to his financial affairs.

Carol was more amenable to the idea of adventure since she and David had travelled the world together, but this suggestion threw her into a nervous spin. This time the plan involved their young girls, and she was not sure how she would cope. Her comfort was that they owned their home, so she knew they could always come back. She quickly moved from her first, panicked reaction of 'Why would we do this?' to the realisation that it might be fun, and finally to the excited acceptance of the challenge. She had a strong sense that it would work out. As she had in the past, she would go for the ride with David.

Almost as an afterthought, Carol was offered the role of running the Methodist-owned Gordon Symonds hostel at Winnellie, near the airport. Before Cyclone Tracy, it had been a city home for Aboriginal people visiting from the bush. Now it would be home to work teams from across Australia as well. Carol had no idea when she agreed to the move that her task in the year ahead would at times be more arduous than David's.

The move to Darwin was impetuous and risky, just as David liked it, but he spared little thought for his family. 'Carol agreed to come, but I wasn't particularly good at thinking through the implications for others,' he admitted. He started working out how he might unwind the business interests he had spent twenty years building. He saw himself as going from one job to another, rather than as starting out afresh.

To the bewilderment of his work colleagues and the architects he had built a good working rapport with over a decade, David finished his current contracts and refused any new work. He completed the break by selling or giving away to those around him all but his essential equipment.

In later years, when he sat back to reflect on this period of his life, he labelled the process as reaching the 'economics of enough'. It was a turning point: he could decide to pursue great wealth or take the more modest success and wealth he had and employ it for social benefit. He decided to take his chances outside the security of the businesses he had bought and sold since his mid teens.

By the time David moved to Darwin with Carol, Tasha and Rachel mid way through 1975, they were largely free of business commitments. The rental income from the four flats behind their house gave them spending money, and the Uniting Church provided food and accommodation, allowing them both Carol and David to work as volunteers. Initially their friends Vic and Marion Henshaw moved into the Randwick house and took over the job of collecting rents.

David was soon on the road, flying from city to city around Australia, addressing church congregations about the Darwin rebuilding program. His presentation skills were rudimentary. His schooling and the homes he had lived in as a boy had offered few opportunities for public speaking. He was awkward, and preferred to sit in a back pew than to stand out the front. Yet his sincerity caught the attention of those he addressed, and his quiet manner drew people to him. Speaking to groups was a means to an end and the result was a steady stream of volunteers to work in the northern city. Before long, he had ten crews of twenty five each, working on twelve properties at a time. When a team arrived in Darwin, David co-ordinated the materials they needed, organised the budgets and allocated the work.

Darwin was David's first taste of development, a time to learn the basic lessons that would shape his later work. Many people wanted to import everything new and shining. Going back to the lessons of his Sedgley days, David hunted through the piles of rubbish instead, searching for materials that could be recycled into rebuilding projects, just as he had fished around for bike parts in the rubbish around Masterton. 'We'd try to pick up any window frames that were lying around then stockpile and catalogue them and use them when we were doing someone's property.'

In an oppressive heat, Carol embraced the challenge of playing host to forty people at a time passing through the hostel. She wore the inflated title of hostel supervisor, which meant scrubbing the floors, doing the washing and, after a cook from the work party left, cooking as well. She had some help with cleaning from a local girl, Gunjong, and later a friend named Grace Hocking arrived from Melbourne to help cook.

Tiredness was the only occasional reminder of the illness she had fought off. There was too much work at hand to be introspective. Carol found the variety of her days interesting and confidence-building. The hostel was like a theatre, with a full cast of characters coming and going each week. One week a group of Japanese tourists from a cruise ship might come to stay and the next it could be a work party and Aboriginal Land Council representatives, or missionaries and translators.

'It was good experience—we were meeting all sorts of people. It was a good training ground. It broadened our horizon and our experience with different nationalities. The kids learned to relate to people as people,' she said.

David and Carol had never experienced anything like the Northern Territory wet season. It was a time of stifling heat and humidity, barely relieved by daily afternoon downpours that caused flooding and often cut Darwin off from the road to the south. Violent thunder and lightning storms opened the skies and cyclones brooding out to sea to the north were common.

Once, a streak of lightning struck a lightning rod on a store

74

behind the main building of the hostel and deflected to the main hostel, hitting it like a bomb, and sending them all to the ground on their stomachs until it seemed safe to stand again.

The Bussau family were rarely alone as a family at the hostel. With David frequently travelling, Carol was left to handle her strong-willed girls alone—plus the ever-changing cast of residents who would witness her parenting skills and offer advice on child rearing. 'Don't speak to your mother like that,' they defended Carol, making it even harder for her to assert her influence on the girls.

The girls loved the times when David was in Darwin. There was a trampoline at the hostel and at the end of the day he taught them the flips and somersaults he had so loved as a young boy. As far as the girls were concerned, he could inject excitement into the most ordinary events. The cyclone had gouged deep potholes in the road leading up to the hostel. They were so deep and wide that when rain poured down it turned them into small baths that could swallow a car wheel up to its axle.

As the sun emerged after a storm one day, David called Tasha and Rachel, 'C'mon girls, we're going for a swim,' and they eagerly followed him outside and down the palm-lined drive. There the trio stripped down to their underwear and splashed around in the tepid water of the pothole, sliding the muddy sludge around in their fingers and toes.

One piece of unfinished business pulled David back to Sydney on many occasions over the next year, reinforcing his reasons for leaving. A client in Point Piper, one of Sydney's most expensive suburbs, had cheated him out of thirty thousand dollars on a building job and David took the man to court, something he had never done before. He agonised for weeks over the morality of taking legal action. In the end he decided it was an injustice that could not be left unresolved.

The client tried everything he could to duck his obligation to pay David. When David flew from Darwin for a hearing he was met with, 'My client is sick and can't appear today' from the man's lawyer. Eventually David won the case—and put the building business behind him, apart from one tile supply business he owned in partnership with Ken Needs.

By the end of 1976, almost two years after the cyclone, the city of Darwin was again finding its feet. Many thousands chose not to return, putting the tragic episode behind them and moving to cities far from the cyclone belt. Those who did return brought life back to the city. The houses growing out of the ruins were now stronger, built to outlast future battering. Residents came back with new resolve.

The time in Darwin had been good for the Bussaus. 'I saw it as a time of building the family and bonding. You share experiences closely when you are isolated,' David later reflected.

Carol had worked hard, and she worried that in the crowd of interesting and broken people crossing the threshold of the hostel, Tasha and Rachel had at times missed out on her attention. She hoped their next move would be less demanding. By now David had completely lost his appetite for building businesses just to make money. Life in Darwin had shown him that his creativity could be well used outside the business world—and with much more personal satisfaction. By gradually selling his business interests he could set himself up to be self-supporting. They could do what they wanted within the constraints of the girls' formal education.

After fifteen months of living and working in Darwin, he came home to the hostel one day and told Carol, 'I think our work here is reaching its natural end.' The rate of rebuilding had slowed and money for reconstruction was drying up.

The Bussaus had made lifelong friends and, most importantly, explored the possibility of life without the security of a permanent job, a steady income, or plans for the future. They were happily adrift and aimless, yet aspects of their lives were becoming clearer by the day. They both felt that they had come too far in their lifestyle change to head straight back to the city.

'What do we do now?' Carol asked David. They shared a sense that the adventure was not over. As it turned out, they were not to be left hanging for long. The next door soon opened, and it was one that would forever change the course of their lives.

6

Buried in the Jungle

On 14 July 1976 an earthquake deep in the Indian Ocean sent its deadly shockwaves across the Indonesian island of Bali, many kilometres to the north of Darwin, crumpling houses, temples, schools and hospitals like paper, and taking six hundred lives with it.

It was some months before the two thousand strong community of Blimbingsari in West Bali could take stock of the losses to their village. Mercifully, no one was killed in the earthquake and most of its houses were lightly constructed, with traditional straw roofs, called *alang alang*, which could easily be rebuilt from local materials.

Months after the earthquake it was evident that the lingering loss to the villagers of Blimbingsari was its community heart, the white timber church in the centre of the village. For many years Reverend Doug McKenzie, a Uniting Church Minister in Darwin, had been a faithful friend of the Balinese Bishop, Dr Wayan Mastra, and others in the tiny Balinese Christian community that lived in Blimbingsari. He kept in close contact with Wayan and helped where he could. He knew the sufferings of the people of Blimbingsari. In changing religion from Hindu to Christian they had lost their culture and their land, and been ostracised by their fellow villagers. This small Christian group, led by Made Rungu, were forced to resettle in the forests in the dry west of Bali in

1939, along with other minority groups. The governing powers had expected them all to die, if not from malaria, then from snakebites, or lack of water. In spite of the odds they had survived.

Following the earthquake Wayan came to Doug for help. He wanted to replace the former enclosed timber building, which had been stiflingly hot and uncomfortable, with an open, Balinese-style church where his people could meet and express themselves with the instruments of their own culture—with the interlocking rhythms of the gongs, cymbals, drums and xylophones of the gamelan orchestra, and with the traditional dance dramas so treasured by the Balinese.

When Wayan asked Doug if he knew of a builder who could help them, Doug suggested David. He knew of no one better suited to the task.

David's response was swift and unconditional. 'Yes, we'll come,' he said, before he considered the danger, disease or logic of taking two young girls to live in a remote village surrounded by jungle. The community had no money for rebuilding their village and David knew it could be costly to take his family to Bali. He would have to pay for building materials and support his family on savings for as long as it took. Yet he found it exciting to blindly answer a call for help. This was his first real exercise in faith. The many unanswered questions appealed to his sense of adventure. How could they get the building materials for a big project into a village that was fourteen kilometres from a proper road? And where would they come from? How could David direct a building project if he couldn't read the plans written in Bahasa Indonesia or communicate with his work team in Balinese?

The retreat from Darwin was far from smooth. David handed over his job in Darwin, while Carol worked frantically to find and train a replacement at the hostel. The enormity of what they were doing showed up in the details, as Carol rushed through her long to-do list, trying to stay calm. She fell into moments of panic and uncertainty about the future in Bali. Friends warned her that village life would be a challenge for a western woman. She was prepared for the worst of conditions. In her mind, they would be living in squalor, in a dirt-floored bamboo hut. It's all very well for Dave to race off in this direction, she thought as she packed the cleaning aids and medical supplies among her personal possessions. The move did not come quite as naturally for her. Still, she wanted to do it. A friend's offer to adopt the beloved family cat fell through at the last moment, and the day before they left, Carol left the cat with the local vet, uncertain of its fate, sobbing all the way back to the hostel.

Then there were the health issues. Injections against smallpox and cholera that should have been a non-event became suddenly important the morning they were booked to fly from Darwin.

'Dave, look at Tasha,' Carol gasped when their seven-year-old came into the kitchen for breakfast that morning. There, planted right in the centre of her nose, where the day before there was only a small scratch, was a huge, festering smallpox sore to match the one on her arm.

'I'm not sure we can arrive with that,' David told her. They dashed to the Health Department, where a doctor pulled out the ugliest needle Carol had ever seen and jabbed its point deep into Tasha's buttock. Then he repeated the procedure on the other buttock.

Tasha screamed in pain. If Carol felt sick at the sight of it, she couldn't imagine how painful the needles were for Tasha. She wondered if this might be the first of many woes to engulf them. She was surprised when the doctor urged them to go to Bali that day.

'She'll be fine. She's no longer contagious,' he reassured her.

Within two weeks of the phonecall, the Bussaus walked out of Denpasar airport, exhausted from the effort of leaving Darwin. They spent the first few days sleeping, walking along the beach, and slipping back to their rooms for more sleep. Also the Balinese knew exactly what the red spot on the little girl meant. They tried to be polite to the newcomers, but there was no hiding their repugnance, and they kept their distance.

A new spiritual reality was unfolding for Carol. Around Sanur Beach, where they first stayed, she was overwhelmed by the intensity of the smells, the smoke of fires burning near the rice paddies, the incense smouldering, the rotting offerings alongside the road, the pungent frangipani. The faces on the intricate carvings and stonework of the temples by the road found their way into her subconscious mind, and during the first night as she slept they became larger, more grotesque, and rushed at her in taunting waves, invading her sleep.

Jalan Legian was the main thoroughfare through the surfers' hangout of Kuta Beach. Even in the early days of tourism in Bali, Jalan Legian teemed with beeping motorbikes and small cars, all jostling for a place on the road with no regard for lanes or rules. Along its footpaths lay mangy dogs with disfigured hips and limbs resulting from failed attempts at crossing the road. Tanned, white-haired foreigners, mostly Australian, revelled in their freedom, riding bikes without helmets, eating cheap seafood and Balinese approximations of western food, snacking from the mobile vendors and warungs, and spinning out on hallucinogenic mushrooms at night.

It was not hard to see the attraction. Young tourists could stay in a losmen right on Kuta Beach for only a dollar a day, with a Balinese breakfast of pineapple, bananas and syrupy tea. Sandy trails led from the beach up to Jalan Legian and the small bamboo-sided restaurants that lined it. The 1970s were the beginning of a revolution for the small island that had for centuries withstood the advances of Arab traders and Dutch empire builders. The Balinese were losing their innocence and the clever locals were climbing onto the tourism wave.

There was certainly no window-dressing for the tourist, no covering the face of poverty. An air of desperation clung to every small transaction that helped feed the children for that day. As the Bussau family made their way from their accommodation at Sanur Beach to the small hotel, the Wisma Mastapa, at Kuta owned by Wayan Mastra, David was troubled and confronted by what he saw, but couldn't see a way around it.

Wayan Mastra already recognised the direction in which Bali was heading, and he wanted to have a part in the new prosperity. To him, it was self-serving of a colonial lord to keep the people in poverty and without power, and only educate the Balinese ruling class.

Wayan came from a poor village called Sibetan on the slopes of Gunung Agung, Bali's holiest mountain. He reached school age soon after the Japanese occupation during World War II; this was the first time education was offered to poor Indonesians and not just the ruling class. Wayan was able to go through both elementary and secondary school, and then on to college in Java where he was influenced by Christian teachings and converted from Hinduism to Christianity. This was such a radical step that it was several years before he admitted his conversion to his parents in Sibetan; they might also be ostracised because of his decision.

Wayan then gained a scholarship to a university in the United States, where he studied towards a doctorate in theology. During his studies, he formed a strong conviction that the church in Bali should not simply be the object of charity, receiving handouts and second-hand clothes from the wealthy west, but should be able to prosper through hard work and give freely to those in need. He could not see the point in the 'poverty theology' that Dutch missionaries had preached to the poor. Wayan was also watching the economic miracle of Singapore in progress—he knew business was a key.

In 1972 Wayan bought a piece of land near Jalan Legian with his savings. He built two basic cottages. By 1976, when the Bussaus came to stay at the Wisma Mastapa, he had expanded his hotel to twenty rooms and built tranquil gardens, typically Balinese in their artistry, with splashes of bougainvillea and weaving streams. Wayan and his wife Ketut were peaceful, warm people, and the Bussaus felt they were among friends.

Wayan took it upon himself to educate the Bussau family in the culture of Bali, and for days he showed them various facets of the island's religion, art and dance. They watched the delicately executed movements of Balinese dancers whose eyes slid from side to side while their hands curved and flowed in slow, symbolic gestures. They visited the temple of Besakih on the slopes of Gunung Agung, the mother temple for all Hindu Balinese, and saw silversmiths in Celuk weave fine strands of silver into intricate bracelets, necklaces and earrings.

High in the mountains of Ubud, they saw steaming ravines plunging down to pure rivers, and monkeys chattering in the trees above. They saw interpretations on canvas of the chiselled green rice paddies they had travelled past. They gained a surface understanding of the Balinese culture and how it pervades every small action of the Balinese people, how they lived with the good and evil forces which, under the Hindu Dharma, were kept in balance by daily offerings to their gods.

Then it was time to start work. The village of Blimbingsari was well off the only road link between Denpasar and the ferry to the crowded island of Java. From Denpasar, the road to the west wove around sculpted paddies, with browned Balinese farmers moving slowly along the curves of new rice plants, then past rows of waves breaking evenly onto pure white sand, and ancient temples poised high above the ocean.

Trucks, cars and motorbikes attacked the twisted road at a speed worthy of a freeway. Cars were often on the wrong side of the road and the potholes were large enough to consume a motorbike. The last fourteen kilometres, from the Negara road to Blimbingsari, were unpaved and accessible only by four wheel drive or motorbike. Most Balinese came by ox cart. Little shacks lined the road—this was where new arrivals from Java, mostly Muslim, had first planted themselves. The Negara area was a potpourri of faiths, with Hindu, Catholic, Protestant and Muslim villages side by side. In this dryer, poor part of the island, so different from the lush south-eastern corner, there were snakes and rumours of tigers in the forests, and the bigger danger of starvation if the rains didn't arrive.

Most villagers had no choice but to walk from Blimbingsari to Melaya, six kilometres away, or to Negara, a half-day on foot, if they needed food or household items that weren't available in the village. Daily, they padded in bare feet along the verge beside the track to the main road.

When the Bussaus arrived in Blimbingsari, some months after the earthquake, the village still bore the signs of destruction. Many of its flimsy houses had been patched and repaired so that they were liveable, but other buildings lay in ruins.

Reverend Ketut Arka, the minister in Blimbingsari, and his wife Rene were there to meet the Bussaus when they first drove into the village. Others poured from their houses as word spread of the arrival of the Australian family who had come to help them. Curiosity about David in particular had been mounting. 'He must be from the CIA,' said one suspicious visitor from Denpasar, who couldn't imagine why David would bring his family to help and expect nothing in return. Now, the intrinsic Balinese shyness took over, and the villagers stood by, smiling.

'This is your home. We hope you will be comfortable here,' Arka told David and Carol, pointing up a rise to a white stucco-walled house with a thatched roof. Carol's heart soared. It was far beyond her expectations. The cottage looked charming compared with the image of a bamboo lean-to she had prepared herself for.

The Bussaus' new house was right beside the *asrama* or hostel which was home to 200 disadvantaged children, some orphaned and others with families too poor to pay for their education. Though small, it had three bedrooms, the main one with just enough room for a double bed, along with a living area and a small kitchen. Its floor was waxed grey concrete, making it cool on the feet and easy to clean. In the bathroom was a big concrete tub called a *bak* filled with cold water, scooped out for the daily bath or *mandi*, and a squat toilet.

The older children from the asrama had the task of keeping the Bussaus' bak filled with water each day; they formed a human chain from the well in the centre of the village to pass the buckets along its streets and up to the hill and into the house. When the water table fell and the wells in the village dried up, the children fetched water from the river, four kilometres away.

The daily water-carrying ritual became a source of both frustration and amusement to Carol as she tried to conduct correspondence lessons with her daughters each morning. A procession of toothy smiles marched past the window where the girls sat, each one greeting Tasha and Rachel with a mischievous 'Allo, allo, allo'.

At first it was hard for Carol to settle into village life. There were smiles and handshakes, but she was alone, and without the means to communicate her feelings. The children needed her to care for them too and she was feeling pressure to start their home-schooling. Some days she was exhausted by the effort of just trying to communicate with other people. 'What am I doing here?' she asked herself on those days.

With only a single-burner kerosene stove in her kitchen she had no way of baking a cake or making a small gift that might

83

break the ice so she could build a friendship. She decided to simply wander in the village, using her few words of Indonesian, smiling and gesturing where her words failed her. 'I didn't have anything to give other than to be friendly,' Carol recalled.

Her behaviour endeared her to the people of Blimbingsari, who soon overcame their shyness. Warm friendships flowed. Rene Arka would become a pillar of support for Carol, and they often shared cups of tea in each other's homes in the afternoon. Carol came to have an important role in village life—that of English teacher. The people of Blimbingsari knew the outside world would soon encroach upon their quiet lives and they were eager to learn the new language of tourism.

One morning during their first week in the village, the Bussau family awoke to the smiling face of Ketut Wasiati. She stood shyly in their kitchen, awaiting instruction. She was a gentle, gracious girl, with beautiful, glowing skin. 'Ketutwas', as they called her, had grown up in the village then gone to Denpasar to do a course in domestic studies. She was now twenty, and the job of *pembantu*, or helper, to the Bussaus, was her first paid employment.

It was awkward for the Bussaus, who were equally shy about having a helper. 'We don't need any special treatment—we want to live like the locals,' David told Arka, who had hand-picked Ketut Wasiati as the most qualified person for the job. But their hosts knew better. The Arkas knew that the labour-intensive grind of buying food, hand-washing and cleaning, and cooking on a small kerosene stove would put the newly arrived family under too much pressure. Carol and David soon realised that the Arkas were right. Life would have been punishing without Ketut. Every second day she left at five thirty in the morning to make the journey to the markets in Melaya to buy food and vegetables for the household. She made breakfast for the family, and while Carol taught the girls each morning, she cleaned the house and laboriously hand-washed the laundry in a small tub. She then prepared a lunch, the main meal of the day, of favourite dishes like Balinese red bean soup, chicken curry, fish, and vegetables. And rice, there was always rice.

Ketut was loving and kind to Tasha and Rachel. Many times each day she patiently put away the toys they spread all over the living room floor. Making a mess was something the village children would never do, even if they had toys to play with. She was gracious about cultural blunders, like passing something with the left hand, and with the barrier of language that stood between them. Over the year, David and Carol came to know every member of Ketut's family, including her grandparents. They learned how much sheer hard work was required when almost everyone in the village survived by subsistence farming. Apart from a nearby *warung*, or small shop, there was no cash economy. The villagers grew just what they could to live on: just enough chickens for eggs and meat, just enough rice to feed the family, just enough vegetables, fruit and coffee for their own use or perhaps a little more so they could trade with a neighbour. A life of subsistence meant the village children had jobs to do before and after school. There wasn't much time for recreation.

Nor was there much future for the young people in the village. The modern economy was reaching Bali, and the new international airport down near the eastern end of the island was bringing with it a wave of change. In the schools, young Balinese were learning all about life in the 1970s, while their own lives were still rooted in a centuries-old subsistence lifestyle. Since the earthquake destroyed the village *gudang*, or meeting place, and the church, there was nowhere for the *banjar*, or village council, to meet to discuss community affairs or for all the villagers to come together to celebrate.

Life in Blimbingsari was a time of unprecedented freedom for Tasha and Rachel. They could wander into the rice paddies, mud squelching between their toes, stopping to greet a toothless *dadong*, a great-grandmother, as she sat rattling tins to scare away the birds. In the fields around the village, there were frogs and rats and mice and snakes to pursue and hours of play with the children from the asrama after their school day and chores. Often the girls' play was as simple as locking arms with their friends and talking in Bahasa about the wondrous things young children uncover from day to day. Rachel was the wilder of the two, and would gladly forego schoolwork to run to the warung and buy rice sweets wrapped in banana leaves with the few rupiah her father had given her. Tasha preferred to be indoors, and soaked up all her mother could teach her in the morning lessons.

Settling in was simpler for David than for Carol. He had a job to do and he set about doing it. Many of the men working at the site came from outside the village and stayed in a long temporary hut built close to the site. Each morning a team gathered well before the roosters crowed to start the day's toil. The men were organised into six groups of a hundred each, rostered on for just one day each week, so they could still tend to their animals and crops.

From the start, David surprised the men with his hands-on approach. What was the boss doing, working with them like that, especially as he was a foreigner? the men wondered among themselves. But David knew from years of experience in building that working alongside his men always brought the best results. He would set the standard of workmanship. Most of these men came with no building experience and were hungry to learn. No one was keener than the foreman and village organiser, Pak Nyoman Yusef. He was a quiet, thin man, with crooked teeth and a sharp sense of humour. He watched and absorbed everything David did as they worked.

The first hurdle on David's new job almost stopped the whole project in its tracks. The church building was designed to last one thousand years. The plans showed a large concrete structure that had deep, deep footings and rose sixteen metres into the air. Thousands of litres of water would be needed just to mix the concrete. Yet the nearest water source, other than the small wells in the village, was a four kilometre walk away.

'We can't build the new church without water. We'll have to build a dam in the mountains and pipe the water down to the village,' David told the team. It would add months to the building time and soak up much more labour than anticipated, but at the end of the project the village would be much better off with a reliable water supply.

With intense daily use, David's Indonesian language skills flourished and he soon overcame the smaller issues, like working off plans written in Indonesian. He needed to make structural adjustments each day, and without the necessary instruments, he did it painstakingly by hand. At night David huddled by a kerosene lamp, working out engineering details, sketching designs and toying with more efficient ways to mix concrete or do brickwork. He needed to build the structure in a circular fashion, like building a pyramid, and he had no foolproof way of knowing that the spire would be in the middle of the oval-shaped church when it was finished.

The area around Blimbingsari was known locally as *alas rangda*, the dwelling place of the evil one. When the first members of the Bali church relocated to the district from other villages, they saw fires burning at night on the very hill where the Bussaus lived. But always, when the villagers investigated the next day, there was no sign of a fire to be found. Such stories were accepted as a part of life on the island of Bali, where spirits, good and bad, were as tangible to the people as the food they ate. *Dukuns*, the traditional Balinese witchdoctors, were known to spend weeks at long-distance duelling, summoning evil spirits and using them against a foe in another village. At night the villagers of Blimbingsari pulled their shutters down to keep out spirits.

Through the early months, the Bussaus heard of many spiritual encounters in the village and beyond—as down-to-earth westerners they dismissed them as local folklore. When they first moved into the white house, the children of the asrama told them stories of the strange goings-on around the area. One day, Carol heard a group of asrama children, who had been happily playing only minutes before, screaming in pure terror. 'We saw a hag's face,' they said. 'And many hands, without bodies.'

Another day Carol awoke with a feeling of deep depression. Things had been going well on the building site. The concrete had been poured into the cavernous footings and the crews would soon start building the pillars. But today Carol had awoken with a nightmare in her head, and it would not go away. Throughout the day, a shocking picture flashed through her mind. She saw her sweet five-year-old Rachel fall into the deep hole of the footings and strike her head on its concrete base. She felt Rachel was going to die that day.

In her mind she saw David carrying Rachel's slack body up out of the hole. In the long hours of that day she went through all the steps they would have to take. It was too hot to leave her, they'd have to bury her quickly. Would they ever be able to take her body home? Carol went over and over the possibilities until she was exhausted by the strain of it. All the while, she kept Rachel close by, waiting anxiously until David was due back from the site. His strength and stability would help her overcome her irrational fear. Off and on, she prayed all day, but she couldn't shake the dread.

When Carol saw David striding up the hill to their home, earlier than usual, she rushed to the door to meet him. Finally, I can tell him what I have been through, she thought, with some relief.

'Dave, I've had the most dreadful day. I can't shake off this picture in my mind of Rachel falling,' Carol blurted out. She explained her waking dream and how terrified she had been by it, expecting David to comfort her. She felt her hair stand on end just telling him about it.

Instead of moving to hold her, David stood still, a look of alarm sweeping across his face. He looked across to where Rachel played happily with Tasha.

'I had it too,' he said quietly. For a moment they stood staring at each other, trying to make sense of this unseen, unfulfilled event that had had their hearts racing with fear.

'All day I've fought off a picture in my mind where I'm carrying Rachel up the steps here and you're waiting at the top,' he explained. 'I came home early to make sure she was all right.'

The presence of evil swirled around them. They could almost touch it. Were they too meeting the forces of alas rangda? It was far outside their own experience and they knew of no response but to clutch each other and pray to God for protection. Were they meant to run away? They would not. The incident brought out an internal strength they had not had to find before. Together they could do this. They stood firm and steeled themselves to stay and finish the job.

Life in Blimbingsari was the training ground for much of David's later work in development. Despite the isolation of the village, David and Carol frequently made interesting new connections. It was while living in the village that David met Mac Bradshaw, an

American who had started a program called Partnership in Mission (PIM), aimed at bringing together people like Wayan Mastra: ministers who were working within their own cultural contexts. Mac's connections would later prove vital to David's work.

David was still in touch with the network of work parties from the Uniting Church that he had enlisted during the year in Darwin and, in April 1977, a work party from Newcastle arrived to help the community. When they looked around they saw a clear gap—facilities for children. With the purest of motives, David and the group decided to do something for the children of Blimbingsari. There was nowhere for them to gather and play and so a playground seemed the obvious way to help them. Before long, the work party had made a beautiful playground, a sight to make any child's face light up, with swings, a slide and roundabout, built right in the middle of the village.

There was only one problem: the children were so busy doing their jobs of carting water and collecting firewood after school that they did not have time to use it. Besides, hanging around on play equipment just did not fit into their culture; the adults in the village had been too polite to tell the visitors it was a culturally inappropriate kindness. Only Tasha and Rachel could really enjoy it, though occasionally their Balinese friends ventured down to join them.

The playground in the village would eventually disappear, and a communications tower would stand in its place but there were some positive outcomes. The episode made the local people of Blimbingsari wonder if they should be doing more for the children in the village. Why couldn't the children take more time to play? they wondered. David learned the hard way that the first thing to do was consult with the local people to find out their needs. This principle would later help him develop deep and trusting relationships around the world.

There were other, more embarrassing cultural lessons to be learned in Blimbingsari. At the end of one work party visit the villagers and visitors decided to celebrate with a concert. The Balinese had prepared some items for the evening, and soon a small troupe of child dancers shuffled delicately onto the stage, their hair crafted into place and make-up accentuating the beauty of their fine-boned faces. The visitors sat intrigued as the children performed an intricate dance they had learned from their early years, with every darting movement controlled and perfected.

When the performance was finished there was a rush of enthusiastic applause, followed by an awkward pause. The cultural divide left both sides not quite knowing what to do next. The Balinese were shy and uncertain about the westerners in their village—there had been few westerners there before.

When one of the local people beckoned to the audience, Carol interpreted it as an invitation to respond with their own cultural item. She leaned towards David and whispered 'Dave, can you think of something we can perform in return?' David wasn't a dancer or singer, but he had learned a little of Maori culture as a child in New Zealand. We'll do the haka, he thought. He rose to his feet and gathered up the work group—even those who were Australian and had no idea what was involved in doing a haka.

'I'll show you how it goes,' he offered as the visitors prepared to go through the indelicate motions of the haka, the Maori warriors' preparation for war. 'Ka mate, ka mate'—meaning, ''Tis death, tis death'—David pushed out the chant, accompanied by menacing facial expressions and aggressive movements intended to scare an enemy. Nothing could be further from the delicate sweeps of Balinese dance.

When the performance finished there was not a sound to be heard. The gentle village people sat still, wondering what they had brought into their midst. Then they quietly dispersed.

Cultural misunderstanding would emerge again when another work group joined the villagers for a concert. Among the western visitors was a young ballet dancer who volunteered to dance for the audience. The ever-polite Balinese women sat neatly folded onto mats on the ground, wearing sarongs that covered all but their ankles, the men equally elegant and contained. The young dancer rose to her feet and started gracefully moving to the music, in western eyes dancing as beautifully as her Indonesian counterparts. She slowly extended her leg, her toe pointed with just the right amount of curl, in synch with her slim arms and fine fingers. Then she lifted the leg as high as her shoulder, a feat of great flexibility, sweeping it across her chest and down again.

But the Balinese were not ready for some of her moves. 'Aahhh,' came the loud, spontaneous gasps from the Balinese among the audience. They had never seen such a risqué movement and show of flesh. Throughout the performance the locals collectively gasped each time the girl thrust her leg into the air.

Ron Hewitt, an Australian contractor, arrived with his wife Meg in May 1977 to help on the site. Ron was more than just a volunteer builder to David. He was a gregarious character who had been a close friend and mentor to David in the Waverley church. He was older than David and had in some aspects played a fatherly role in David's life. From the minute he arrived, Ron loved being in the village, where he and Meg stayed in the home of one of the villagers. Each day he wrote in a diary the detail of village life, of the cool water scooped each morning from the bak for his bath, the pre-dawn crow of the rooster nearby, the warmth of his hosts. His bright personality drew a glowing response from the Balinese.

The week before, David and Carol had taken the Hewitts on a tour of the island, stopping at the silver factories of Celuk. As they wandered past the glass displays, Ron and Meg paused, admiring a silver necklace with small hearts on it. 'That's lovely, I'll buy that for you,' Ron said to Meg, within earshot of Carol. She was about to step in and say 'Don't buy that here, these are tourist prices,' when she heard a clear inner rebuke: 'Don't interfere.' She turned her back and bit her lip as Ron bought the necklace, a gift Meg would treasure.

By the time the Hewitts came to Blimbingsari the concrete skeleton of the building was reaching up into the sky. Many of the men were working high up on scaffolding, but Ron was working just two or three metres above the ground on a ladder. As the men hammered and scraped, David heard a thud on the concrete floor beneath him. He looked down to see Ron's unconscious body lying below. He scrambled down and found his friend still breathing. Could he have suffered a heart attack and fallen? They had no way of knowing. Soon the whole team was gathered around, and David quickly took what action he could, sending one of the workers for a sheet to keep his friend warm.

'I'll go down to the Melaya road and bring back a car,' Yusef offered, and roared off on a motorbike. Without a car in the village there was no other option. Meanwhile, they had to keep Ron going until they could get him to a hospital.

Word of the accident raced around the village and within minutes Carol and Meg heard the news, though there was nothing they could do but wait for transport. Down on the main road, Yusef had managed to flag a local taxi, a *bemo*, and after what seemed like hours to those waiting, arrived back for Ron.

As they set out on their long ride to the hospital, Ron lay across David's lap, bleeding and faint. David held his friend, trying to comfort and assure him, knowing they might lose him if they didn't get medical attention soon. Ron had lost litres of blood by the time the bemo finally arrived at the nearest hospital.

Here they were met by a cold supervisor. 'Sorry, Pak, we can't take him here. The accident did not occur in this region,' he told David.

'But he could die if he doesn't see a doctor right now,' David pleaded. He was desperate, appealing to the man in every way he could think of, but the man was unyielding. There was nothing to do but try another hospital. They sped along the main road to a hospital closer to Denpasar, but Ron slipped away before they could get there, dying in David's arms. At the next hospital they were directed to the morgue in Denpasar. Several hours later, with Ron's body still wrapped in a sheet, the bemo arrived at the morgue. Here, a doctor examined Ron and wrote in his report, 'He hit his head on the concrete.' An error in translation had the report saying, in English, 'The concrete hit him on the head', a reversal of meaning that allowed the interpretation that Ron was deliberately hit, adding further confusion to a difficult situation.

Meg Hewitt waited with Carol in Blimbingsari for a whole day with no way of knowing her husband's fate. Carol comforted her as best she could. Late that night, many hours after he and Ron had left the village, David came back alone to break the news of her husband's death to Meg. It was surreal. An idyll turned to a nightmare in a moment. The next day Meg travelled with David to Denpasar, in a daze, and soon after they both went with Ron's body on a sad flight home to Sydney.

Still, though he was shaken as never before, David had to return to the village and convince his team of workers to press on. For two weeks, none of the workers came near the site. They were convinced there was an evil spirit on the building. Day after day, David went up on the scaffolding on his own, to show them it was safe. Then one day, a young Hindu boy named Made Wenton joined David, and the others slowly started to trickle back. Soon, they came to see that finishing the building would be a way of honouring Ron's memory.

On a visit back to Sydney earlier that year, David had bumped into a young fellow named Leigh Coleman on the street. Leigh was the shaggy-bearded renegade who had regularly turned up at the Waverley church with his bike gang, to hustle at the snooker tables in the hall where David ran the local youth group. He had worked as a labourer on several of David's building sites. The two fell into easy conversation.

'What are you doing with yourself these days, Dave?' Leigh asked.

'We're living in Bali, in the jungle, doing a bit of building,' David replied, in a typically understated way.

'Do you need a hand up there?'

'Yes, I could really use a hand. There's a lot to do,' was David's reply. There were no numbers exchanged, or dates or times discussed, no firm undertaking on either side.

Not long before his encounter with David, Leigh had returned, disappointed, from a journey to India to 'find himself'. He had tired of running his motorbike business and was at a crossroads in his life, just as David had been two years before. Whatever Dave was up to in Indonesia, it seemed more promising than going back to the rut of work and drugs he had fallen into, Leigh thought. Besides, Leigh owed David a favour. David had helped him out with ideas and introductions when he'd needed some credibility to set up his business in Sydney. With David's backing to kick him off, Leigh had run a successful motorcycle business, with three showrooms around the city.

Leigh came to Bali by a cheap but circuitous route. He flew to Perth, then jumped on a Russian cargo ship, the *Turkmania* from Vladivostok, travelling as far as Singapore. He then went overland across Java to Denpasar, where he hired a motorbike and rode out to Blimbingsari.

When Leigh arrived, David had just left for Sydney with Meg Hewitt and Ron's body. Leigh moved into the third bedroom of the little white house. He came for a couple of months but stayed for over a year. David assigned Leigh to the dam-building team, which meant being up before dawn each morning to meet other workers in the village centre and making an hour-long trek through forest and jungle up the mountain to the dam site. Most days David stayed with the men working on the church, road and bridge projects down in the village; he only visited the dam on his motorbike from time to time to supervise progress.

At the dam, the men worked from sunrise to sunset, but they always stopped for a long break as noon approached. They cooked their lunch and brewed strong Balinese coffee over an open fire, then settled under a tree for a nap until the harshest heat of the day subsided. The mountain was regarded as an evil one by the Balinese because there was no water flowing from it. The mountains with good spirits had streams that became rivers. The dam they were building would collect water in the rainy season to see the people through the dry months.

Though quite small, the dam itself was a complex piece of engineering. It was built into a volcanic gorge and, to secure the structure, the team drilled right through the volcanic rock and pumped a slurry of concrete into it so that the water couldn't leak under the dam. They then built an earth-filled dam with an impervious clay core and covered the whole thing in reinforced concrete. Not even a flood would have brought that structure down the mountain into the villages. Every piece of material—all the cement and pipes and other materials needed, and even the electricity generator—had been lugged up the mountain on the men's backs.

It was hard work, but not without joy and hilarity. Once, as the men lounged about resting in the heat of the day, a bull ant crawled up the inside of Leigh's leg and planted its sting in the most tender of places. As Leigh hopped around in acute pain, his eyes welling with tears, Yusef rattled with laughter. 'He's gone to visit the king, Leigh,' he hooted. Leigh could only laugh along, despite his agony.

Arranging materials for any of the building projects meant a five day round trip in a hired truck to Surabaya or Bandung in East Java. Sometimes David took Yusef along for the twenty four hour journey across the Bali Strait to Ketapang then up to the industrial cities of Java. Once there, they hunted out materials or found themselves sitting, at times waiting for days, while bolts or other vital materials were made to order. On one occasion David planned to go with just Leigh and made arrangements for a four wheel drive vehicle to collect them at ten in the morning on a designated day. The men waited and waited that day, and were vigilant the next, but it wasn't until two days later that the driver and car arrived for them. Moments before departure several friends appeared, bags packed and ready to travel with them to Java, leaving them no choice but to crowd the unexpected fellow travellers into the vehicle for the long journey.

With every inch of the old car crammed with flesh and luggage, a strange bug started to take hold of Leigh. Along the road to the ferry, his temperature rose and the crush of bodies removed any fresh air that might have helped with the waves of nausea. The ferry ride allowed him space but no reprieve from his sickness. By the time the group arrived in Surabaya, Leigh was as wet as a rag and in a sorry state. As the others dispersed to the homes of friends or relatives, David quickly moved himself and Leigh from the cheap accommodation they had booked into a comfortable hotel where Leigh could recover for the return journey to Bali. This sickness was one of other illnesses—including malaria, typhoid and a variety of stomach bugs—that Leigh endured during his time in the village.

In the forests near Blimbingsari were people called *contrakan*, who lived outside the villages and foraged or killed wild animals to survive. They were brought to the area by the government from small islands nearby and were paid a pittance to cut down the teak forests for export. Once the forests were gone, the people were left without jobs—they were desperately poor. At night they could be heard in the forest, cutting up small logs to sell around villages as firewood. The contrakan children were visibly undernourished, with pot bellies and skinny little legs, and it was only the strong among them who survived. One family in the forest had just one surviving child of the thirteen they had borne. They had never had access to a doctor, and the babies rarely made it past their first year. Families like this were so desperate they would give their children away to keep them alive.

One day on the way to the dam Leigh saw a group of contrakan standing around a wild pig they had found and slaughtered. As he moved closer to talk to them, he looked at the pig, and there, writhing around its innards, were hundreds of maggots.

'You shouldn't eat that, it's no good,' he told them. But they were so hungry they ignored him. They took the diseased pig away and later shared it among other families.

Nevertheless, the strongest of these forest people were up at the dam site every day, moving rocks and later laying pipes, and they were rewarded for their efforts. After a year, the water flowed from the dam—it went first to these people, then to a Hindu village close to the mountain, and finally to Blimbingsari. The results were dramatic. With a secure water supply, the villagers could produce much more food, and even think about selling some, where before they had only ever had just enough to survive. The forest dwellers could think about cultivating their own food. In Blimbingsari, there were now two rice harvests a year instead of one.

The government was so delighted at the visible improvement in the standard of living for the people in this remote part of west Bali, that it built a new road into the area as a reward. When electricity came to the region, Blimbngsari was the first village to be connected. The village was then awarded a prize by President Soeharto for the most improved rice production in the country.

Yet there were still many concerns. Health care was the most obvious and, after meeting with the village leadership, David agreed to fund a mobile health clinic with a paramedic and two nurses. The nurses travelled from village to village in the district on their bikes, dispensing much-needed advice on health matters and family planning. So great was the need that they met with a long line of patients in each village they visited on their rounds.

Of most concern to David was the lack of economic activity in Blimbingsari and surrounding villages. If the young villagers could afford to leave for an education in high school and university in

Denpasar, or even Java, there was little for them to do if they returned to the village, even with its new roads, new bridge, new buildings and water supply.

For a year, David had been consumed by the daily issues of building infrastructure. The structural part of the building was now almost complete and the Balinese artisans would soon start the laborious job of carving its stone and timber adornments and weaving its *alang alang* roof. But he felt that the task was not yet complete. There was still the problem of poverty and lack of economic opportunity. His own experience and observation of the way 'development' worked at the time told him that charity was not the answer. He had already worked his way out of that place, and knew the value of dignity and the satisfaction of personal achievement. He started wondering about ways to create jobs, and he always came back to what he knew from his experience. Small businesses could do that.

As the family's time in the village was drawing to a close, a bigger picture was emerging for David. He was thinking much more about longer-term benefits of development, things beyond roads and buildings. He and Wayan were about to embark on a life-changing experiment.

7

Stretching Out

Pak Nyoman Yusef, the foreman on the Blimbingsari building site, was a hardworking man, motivated and keen to improve himself. He held an esteemed position within the village hierarchy, sitting on a committee of village elders making decisions aimed at benefiting the whole community. He proudly carried out his job of organising teams of workmen for all the projects around the village. On the days when he was not working on or organising the construction teams he ran a small business selling coconuts, cutting his way through the tangled undergrowth behind his home into groves of slender coconut trees.

Yusef was slight but strong, and plodded with his ox along the jungle paths criss-crossing the side of the mountain collecting coconuts, and then back to his tiny house, where he hacked at the sinewy husks with a machete. Every few weeks, when he had built a tall mound of coconuts behind his hut, buyers arrived from Melaya to collect the fruit and ship it up to the factories in Java for oil.

'We'll give you 5000 rupiah for the lot,' they offered. It was a pittance, but still money in his hand. How else could he earn an income? He knew he had no right to bargain for more.

Yusef was, like everyone else in the village, from the church leaders to the *kepala desa*, the village head, living from hand to mouth and vulnerable to every misfortune nature served up. In a dry year, when the rains arrived late and their crops shrivelled, the villagers were at the mercy of the moneylenders in the larger towns to tide them over until the next year, when they hoped to repay the loan.

None of this was lost on David. He came to Bali with a simple, western view of poverty. It was only lack of resources that brought about hunger and poverty, wasn't it? During the year his perception of poverty had been recast. The poor became friends and co-workers as he moved between villages and islands to work on small development projects and talked with people about their lives. The realities of poverty were stark and shocking, its causes complex and even endemic.

David was surprised by the number of people he met, mostly in Java and Sumatra, who were locked into cycles of generational debt. Parents with young children had already condemned them to a life of hard labour, just as their own parents had done to them, and their parents' parents before them. Hardest to accept was the fatalism and sense of futility he encountered about the debilitating debt and even the harshness of daily life. 'We're not going to live long anyway, so why worry?' was the message he heard.

David returned from his travels outside the village with stories of poverty that brought Carol to tears. After the girls had gone to bed they often sat up late by the kerosene lamp in their cottage, talking of the plight of poor Indonesians.

'Is there a way out?' Carol asked sadly.

'It seems to me the people have lost all hope. They see little purpose in life,' he replied. 'No one I've met is making plans for the future.'

It troubled David that the hardworking people of Blimbingsari, whom he knew well and respected, shared this malaise. They bravely faced each day in their poverty, locked in a daily struggle for survival and unable to plan beyond the next day. Their prospects were now vastly better because they had roads out of the village and bridges over the ravines, so they could get their produce to market, and a water supply meant they could produce more food to sell in the market. They were proud of their clean and efficient village. Yet how could they look to the future when the spectre of moneylenders hung over them, waiting to profit from their need? When Wayan visited the village the two men spent hours discussing ways the community could help itself. There had to be a solution to this economic dead-end. 'We need to give money to people without them becoming spoiled, so they have to return it, like revolving funds,' Wayan said. David agreed wholeheartedly with this approach. His business background told him that loans rather than straight charity would be more beneficial and dignified in the longer term. Many years before, the church had started a revolving animal scheme, where the villagers received goats, pigs and cows to raise and fatten, sharing the income on their sale. Wayan now wanted to teach them farming skills and help train young Balinese for the tourist industry. His ideas became an early and defining influence on David.

Just as importantly, David's entrepreneurial approach influenced Wayan. David provided the business brain. Wayan had found in David and Carol a couple willing to help without conditions, a couple with financial resources they now offered to share. 'If you can identify some people with good business ideas, we will find the money,' David volunteered to Wayan. 'We can surely generate some work for other people in the village.'

The first loans he and Carol made were large, in the thousands of dollars, much more than a bank would ever have lent anyone in the village—if they could have qualified at all. One of these first loans went to a local man named John Panca. He was bright and enterprising, with the foresight to see just how important tourism would become to Bali in the years ahead. He used the loan to set up one of Bali's first travel agencies—and he had big plans for future expansion.

After a series of substantial loans, it became clear to David and Carol that they risked exhausting their resources if they only gave large amounts. With smaller loans they could help more people and reach those who were even poorer. A series of smaller loans soon flowed, each one going to someone David and Wayan knew would build a business and employ others. They were resourceful people who came to Wayan bubbling with small business ideas that could improve their lives; some involved tourism down in the Kuta area. David was assured that Wayan had a close feel for the needs of the people around him.

Yusef was among the first of David's friends to receive a smaller loan, for one thousand dollars, but he and the others would never have known the money came from David. As far as they knew, it was a loan from the Bali church. David knew intuitively that for the lending to work, he needed to be sensitive to the community's own authorities. Each village had a hierarchy that commanded respect. In a nearby village one lowly ranked villager had watched helplessly as those higher in the chain of command destroyed his new bicycle in a jealous rage. The last thing David wanted to do was create jealousy and division among his Balinese friends, or to force his western ways onto people he knew could find their own answers. Working in the village had tempered David's fierce independence. As he struggled to communicate with the men on the site through the early days he quickly learned that nothing in this community would happen without teamwork.

Yusef's excitement was barely containable when he received his loan. It was more money than he had expected to see in his lifetime. The jungles around Blimbingsari were overflowing with coconuts that fell and lay wasted on the ground before they could be collected, and he dreamed of having the means to build a stockpile so that he could sell when prices were higher.

He set out for Denpasar in search of a truck, and settled on a beaten-up one with high, red, peeling wooden sides that had already bumped along Bali's rough roads for many years. It was perfect. He imagined the hundreds of coconuts he could pile into it. He proudly arrived back in Blimbingsari, one of the few men in the village with his own vehicle. He now needed employees to cut and pull the husks off the fruit, to sort the good from the bad, and to load the truck so that he could drive across to Java (by ferry) to the large copra-processing plants. A whole new future opened up to him. His business thrived, and others brought their coconuts to him to sell.

The lending grew through relationships. David was discreet. 'If Mastra asked me to make the loan, I did it. I wasn't held up as the big white saviour who arrived in the village with a lot of money to lend.' In the early days he gave no thought to monitoring and reporting the impact of the loans, or even to how extensive the changes in a person's life might be when they had even a small degree of economic security to fall back on. For now it was personal, just David and Carol helping out a few friends. Yet even early on there were signs that the experiment was working.

David saw a change in Yusef over the year they laboured together. He saw his confidence grow as he accepted responsibility in his role of foreman on the building sites. The more Yusef recognised his own skill in organising people, the stronger and more assured he became. By the time he received his first loan, Yusef was ready to stretch himself, to look to the future, to take personal and business risks he would never have considered a year or so before.

The work with Wayan was only starting when it was time for David and Carol to leave Blimbingsari, just before Christmas 1977. With the clinic and the dam, and roads and bridges rebuilt—David's part of the church finished—the task they had set out to do was complete. They now needed to attend to their lives back in Sydney. David still held a partnership in a tiling and building supplies business, and with the construction industry at home suffering economic decline, its viability was in question. He expected to close it down when he returned home.

The entire village came down to the village meeting hall for the Bussaus' farewell, the women dressed in the traditional Balinese ceremonial dress of soft *kebayas* over neatly secured sarongs. They were slender and graceful, and came offering aromatic delicacies laid out on a square of banana leaf. The men marched in proudly in their long shirts and earthy batik sarongs secured by a yellow sash or *saput*.

The Blimbingsari community had seen more progress in their village in one year than in many decades before. How could they ever thank the Bussaus and the many other Australian people who had visited to help? Made Rungu, the erudite father of the community, the man they called 'the Moses of Bali', sat back quietly and watched, content to see his people with new hope, moving into new ways. He too had grown fond of David and Carol and their young girls.

David and Carol were sad to be leaving Blimbingsari. They knew there could be no going back to the first, electrifying taste of the unknown world they had experienced just a year before; nor could they recapture the simplicity and warmth of village life. It was a sad moment for Leigh too, though he planned to stay on in the village for some months to help finish the projects.

Even as they left, the Bussaus knew that Bali was part of their future, that the bond with their Balinese friends was strong and lasting. In fact, David's role was still in its infancy. Some months before, he had started working on his next project, a meeting room and accommodation for a hotel training school at Dhyana Pura, down on the beach in Seminyak, close to the tourist hub of Kuta.

'I'll come back and help finish that project,' he promised Wayan.

Back in Australia, David and Carol wanted to formalise the way they used their finances by setting up a vehicle for giving. In 1974, Carol's close friend Judy Brown, a fellow teacher, had died and left her $9000. Instead of spending the money, Carol put it aside, intending to use it on education, as a legacy to Judy. Now, David and Carol decided to use Judy's money as the seed for a charitable trust that would allow them to move ahead with the development work they had started in Indonesia. Maranatha Trust was founded in 1979. Within two years, the Bussaus had sold and transferred all their assets, other than their own home, into Maranatha. David brought in Ken Needs, an accountant and former partner in the tile business, and his wife Lynn, as the third and fourth trustees of the foundation. The trust would sustain the Bussaus for some time.

After Blimbingsari, they knew how happy they could be with a simple lifestyle. They had never been extravagant people who yearned for holiday houses and expensive clothes. They now made a decision to invest their money and talent in this work, their calling. It would be more than a job or an act of altruism. It was a way of life, and there was no going back. The Bussaus' friends could see the change in them that had come about in just two years, since the move to Darwin. David was now focused on development and, although the details were still to be filled in, quite sure of his direction in life. Carol arrived home with new confidence. She had overcome her illness, run a hostel in Darwin,

103

home-schooled her daughters and taught young Balinese in an isolated village, each time confronting her own fear that she was not up to the task. There was little that would faze her now.

David soon found a well of interest from friends and acquaintances in his fledgling development work, with small amounts of money coming from many quarters. His own passion and integrity shone a light on the plight of poor Balinese and this unusual way of dealing with their poverty.

David and Wayan were in contact throughout 1978 as the Bussaus prepared for a longer break from Sydney. They all agreed that the family would soon return to Bali and David's first task would be to supervise the building of the Dhyana Pura conference hall. In the meantime, David and his friend Garry Cairncross, a draftsman, came up with a detailed plan for the training centre. Along with the conference hall, it included student and staff accommodation, restaurants, classrooms and a workshop.

David was mindful of not pushing himself onto the Balinese, prefacing the finished plan with the following statement:

The intent is to provide a skeleton structure and broad outlines only so that 'Dhyana Pura' can determine its own method of implementation and operation. It would be presumptuous of me to attempt any other role than this.

David's attitude was a refreshing change from the heavy-handed and paternalistic approach colonial powers and missionaries had often taken in previous centuries. He instinctively knew not to force his own thoughts onto his Balinese friends. He would suggest and encourage rather than push.

When the Bussaus returned to Bali at the beginning of 1979 it was to a newly-built thatched cottage at Dhyana Pura, a tropical enclave two hundred metres from the main Kuta Beach thoroughfare, Legian Road. It was along a dirt walking track, past water-filled rice paddies. Ten years before the whole area had been paddies, but when tourism drove up land values many rice farmers exchanged beachside farming for terraces higher up the mountain, or set up their own small businesses with the proceeds from the sale of their land. Dhyana Pura was still a sparse collection of buildings scattered across the twelve hectare site, but the conference hall and new accommodation for hotel guests and students were soon underway.

The small tiled verandah at the front of the Bussaus' cottage became a meeting point, a place where friends gathered in the evenings to talk and catch the sea breezes and magnetic red sunsets on the horizon beyond Kuta Beach. Within weeks of arriving, Tasha and Rachel had collected a pet monkey and adopted a mangy old dog called Snowy, which would engage in vicious fights with other mangy dogs outside the family's cottage.

No one could have anticipated the extent to which the western world would embrace the uncrowded volcanic beaches and sacred mountains of Bali, but Wayan Mastra and others were anticipating an influx, and he knew that tourism training was needed to build employment opportunities for Bali's young people. It was a gamble. What if tourism in Bali didn't take off?

Word spread quickly that a tourism training school, one of the first on the island, was starting up at Dhyana Pura. Young people streamed in from around the island, excited and keen to be part of Bali's future. Most had scant knowledge of the world outside their village; their homes had dirt floors and squat toilets, if they had them at all. This training could lead to jobs in hotels, restaurants and airlines, and opportunities that had been beyond their reach until now. Some of the young people the Bussaus knew from Blimbingsari, from the village school and the orphanage beside their small home, now came to work or train down at Seminyak.

There was great excitement when gentle Ketut Wasiati, the Bussaus' pembantu in the village, arrived to learn to be a kitchen supervisor. There were others. Ketut Suwirya, the young economics graduate Carol had coached in English in the village while he cared for his sick father, had jumped at the chance of training in hotel management. Made Wenton, the young boy who defied evil spirits in Blimbingsari to return to work after Ron Hewitt's fatal accident, was back by David's side, this time training to be an electrician. Ketut Waspada, son of Made Rungu, the village founder, and newly returned with a doctorate in theology from Germany, became the first manager of the Dhyana Pura hotel training school. He later had the satisfaction of seeing his students spreading out into good jobs across the tourist industry, meeting them on planes, and in management of international hotels. Eventually the school would produce three thousand graduates each year.

Although still only in their thirties, David and Carol assumed the role of unofficial guardians to the young people. Over the next two years they continued to sensitively meet the needs of those around them, as they had in Sydney, quietly financing study in Java for a young woman here, or a piece of land for a newly-wed couple there, without keeping tabs or putting expectations on those who received their generosity.

David now took the hands-on job of managing Dhyana Pura. There was so much to teach the students. Some took to garden-ing, to room cleaning, or front office management. Those like Made Wenton, with a maintenance bent, learned about electrical work or plumbing or carpentry in the workshop. Teams of skilled helpers arrived from Australia to volunteer their expertise.

If Carol thought her new life by the beach in Bali might be leisurely, she soon found otherwise. She set up a routine of teach-ing Tasha and Rachel their lessons in the morning then moving on to training sessions and language lessons for the tourism students later in the day. Her life became a balancing act between her com-mitment to the girls' education, to the students, and to meeting Tasha and Rachel's need for fun.

The sound of the waves breaking just metres away on Kuta Beach and the laughter beyond the cottage lured the girls' atten-tion from their lessons, yet Carol stood firm. She was determined to keep a close eye on Tasha and Rachel. The beach was notori-ous for dangerous currents that could pull weak swimmers out of their depth. Some years before, Wayan and Ketut Mastra's seven-year-old daughter, Ketut, drowned when currents in shallow surf pulled her out to sea, after ripping her from visitors' hands on either side. The story terrified Carol.

At first Carol became involved in the aesthetics of the new hotel, hanging curtains and decorating rooms. Then she took on the task of training the students to western hotel standards. She knew that if they were to be part of the new tourism industry, they needed to learn to clean bathrooms to the level tourists would expect, to hang a towel in a certain way, and to be attentive to tourists' needs. She showed them how to make up the beds with perfectly squared corners, to clean toilets with disinfectant, and to use different cloths for the toilet and basin.

The young Balinese were relaxed and amiable, open to learning, but often saw little use in fastidious details like dusting. 'We never have to dust in the village,' they sometimes laughingly challenged Carol. She would find them giggling and talking, the duster waving around in the air, rarely brushing the furniture. 'Ibu Carol, what is wrong with this?' She could see their point, but she persevered, calling on her teacher's patience.

In the hotel dining room Carol pulled out her favourite recipes to set up the western menu that would be demanded by less adventurous tourists. She taught simple cooking techniques to the trainee chefs and showed restaurant staff where to place knives and forks and napkins on a table. She trained those preparing the food not to wash the lettuce and tomatoes in unboiled water. Each afternoon she tutored them in the basics of English, working out role plays about every aspect of the work, from providing room service and greeting guests at reception to waiting on tables in the restaurant.

One young man, Gusti Tri Jata, an eighteen-year-old from a village near Penataran in the north of Bali, was training to work at the front desk. In his tiny village, the only prospect for work was labouring in a coffee plantation.

'Now Gusti, how would you greet a man arriving at the hotel before lunch?' Carol tested him.

'Good morning, sir,' he replied awkwardly. Like all Carol's students, Gusti was good-natured, laughing his way through his fumblings with the strange language.

'Ibu Carol, I'm going walking walking now,' he once said to Carol, making a literal translation of '*jalan jalan*', the Indonesian words for walking. When he realised his mistake he collapsed, giggling. Another time he instructed a guest to make his way to his room 'by feets'. Later, when he started paid work at the Dhyana Pura reception, he found an ingenious way around his language problem when English-speaking guests arrived. He tucked his two young Australian friends, Tasha and Rachel, under the front desk so that if he struggled with a word they popped up, like small ventriloquists, to help him out.

Before long there was a steady flow of conferences at Dhyana Pura, putting pressure on David and Carol to prepare everything on time. David often rose at five in the morning to clean out the conference room from the day before. If someone was sick in the village or it was a holiday on the Hindu calendar the staff disappeared, leaving David and Carol to fill the gaps.

'There was constant pressure to get the students performing at a reasonable level, to upgrade standards,' David says. 'Doing things within a certain time frame was a difficult concept. It was a matter of holding their hand and working through it.' He set up a system of clocking in, to overcome the entrenched Balinese concept of rubber time.

In the early days he went from door to door in the mornings to get the students into the habit of being punctual, calling 'Selamat pagi, Made,' or 'Wake up, Ketut.'

Far from grumbling, in their eagerness to learn they deeply appreciated David's morning intrusion. 'We're coming, Pak David,' they called back cheerfully.

Though she had enjoyed life in Blimbingsari, Carol had experienced lonely times when David was away or working. Dhyana Pura was an entirely different place. Australian work parties and other helpers flew in regularly to help with building and teaching, and the popularity of the conference centre was growing. She was surrounded by interesting visitors and good friends among the Blimbingsari crowd and the pastors' wives. The girls had many friends among the children around the guesthouse and loved it when Australian visitors arrived with children, venturing out into the reception to size them up. Would they be fun? Would they enjoy the same games? Their eyes lit up when one family from Sydney, the Holdens, came with two children of a similar age. Visitors meant they might go to Poppies restaurant down at Kuta for dinner, where they scrambled around under the table, or explored the ponds and streams and bridges of its gardens, as the adults talked and talked. Usually they ended the night curled into an adult's lap as the group kept talking.

Occasionally, there were Sunday visits to big hotels—the Bali Beach at Sanur, or Legian Beach Hotel just along the beach from Seminyak. Here the girls played games in the pool for hours with their father, ate ice cream and ended the day's outing with a plain western meal.

Midway through 1979, Gary and Di Cairncross came to stay at Dhyana Pura with their children Glen and Catherine. While Di and Carol stayed at Dhyana Pura with the four children, David took Garry across to Sulawesi, the large odd-shaped island to the north-west of Bali, to meet a struggling community of Balinese transmigrants, a group moved to the island by the government in the 1970s and 1980s to ease the overcrowding of Java and Bali. Some of the transmigrants had come through Blimbingsari for training before being shipped off, armed with shovels and other farming implements so that they would not starve. David wanted to see how he might help them set up small businesses in their communities.

Garry soon found himself the butt of David's humour. At the airport in Ujung Pandang in south Sulawesi a group of young girls pointed and giggled in Garry's direction. 'Hey, they fancy you,' David smiled. He knew they were fascinated with Garry's hairy arms, clearly on view in a short-sleeved shirt. David soon caught on to the action and announced in Indonesian, 'Namanya Pak Rambut,' which brought more fits of giggles. He had told them Garry's name was Mr Hairy. At the next stop, Palu, a group of community leaders broke into laughter when David introduced Garry again as Pak Rambut. It broke the ice, and they too warmed to the affable Garry.

The drive from Palu, a bustling regional centre, to the sparsely populated Parigi region on the west coast of Sulawesi was a dangerous one. It involved four hours of violently winding, landslide-prone roads in an old Land Rover with three bald tyres, a single headlight, and only one brake.

'You sit in the front,' David directed Garry before they started out from Palu.

'No, it's OK, you have the front, Dave,' Garry replied.

'No, you're the visitor, you'll get a much better view down the valley from the front,' David insisted.

They were just a kilometre from Palu when they had their first puncture. From there it only got worse for Garry. David had thoughtfully positioned him where he could see the view, but

Garry could only concentrate on the two hundred metre drop into a vine-tangled ravine just a metre to his side. Meanwhile, David placed himself diagonally opposite in the back seat to balance the car, and drifted peacefully off to sleep.

David now had even less leisure time than he'd had when running his own businesses in Sydney. Building the conference centre and then helping to manage the day-to-day operations of Dhyana Pura were just two of his roles. Small projects continued out in Blimbingsari, and he travelled back and forth to the village each week to oversee some aspect of the building. At the same time, the small lending programs he and Wayan had started were accelerating so quickly that David and Leigh, who by now had moved down to Dhyana Pura, scrambled to keep up with the demand. If the lending continued at this pace it would devour most of their time.

An explosion of other projects drew out David's creativity in new ways. Wayan had earmarked dozens of villages to be connected to water supplies. Wayan's own village, Sibetan, on the slopes of Mount Agung, was among the villages David first worked with; another was Segar, a remote mountain community in the driest part of the island.

With the dam finished, David wanted to involve Leigh in some of the other development work that was coming up. Most villages in Bali could be reached within a few hours, yet Segar was a taxing full day's hike from the road, along a track that defiantly hugged the mountainside—and was too narrow even for motorbikes. David and Leigh arrived in Segar late in the day, hungry and thirsty, and were met with a desperate scene. David had visited many poor villages in his time in Bali, but nothing compared with this forgotten place. It was eerily empty. Where were the goats tethered to poles and the chickens pecking the ground?

The village was a sparse collection of dusty-floored mud huts, with little else. There were none of the skinny, mangy dogs that were so common in every other part of Bali. As they looked around they noticed that nearly every adult in the village of Segar had a bulging goitre extending around the neck like a rubber ring, a telltale sign of poor nutrition. And where were the young people? Later they discovered that most of the younger members of the community left for larger towns as soon as they could.

Though desperately poor, the village head was a dignified man who welcomed David and Leigh as brothers. He was intrigued when he heard that foreigners were coming to help bring water to the village. Most people in the village had had little or no contact with foreigners and had not heard much about the wealthy other world these men came from. This miserable grouping of huts was their world—David and Leigh knew better than to tell them about their own world.

On the night of David and Leigh's arrival, the villagers prepared a welcome meal with the few resources they had on hand. Through waves and smiles—and with some help from David's knowledge of the Balinese language—the village leaders invited David and Leigh to sit down with them on the ground. Both men sensed a heightened level of anticipation among their hosts, and were soon to discover why. The village would celebrate the arrival of the two men with a rare feast.

'It is our custom to share our delicacies with visiting village heads,' the kepala desa proudly explained to David. In Segar, the hormone sac hidden safely in the dog's skull was the most prized of delicacies. The villagers all longed for the taste of the roasted dog, but it was offered first to David as a sign of esteem, followed by the village leaders.

'*Terima kasih*,' David thanked his hosts as he graciously accepted his portion. He swallowed the piece of slippery sac as quickly as he could without seeming rude, making sure his face remained expressionless. All the while, he tried desperately to keep his mind on matters other than the smell of burning dog's hair now permeating the village. With the main course behind him, David thought he was in the clear. He was wrong.

Dessert was a sweet custard made with the larvae of large spiders bred in the village for eating. Still, spider's larvae was a more pleasant and sweeter option than a piece of dog's brain.

The welcoming meal did not put Leigh off. 'Leave it to me, Dave,' he responded when David asked him about running the project at Segar on his own. For the next four months Leigh lived with the people of Segar, working each day at installing a hydraulic ram pump and piping so that they could bring water into the village. Leigh lived in the worst conditions he had ever experienced: in a windowless mud hut, with a dirt floor and bamboo slats for a bed. When he closed the wooden door, day or night, he was plunged into an oppressively hot, pitch black cave, where only the spiders felt at home. There were days when he thrashed with fever on his merciless bed in the dark, sick and alone, but he remained, determined to finish the job.

His own suffering, he felt, was insignificant beside that of the villagers. The people of Segar died around him at a pitiful rate. Each day they ate only rice and perhaps one vegetable. The protein in their diet came from the dried fish they procured occasionally from people passing through from the coast. Water was a tangible addition to their prospects. If they used the water to grow more vegetables, they could trade a surplus for meat and fish; they would slowly become stronger, and able to think beyond daily survival.

David ran at a frantic pace, never pausing to philosophise about the work he was doing. When a village project arose he jumped on his motorbike and went to meet with the village leadership; soon there would be a plan of action. He then hit the phones to raise financial support, throwing his own money in to make sure it happened.

Leigh was proving a loyal and trustworthy offsider. After Segar, David knew Leigh could manage his own water project in Bali, from the planning stage through to raising the money needed and physically bringing in the water. The project David offered Leigh was small, but Leigh felt the weight of the responsibility. Before he started, the Australian Council of Churches (ACC) asked David to evaluate a series of programs it was running in Java, and Leigh joined David on the trip.

Away from the hectic workload of Bali, Leigh saw a small window where he might be able to to soak up some of David's accumulated experience. Since arriving in Indonesia, he had seen his former boss gain growing respect in the development field. Governments, churches and private sector now sought David's opinion on big-ticket development projects. He watched David develop his own style of leading from behind. He could see that David was stretched far beyond any of his life experience. David

top: Sedgley Boys' Home, scene of David William's early escapades and his home from the age of twelve to seventeen. Sedgley was a small working farm on the edge of Masterton in New Zealand, where the boys learned to work hard from an early age.

bottom: One of David's school photos from Wairarapa College in Masterton. He is in the centre of the back row.

top: David with Rocky Bussau, his adored younger 'sister'. Rocky was heartbroken when David and her parents became estranged.

bottom: David (centre front row, holding ball) was a talented sportsman, excelling in soccer and cricket. He captained many teams while at school.

top: The wedding day, 8 May, 1965. Carol Crowder, who was unwell on the day, struggled to make it to the altar.

bottom: David and Carol leaving New Zealand for Sydney by boat in January 1966.

top: Cyclone Tracy devastated the northern city of Darwin on Christmas Day, 1974. David quickly gathered a team together to help with the rebuilding process.

bottom: Eighteen months after leaving Sydney for Darwin, the Bussau family (from left Carol, Rachel, Tasha and David) moved on to the Balinese village of Blimbingsari, where David helped rebuild a local village damaged by an earthquake.

top: The girls loved Balinese village life. Ketut Wasiati (second from left), the young girl assigned to help them, became a part of their family.

bottom: The opening of the dam in Bali was cause for celebration. Ready access to water saved hours of carting by hand and ensured more frequent and reliable crops.

top: Pak Made Tegeg (left) was a poor potter who lived with his wife in the Balinese village of Kapal, near Denpasar. He first received a loan for 100 000 rupiah (US$110) in 1983 to make more pots, the first of sixteen loans. He now employs more than one hundred people from his community.

bottom left: David often spent his days travelling by bike from village to village to work on water and other development projects.

bottom right: Leigh Coleman frequently travelled with David in the early days and was often the operational person who assumed responsibility for the programs.

top: Pakistani kiln workers could be indentured to the kiln owners for many generations. David developed a project to release the workers from bonded labour, while providing health services, education and the means to build and own their own homes.

bottom: David was a regular visitor to Pakistan throughout the process of setting up the kiln project. Developing a program could take months of consultation.

top: Pak Nyoman Yusef from Blimbingsari was one of the first to receive a loan for his coconut business. He now processes 300 000 coconuts each month.

bottom: Priyadi Reksasiswaya joined David in the development field as an agricultural science graduate in 1981. He was David's first protégé and the person who drove expansion through Indonesia. He inspired many around him to help their poor countrymen and women.

was winging it, learning on the job once again, and in difficult and challenging circumstances. Leigh wanted to know his secret, so that he could apply it to his own project.

He prepared himself with a pen and paper one morning over breakfast in their Jakarta hotel. The next day David was flying to Sumatra for consulting work and Leigh was heading back to Bali. When David arrived at the table in the crowded dining room Leigh was ready. In rapid fire he asked, 'David, what's the formula? What is the first thing you'll do when you get off the plane? Who do you talk to and how do you plan it?'

David sat quietly for a few minutes then replied, 'Well, Leigh, it seems to me that you've got to learn to be sensitive.'

'Well, yeah, sure. What's next?' Leigh bounced back, still waiting. That was all David would offer him. He left for Bali puzzled, but the words 'be sensitive' kept coming back to him as he discussed the water project with the villagers. He found himself becoming more open to the villagers and their culture, more likely to sit back and ponder 'What do these people really want?' instead of simply solving the problem for them.

By now Leigh's life had completely changed course. He had lost interest in his former lifestyle, where the pursuit of better drugs and faster motorbikes had seemed to be his highest goals. Even the financial rewards of the businesses he ran in Australia for six years bore no comparison with the excitement and enjoyment of helping the Indonesians.

'What do you want me to do?' Leigh asked Wayan Mastra. As always, Wayan knew exactly what he wanted. 'Our people don't know how to do mechanics. Many people are now buying motorbikes—we must train them to look after them,' Wayan replied. Soon after, Leigh returned to Australia, trawling Sydney for manuals, tools and bike parts to haul back to Seminyak. He rented a small house in nearby Legian and set up a mechanics training school near the front of the Dhyana Pura site.

The mechanics school tested Leigh's patience to new limits. He was a laid-back hippie most of the time, but this was too much. The concepts, the tools and the technology of motorbikes were all foreign to young boys coming out of villages, and they often bungled their way through his tuition.

'They knew nothing about motorcycle maintenance, and that's an understatement,' Leigh recalled. One day Leigh lost it altogether. A student slipped as he shoved a screwdriver onto a delicate thread and it snapped off, rendering the motor useless.

'If you're not going to concentrate on what you're doing you may as well throw the motor out the window,' Leigh yelled in frustration before picking the motor up and doing just that. His angry outburst met with trembling silence from his students. Such emotional displays were entirely outside the bounds of Balinese culture.

More rewarding were the small loans he had started to make with his own money. Inspired by the effectiveness of the loans David was making, Leigh decided to follow his example. Leigh was well known among the locals of Legian. Most mornings he sat over a sweet Bali kopi chatting with the young business owners along Legian Road. He had come to know a batik painter named Cok who taught Balinese painting to young villagers in his studio at Kuta. Cok's dilemma was that his paintings were not selling, and he was so poor that he could only afford to eat one meal each day. Leigh could see Cok was not doing well. He suggested to Cok that he sell some Javanese batik as well, and on Leigh's next visit to Java he bought some Javanese paintings for Cok to display. They were snapped up within days by eager tourists.

'I'll get the welding guys at the mechanics school to make some displays so you can sell more,' Leigh offered. Cok was excited. He could see the potential for his business: that it could allow him to eat and continue with the Balinese-style painting he so loved. Next, Leigh took Cok to Java, where they met with local artists to discuss a regular supply of their paintings to his business in Bali. Leigh gave the artists $500 for materials and asked them to send their paintings to Bali in the quieter times, when they were not selling to tourists themselves. True to their word, a steady flow of paintings started to arrive in Kuta. Cok's business prospered beyond his dreams. He was among the earliest Balinese to bring the art of Java to the beach-loving tourists of Kuta, and saved he enough money to study law.

Though they were action-packed, David and Leigh would later reflect on the Dhyana Pura days as a carefree time. They were a knockabout pair, cowboys in the development field who were viewed with suspicion by those in traditional development circles and the missionaries they met. They were independent, funding themselves and not representing any organisation. They did not fit in anywhere, and yet here they were, espousing a view of enterprise development that seemed overtly commercial. They talked of loans, not grants. They were talking about repayments and interest when people were hungry. David was an anomaly in the late 1970s and early 1980s. He was one of the few people in Australia with hands-on expertise in development, and the only person to be working on micro lending. David could feel his creativity coming to life in a new and exciting way. His abilities had never been stretched in so many directions, and he was loving it. Still, he had no inkling of how quickly and how far this work would take him in the years ahead.

8

The Road Out of Poverty

By the end of 1979, David's underpowered motorbike was his constant companion. He spent long days zipping between water projects in outlying villages and building sites, coming back to Dhyana Pura at sunset. He was at once managing, training, building, financing, supervising and consulting. He relished being able to respond wherever he was needed.

The lending fuelled his imagination most of all, but in charging ahead in the direction of loans rather than charity, David had come up against stiff opposition. Infrastructure was an easier language to understand within the development world, something for the collective good of the community. Affluent governments and churches would fund schools, wells and hospitals. David's approach of economic empowerment promoted individualism. To some it was heretical to be linking the 'filthy' world of business and wealth creation, surely the very system that now subjugated the poor, with a solution to poverty. How was that charitable?

Though he did not know it, David was not entirely alone in his thinking. In other parts of the world other people were coming to realise that a handout system was not working. By the end of the 1970s, Muhammad Yunus had made his first small loans in Bangladesh, the beginnings of the Grameen Bank. In Latin America, a small US development agency named the Institute for

International Development Incorporated (IIDI) was funding business people through joint ventures, and ACCION International was setting up lending groups.

There was no denying that the loans were helping people out of poverty in a remarkable way. Pak Yusef had not looked back. He made his repayments and worked hard to build his coconut business. He enjoyed the dignity of being a self-employed. He did not want a handout. If his business thrived, the benefits could reach out into the community in the form of employment of others and increased spending.

Another of David's work colleagues, Pak Wayan Pegug, was also showing how much a life could change with some capital to work with. Pak Pegug was a labourer who had helped dig the foundations of Dhyana Pura. A hard worker and ambitious, as a small boy he had worked with his mother in a tiny warung where she sold food. Wayan set up his own small business alongside his mother's, selling gasoline and *es lilin*, an ice cream adored by local children. He had always thought that he would have his own business when he grew up.

Working at Dhyana Pura, Pak Pegug became a keen observer of David's approach to building, and David soon noticed his aptitude for the work. David also recognised the entrepreneurial spirit in Pegug. Here was a man eager to change his circumstances. David took Pegug under his wing, teaching him about arranging budgets, meeting deadlines and encouraging him to have confidence in his own ability. 'You've got to build up trust with your clients,' he told him. 'That means being honest, finishing the job when you say you will, and making sure it is on budget.' Then David demonstrated his own confidence in Pegug's ability by funding, along with American investors, a loan of two million rupiah, US$3500 at the time, so Pegug could set up his own construction company, CV Christina.

Two million rupiah was a king's ransom to Pegug. It paid for materials for his first job and petrol for the car, and allowed him to set up a line of credit to buy materials for other building contracts. Before long the first contracts rolled in and he could hire others to work for him. In the early days, no one, not Pegug nor David nor Wayan Mastra, could have foreseen where the first small building contracts would lead. Contracts to build churches, schools, shopping centres on Bali and neighbouring islands, and jobs for well over one hundred people, were all to follow for Pak Pegug. All four of his children received a university education. No one knew it at the time, but Pegug was an indicator of much bigger things to come. In the next two decades, Pegug's story would be repeated a million times, on a smaller scale, right around the world.

Even before the small loans, Wayan Mastra and other leaders of the Bali church had been active in helping the poor. The church owned a farm in the village of Kapal, an hour by bus from the island's capital city, Denpasar, which housed animals for a revolving animal scheme. The Kapal farm was now expanding to become a training farm, where poverty-stricken church members and others from the area could come to learn farming skills that would allow them to become self-supporting.

Rows of banana and mango trees lined one side of the farm, with rice in wet paddies, ponds for fish farming, and shaded beds for mushrooms on the other. There were daily lessons on how to raise goats and pigs and rabbits. Eggs from the thirty thousand chickens housed on the farm helped cover running costs. Any profit was ploughed back into the programs. Later, as David travelled more widely, he returned with new methods and farming technologies, such as the latest grain-drying and storage techniques. Then came joinery and engineering workshops.

By the time the Bussaus returned to Bali in 1979, the Kapal facility had become the focal point for the small business loans, with numerous villagers seeking funding for small businesses.

Late in 1979, a curious visitor came to the Kapal farm for a meeting that would change the direction of David's work. Hillary de Alwis, a Sri Lankan driven from his homeland by civil strife, had heard of the loans program while on holiday in Bali, and arranged to meet David at Kapal to see it for himself. Hillary was the Jakarta representative of IIDI. In 1971, IIDI had started a venture in Latin America with a similar aim—to help families out of poverty through their small businesses—and had found it similarly effective. IIDI's first loan went to a man named Carlos Moreno, who ran a spice and tea business in Columbia. That first venture was a resounding success, with Carlos able to repay his loan inside two years and hire eleven new employees. Ten years later he sold his business and retired on the proceeds. Hillary had not heard of anyone doing similar work until he stumbled across David.

There was another facet to Hillary's interest. To retain a presence in Indonesia, IIDI's visa and USAID (a US government aid body) funding required the agency to become involved in building infrastructure such as bridges, dams and schools. Hillary had excelled in making high-level contacts for IIDI in Indonesia, and had signed IIDI up to build a new hospital and school in Sumatra and some large water projects in Java. On his return to Jakarta from Bali, and with the enormity of these tasks in mind, Hillary phoned Barry Harper, his boss in the US. 'I've met an interesting Australian in Bali who might be able to help out as a supervisor of the government projects. He's also making a success of small business loans,' he reported to Barry, who soon hot-footed it down to Bali to enlist David's help.

Not long before, Barry Harper had left the affluence of the business world for third world development. He was one of a group of American businessmen influenced by the teaching of missionary Paris Reidhead on the need for economic empowerment in poorer nations. Paris had returned to the US from Ghana some time before, fired up with the idea that the best way to help poor entrepreneurs in the developing world was to transfer knowledge and business skills as well as finances.

Barry had just taken the helm of IIDI from Al Whittaker, former chief executive of the Mennen Company in the US and before that international president of the multi-national company Bristol Myers, a position that brought him into contact with poor communities when he visited the company's operations. Al had moved on to chair the board of IIDI, and he was another who had decided there was more to life than making money. Paris' thoughts on poverty, and the shocking poverty he had seen through his work, had inspired Al to action.

When Al's wife Marion challenged him at breakfast one day in 1970, 'How long are you going to continue making rich men richer?' he knew his time had come. Soon after, he resigned from the company, and he and Marion sold their home and moved to

Washington DC, where they would be close to decision-makers and more likely to be considered for development grants. Like the Bussaus four years later, Al and Marion lived on their own savings and investments rather than taking a salary. IIDI's earliest funding came from the sale of Al's company shares. Later, as IIDI grew, an independently wealthy businessman, Dan Swanson, made a major financial contribution.

David and Barry discussed the IIDI projects as they wandered along Kuta Beach. This was the venue for many of David's most significant meetings and deepest discussions.

As David and Barry talked, David could see that IIDI needed help with the large development projects it had promised the Indonesian government. He agreed to take on the challenge. David then made frequent visits to Jakarta to consult with Hillary, to meet with government officials and work on building designs with local engineers and architects. He commuted from Bali to the project sites to offer technical advice and push the jobs to completion, while still working on his own projects.

By 1980 the informal lending programs in Bali had grown substantially. Smaller loans had proved more effective and almost one hundred people had received credit, with the average size of the loans being around one hundred dollars. Some of the short-comings of the first loans had been addressed: more effective screening processes were in place, and the borrowers' capacity to repay, their work experience and business knowledge were also now considered. The structure of Balinese society worked well for small loans. Its communities were built around the clan, and family groupings within the clan, rather than the individual, as in western cultures. The clan was cohesive and strong. David learned early never to bypass its leaders, so lending always came with the agreement of the heads of villages and clans. Balinese Hindus took the repayment of debt seriously, because in their belief system, dying with debt could impede the spirit's transition to heaven.

The micro lending scheme evolved as David addressed other issues. At the time, people associated the church with charity and handouts. When loans went to church members, it could be harder to get repayment. If micro enterprise development was going to develop further, there had to be a clear distinction between the lending and charity. The programs had to be crystallised into a separate structure, run along business lines for small business people.

Ibu Nyoman Yulia, a gracious young woman who worked with the Bali church, joined as administrator of the programs, the first employee of an indigenous foundation devoted to starting small businesses and small development projects. Maha Bhoga Marga (MBM), meaning 'The Way to Prosperity', was founded in 1981, with a grant from IIDI and support from Maranatha Trust, David and Carol's foundation.

From the start, MBM had clear goals: 'to foster a spirit of self-reliance among those it assists. MBM beneficiaries enjoy an intangible pride of ownership, control over their families' and communities' welfare.' Though many non-government organisations were active in Bali, MBM became the first to provide small business loans. David was MBM's link to outside funding and support.

Meanwhile, David had handed over his management role at Dhyana Pura to Pak Sus, a savvy man in his late forties. He had worked as manager of a large hotel and as head of catering with Garuda Airlines. With a great understanding of tourism and hospitality, he was ideal for the job.

Pak Sus had a son in his twenties, Priyadi Reksasiswaya, who lived in Java, studying agricultural management at Bogor Agricultural University. David soon spotted Priyadi as a prime candidate to manage MBM. Yet Pak Sus had reservations about the position. Why take a lower-paid job when his qualifications guaranteed him a solid government position and a comfortable future?

Nevertheless, Pak Sus realised that Priyadi would probably end up in the job, so he turned to David. 'David, I want you to walk beside my son, Priyadi. Please take care of him and make sure he is not hurt.' In Balinese culture, asking another person to take responsibility for a child was a serious step; this was a job David needed to consider carefully. Pak Sus was asking David to step into Priyadi's life as an authority figure, and Priyadi in turn would be bound by his culture to respect David. David considered the request before coming back to Pak Sus with his reply: 'I will take care of Priyadi.'

Weeks later, Pak Sus had a massive heart attack and died in hospital. David threw himself into training Priyadi for the task ahead and Priyadi took up the challenge of serving poor Balinese as one born to it, knowing he could fall back on David for advice.

He and David became a formidable team. At first, David came up with the concepts and funding, and reported back to donors at the end. Priyadi drove the projects to completion. He had the humility to melt into a community, to sit down with village elders and quickly ascertain the needs of poor people in villages around the island.

Though financial self-determination was the goal, the entry point was not necessarily immediate credit. Thrusting capital into the hands of poor, uneducated Balinese villagers before they understood the development process was counterproductive. There were sometimes many steps required before a community was ready to receive small business loans. As David had done, Priyadi got to know the community, built trust and identified the natural leaders among the people—those who had integrity and could manage a credit program.

Priyadi soon became an expert in initiating the development process. 'What does your community need?' he would ask when he sat down with the village council.

'We need clean water. We can't grow crops because we spend our days carting water,' was often the reply. David had already experimented with different ways of bringing water into a village. Those on the lower hills could be fed water through a simple piping system using gravity—this kind of system had been set up in Java. He had recently been experimenting with a hydraulic ram pump that could compress the water and force it twenty metres uphill without the need for electricity. Whichever method they used had to be simple, with low maintenance.

'OK, let's start with water,' Priyadi would answer, and dialogue within the community would be ignited. In the town of Singaraja in Bali's dry north, this process led the community from a simple water project to an irrigation system and then into grape-growing, a new industry on the island.

Many times a community wanted to jump ahead a few steps and Priyadi had to persuade them tactfully to take a more ordered approach: 'Right now you need a road to your village, so that when you receive loans for businesses you will be able to transport your goods.'

In the early days of MBM David spent a quarter of his time with Priyadi, teaching him to speak the language of foreign aid, to write clear and appealing proposals that could be sent to donors. 'I taught him how to relate to westerners, particularly western donors, and how to write project proposals to westerners in the type of language they wanted to hear, how to evaluate the projects through data that westerners would relate to. He learned by osmosis how to relate to the donor community,' said David. 'Once he had the bit between his teeth he didn't need me anymore. He just took off.'

Occasionally, Priyadi called on David's lateral thinking. With MBM's farm training at Kapal, a large number of the loans were related to Bali's backbone, agriculture. Poultry farming had proved popular with early clients and thousands of dollars were invested in the industry through the loans. To make the loans more efficient, MBM started organising individuals who wanted to work in a particular business into groups and lending to the group. Chicken farmers made up many of the first groups, and they were going well when disaster struck. A large Javanese poultry producer swooped on Bali, flooding the market with cheap chickens. This immediately depressed the price of local chickens.

Priyadi had a huge dilemma. How could the poor Balinese clients, who had borrowed perhaps $50 each to set up their small poultry farms, ever compete with this producer? It was costing them more to keep the chickens alive than they could now sell them for. How could MBM keep lending to other clients if the first loans were not repaid? The program's success depended on receiving the money back and lending it to the next borrower. Disaster was imminent.

'I don't know what to do about this,' a distressed Priyadi told David. 'Our chicken farmers will be ruined.'

David went away and thought about it. How could the farmers wait this one out? It wasn't long before he came back with a simple solution. 'We could snap-freeze the chickens and wait for the prices to go up. And if the farmers band together and sell their chickens as a group to the hotels, a thousand at a time, then we can stand up to the Javanese poultry farmer.'

At Dhyana Pura there was a disused storage area behind the huge laundry that could house the freezers. It had laneway access at the back and a small space, tucked away from public view just inside the gates, for a chicken abattoir. Soon the farmers lined up in the laneway with their chickens, ready to go through the process of slaughter, cleaning, plucking and snap freezing. As a collective, the MBM group was a large producer. They had staved off ruin until the next blow.

For two years the Bussaus had been making the milk run every six months to Singapore to renew their visas. Without residency, it was the only way David could work.

A few slow days by the pool in a comfortable hotel were a respite from the hectic pace of work in Bali, but it was time David did not have to spare now. His development activities were expanding as his reputation spread. Already requests were coming from Christian aid agencies in Europe. Could he fly to Israel to assess the viability of a hospital at Nablus? Could he meet with doctors in Nepal to talk about their health clinic? Sometimes the projects needed funding; at other times they needed design or consulting help. 'Would this project work? Is it being efficiently run?' donors asked.

If the consulting work took off, David would have to travel extensively. He needed a more accessible home base—preferably close to an airport, and with better communications. When David and Carol bought the house in Randwick it was not with travel in mind, but here they were, looking for a convenient base, and they already owned a home that was a short drive from an international airport—though a minimum five hours' flight to his nearest place of work.

It was also time to think about the girls' future. At ten years old, Tasha was nearing high school age and Carol was concerned that home-schooling would leave her behind her peers in her studies. Tasha had fallen in love with Bali. She'd have stayed forever among her friends at Dhyana Pura, where the entire complex was her secret garden. She and Rachel ranged the property, popping into the laundry, then the kitchen, then over to the open-sided dining room, assured of hugs and smiles wherever they went. Tasha had started to think of herself as Indonesian. Reluctantly, they decided to leave Bali and move home to Sydney.

David and Carol were often invited to Balinese ceremonies in the home villages of their students and friends. In the last weeks of their time in Bali, David and Carol were invited to a combined wedding and tooth-filing ceremony for Nyoman, a young man from Sibetan they had met at Dhyana Pura, and his fiancée.

Tooth-filing was an important ritual in the lives of young Balinese, a rite to mark the passage into adulthood. The Balinese believed that flattening the top six teeth symbolically removed the 'sad ripu' or six vices—lust, greed, anger, confusion, jealousy and drunkenness—in preparation for adulthood, and that the canine teeth, associated with dogs and demons, stalled their entry into heaven. Most families were too poor to stage an impressive celebration on their own, so in many villages a group of adolescents was gathered together for a combined ceremony, or the ceremony was linked to another big event. Nyoman and his fiancée were both to have their teeth filed before their wedding ceremony.

David, however, had no spare time. He was working hard to finish a series of projects before the family returned to Australia, and setting up lending and other development projects that he would continue to work on from Sydney.

There had been days of preparation before Carol and other guests arrived just before midday for the tooth filing. The night before, a *gamelan* orchestra had played and a puppet show, *wayang kulit*, had depicted the rites of Balinese life. The family's compound had been transformed, with decorations made from pig bladders stretched over bamboo and bent into flowers and other shapes, and there was a temporary *bale*, or couch, set up for offerings.

Carol stood near the back of the crowd as the young couple was carried into the compound wearing their finest clothes and heavy make-up, to be placed on cushioned beds for the filing. Women chanted to the metallic rhythms of the gamelan as the priests, members of the Brahmana caste, stood by with crude metal files.

Carol's senses were reeling. The stifling heat, the jarring scrape of metal on tooth, the strong smells of the food that would soon follow the wedding and the cacophonous music swelled around her. She found it both fascinating and overwhelming. The pain was palpable, yet Nyoman and his wife-to-be lay expressionless, reining in their tongues and eyes and the muscles on their hands so that not even a breath escaped their control. The crowd was on edge until Nyoman finally stood and smiled. The hard part was over, and now it was time to celebrate the union.

After the wedding, Carol visited another young friend from Dhyana Pura who was in Sanglah Hospital, seriously ill with hepatitis. Then, in their last days, their friends treated the Bussaus to a farewell dinner and ceremony at Dhyana Pura. This time it really was goodbye to a whole way of life, and to people who had taught them so much. David and Carol knew they had accomplished as much as they could living in Bali, and that they could now do more living outside Indonesia. Besides, David would still be coming and going, and Carol hoped to come back with him from time to time.

Carol felt overwhelmed by the outpouring of affection from the people at Dhyana Pura. She floated through the elaborate meal, detached, as in a dream. It humbled her that the Balinese would go to so much trouble. Afterwards she was uncomfortable as their friends stood to make speeches of thanks and good wishes. She had never liked being the centre of attention. David was equally uncomfortable. Yet this farewell somehow affirmed the direction he was taking as the right one.

David had found the Balinese, without any material wealth to fall back on, more trustworthy than some of his affluent clients in Sydney. As he had immersed himself in Indonesia he had unknowingly absorbed some Asian thought processes and practices. He could now sit through a discussion between opposing camps without taking a position either way. This would later cause problems for some westerners, who would pressure him to take a position and hold it. He had come to understand consensus decision-making, where the outcome could alter quickly with group discussion, and had learned not to criticise people for changing their minds. He had also learned not to focus on a particular outcome, and not to be concerned if people did not meet targets. 'I found that my agenda wasn't that important—the outcome of any meeting was the bond and relationship that was established,' David reflected. This would make his future work in the developing world more effective—and his clashes with the west more pronounced.

The Bussau family planned to be home in Australia early in 1981. They left Bali in mid-December for Jakarta, where David held a last round of meetings with IIDI and others with whom he would continue to work. Yet another serendipitous meeting led him to Atholl Murray, a scientist, who was in Jakarta meeting with trade officials about a grain storage invention he was working on.

The term 'appropriate technology' was now being heard in development circles. David's rudimentary water ram pump fell into this category, as did other simple technology ideas that could be easily maintained, managed and replicated in communities with few resources.

In Australia, Atholl had pioneered a way of storing grain using impervious membranes that would kill insects and keep out rodents. He was passionate about bringing the technology to subsistence farmers in Indonesia. 'The farmers here can lose a third of their crops in storage, to insects and rats,' Atholl explained to David. Proper storage allowed them to sell their corn and rice when prices were higher, instead of straight from the harvest. He was also exploring ways of drying the grain during the wet season. Atholl had gained the support of the Australian government's research body, the CSIRO, to continue research through Silliman University at Dumaguete, on the Philippine island of Negros. He wanted to apply the technology at a micro level, in villages and rural towns. David and Atholl agreed to meet when they were back in Sydney.

David and Carol flew to Sydney and almost as soon as Carol boarded the plane she was wracked with stabbing pains all over her body.

'What's wrong?' David asked Carol when he turned to see her face grey and contorted in pain.

'I think it's just the pâté I ate before we left Jakarta,' she replied. Even when she tried, she could not lift her head; she cradled it on the tray table in front of her. She still thought it was a nasty episode of food poisoning that would soon pass.

Their friend Lynn Needs met the family at Sydney airport and they went straight to a welcome home lunch prepared by Ruth Moss. Carol tried to be sociable, but it was impossible. David carried her upstairs to her familiar bed. The pain and sweating of delirium grew worse as the afternoon progressed. Later she was rushed by ambulance to hospital. Carol had hepatitis, passed on through food prepared for her in Bali. It was months before she regained her health, and weeks before she could reflect on her remarkable two years in Indonesia.

The flow of life for the Bussaus had changed forever from the pre-Darwin days. Now, interesting guests from every part of the world frequently filled the house. The biggest adjustment was David's absence. David made frequent trips back to Indonesia for MBM, and consulting work now took him further afield as well. It was a difficult transition for Tasha and Rachel. Before Darwin, their father worked hard, but he was always around, either out in the workshop where they could join him or in the house at night. In Bali he worked long hours, but at the end of the day he was often able to take them swimming at Kuta or out to a restaurant. 'He just suddenly seemed to be away an awful lot. We really missed him when he went away,' Tasha recalled.

Tasha also struggled with the shift back to western culture. She missed her young Indonesian friends with whom she could laugh and hold hands without feeling self-conscious. In comparison, she found many of the Year 6 girls at her school nasty and judgmental. Her saving grace was a young Malaysian girl named Anne, whose Malay language was close enough to Indonesian for the two to be able to escape in conversation to the comfort of their foreign world. Rachel, too, found that other girls had already formed their groups of friends and it was hard to fit in. In Bali, other children had eagerly sought her friendship.

Carol was struggling too. She now often found herself a sole parent. For the first few months the effects of hepatitis dragged her down daily. Yet she believed that David was fulfilling his destiny in helping poor people find their way out of poverty; he went on his trips with her blessing.

Back in Sydney, David reconnected with Atholl Murray. Atholl offered David office space to work in until he set up his own office. He was eager to hear David's opinion of a short proposal he had written, introducing his grain storage system to potential donors. Atholl was hurt when David dismissed his slim proposal with, 'That won't do it, Atholl'—but the two then set about writing a proposal that would land the funding Atholl needed to continue with his grain storage project. The friendship flourished.

Later that year David made the first of a series of visits to Silliman University on behalf of Atholl's Grain Security Foundation. It was here that David was drawn into yet another interesting project, one that converted agricultural residue into roofing material. He was now enthralled with the idea of using his building knowledge in a way that could improve the living conditions of the poor. He determined to stay open to whatever challenges came his way.

David now had a completely different way of life. In a short time he had become a resource, a global trouble-shooter who stepped into a situation when things were not working and pulled out when they were running smoothly. From rolling his sleeves up and getting involved in building the dam or hands-on training in the hotel school, he had become a consultant, planning, designing and finding funds for projects.

The picture was getting bigger. In Bali David had realised that supporting individuals bore fruit. He had watched as Leigh took on more and more responsibility and became a development specialist in his own right. Now Priyadi was moving in the same direction. It was clear that he himself could be more effective, and the work with the poor would have a wider impact, if he handed programs over to quick and eager learners like Leigh and Priyadi.

On the lending front, the linkage with IIDI was progressing. For now, IIDI and Maranatha Trust were simply development partners, but later they would converge to become Opportunity International, a global aid agency. It was a marriage of complementary strengths. Al Whittaker had created an institution in the

US to garner support for poor entrepreneurs. He had left a big office on Fifth Avenue in New York City to work from cramped quarters on a strip mall in Vienna, Virginia. Like David, he had never been happier than in this new role. The Americans brought a strategic framework and focus to the work, while David came with the spontaneity and energy needed to make it work.

David liked working with Barry Harper, IIDI's executive director, and they endlessly explored development ideas. IIDI were planning to expand into the Philippines. They were pursuing funding in the US, but were short of contacts and would need a man on the ground in Manila. 'Would you be interested in working with us to transfer the lending methods from Indonesia?' Barry asked David. It was a natural step, David felt. Who knew where it might lead?

'I'll meet you there,' was David's response.

9

The Bigger Picture

When David flew into Manila in October 1981, thirteen years since his first visit with Carol, the city was still as he remembered it, a series of cities melded into one rambling metropolis, a jumble of makeshift squats and apartment blocks and filthy rivers, its people bustling under a miasma of car exhaust and industrial waste. In 1968 David and Carol had been disturbed by the squalor of the poor, and deeply touched by the buoyant spirit of the Filipino people. But that time they were onlookers, simply observing the effects of Manila's population explosion. Between 1940 and 1960 the city's population had more than doubled to four and a half million, as the poor streamed in from the provinces.

Now David came with a belief that economic empowerment and creating jobs, was the best way to help people lift themselves out of their daily suffering in the slums. He knew there was a solution to poverty, but would the strategies that were so successful in Indonesia work in the Philippines? Barry Harper flew in from Washington to meet him. He too came with a sense of anticipation. A good working relationship was developing between the two men. In Bali, IIDI's money had helped MBM expand its loan programs into more villages. David had pulled IIDI out of a potentially embarrassing hole by getting the Indonesian infrastructure projects finished.

David and Barry started by meeting local church people. David set out to explain to them how effective the lending programs were proving to be in Bali at fighting poverty. 'We're finding that our borrowers are trustworthy and reliable in repaying their loans,' he informed the group, who were mostly well-off middle-class Filipinos. 'We believe this method could work very well here, where there is a higher general level of education.' Then he explained his ideas of how small loans might help entrepreneurs and make jobs for others in the Philippines.

Within minutes it was clear that his message had been misread. Some of the group assumed the westerners had come with loans for them and their families. 'It is good that you are bringing in this money for loans. Is it possible that my nephew could apply?' someone asked. It was as if the strata of poorest people did not exist. David and Barry cut the meeting short and dragged their dispirited selves back to the hotel. They would have to walk away from the Philippines if that was the attitude.

That night David shared his disappointment with his friend Mac Bradshaw.

'I can line you up with some great people,' Mac offered. He had good contacts among business people in the Philippines and enthusiasm was soon restored. From that point on, plans went smoothly. The next week David and Barry convened a meeting to outline the plan to set up lending programs in and around Manila. In the room was a small group of influential and wealthy businessmen, each of whom had reached the top of his field. Among them were Professor Ricardo Jumawan who would later become the first chairman of the IIDI and Maranatha Trust programs in the Philippines, and a banker named Aurelio Llenado, known as Jun. All were drawn to the idea of helping their poor compatriots. They would later inspire many others to help in the fight against poverty.

David and Carol's Maranatha Trust, IIDI and the US government aid body, USAID, had negotiated a three-year package to start micro enterprise development in the Philippines. The package was non-repayable and subject to 'matching grants', whereby donated money was matched dollar for dollar by US government funding. 'We have US$300,000 in loanable funds and $90,000 over three years for expenses,' David and Barry told them.

'You mean to say we will be given six million pesos we will not have to repay? The funds can stay in the Philippines?' Jun Llenado was incredulous. It did not take his fifteen years of experience with the Central Bank to tell him this was a ground-breaking arrangement. Finance was second nature to Jun, but this micro enterprise development concept intrigued him. It was not a matter of just lending money; it also involved developing the prospects of the borrowers.

The questions flew. 'How do we know the poor will pay us back? We could be wasting our time.' There was nothing in the Philippines to compare this idea with other than government-backed rural banks.

'How can we charge interest to the poor? They don't have any money,' someone asked. This was a stumbling block to many in the development world, but this was not an obstacle for David. He was clear in his answer: 'We want to make the programs sustainable. We must cover our costs so that we can be here for the poor for a long time.' He had been through this issue in his mind—and with many others—numerous times over the past four years. He remained convinced that straight-out charity was not the lasting answer to poverty. He himself had come from nothing. He had no problem with charging interest to the poor. It was more important to maintain a person's dignity, whether that person was rich or poor.

When the group decided to plunge into this new initiative, it settled on the symbolic name Tulay Sa Pag-Unlad Inc., meaning Bridge to Progress, to be known as TSPI. While David and others initially guided the process, the key to TSPI's ultimate success would be the quality and dedication of its board and executive leadership. Lamberto Meer, a leading Filipino lawyer, became a close and loyal friend to David. Elena Lim, later voted the most successful entrepreneur in Asia by *Asiaweek* magazine, also spent time on the TSPI board. Her own background was remarkably like some of the poor women now receiving loans. She had begun started her career with a market stall, selling tomatoes. By the time she joined the board she was a manufacturer and exporter of cars, televisions, audiovisual equipment and Philippine marine produce—and a generous benefactor, wanting to give back to the country that had enabled her success.

Soon after the first board gathering, Dennis Isidro, vice-president of Citibank in Manila, joined TSPI. As a banker, he could see how it might work, but even he struggled with some aspects. 'We had to think through the concept hard and deep.' They all understood that the project rested on the loans being viable—it was going to be expensive to make the loans, and if they wanted to help people for many years, the money lent had to be repaid. They also realised that the lending would be a hands-on process. 'We had to go out to where the clients were, rather than sitting in an office giving out and collecting the loans.'

David himself became the subject of as much interest as his proposal. Who is this man who has given up his business life for the poor? they wondered. Then Leigh was invited to the Philippines to set up the lending systems and programs. He seemed to be cut from the same cloth. He volunteered his time and expected nothing in return. The board members pondered the motives of the two men.

'They are not pastors, not ministers, not priests, who are called to work alongside the poor. Why would they sacrifice their lives?' Dennis Isidro asked.

'Maybe they have a lot of money to spare?' another offered.

The new board was impressed with their dedication and vision, but David and Leigh would have to prove themselves before they could fully win trust. Jun Llenado, with the thorough mind of an auditor, withheld his judgment until he could see there was no hidden agenda. 'David seems happy to act as a consultant. He is not lording it over us or trying to influence our decisions. That is good,' he concluded.

Over many visits, David encouraged the group, affirming that they were business people who had much to offer the poor in their country, apart from just money. They had often been asked to finance church social programs in poor neighbourhoods, but no one had tapped into their business knowledge to help with the problem of poverty. The church saw helping the poor as its domain, and business as another, separate, world. David saw otherwise. 'Poor people need to learn to do what you know how to do,' he told them. 'God has given you gifts in this field. This is how you can use them.'

In 1981 the Philippines was in political and social turmoil, and rumbling noisily toward a people's revolution. President Ferdinand Marcos (who had been in power since 1965) had just lifted the martial law Filipinos had been living under since 1972, although there were to be few new freedoms. The Communist Party was gaining support among the urban and rural poor, and the Catholic Church, representing the majority of the population, was standing up to the regime.

Throughout the Marcos era, the Philippines was crowded with non-government organisations working to prop up its social structures. As Marcos and his capitalist cronies grew richer, the Filipino poor were plunging into deeper, more desperate poverty. The wealthy lived behind high walls, had guards to protect them, and seemed not to notice the ramshackle huts propped up like playing cards around the perimeter of their properties. Within Filipino society the rich and poor lived alongside each other with almost no social crossover.

It was clear in David's mind that any programs in the Philippines would be different from those in Bali; they would be a Filipino solution to poverty. Any institution lending to the poor in this country would have to be strong, business-minded, and able to survive the upheaval of political change. The Philippines society was built around the family, not the clans as in Bali, and the work would start in the urban slums of Manila, with rural migrants, rather than in well-organised rural villages.

The next hurdle for TSPI was getting sign-off for the matching grants scheme the US government was providing through USAID. None of the USAID money spent in the Phillippines was currently going to the type of project David and Leigh proposed. It would be a hard call, one that would involve convincing the Philippines' USAID assistant director, a gatekeeper of the millions earmarked for the country, to release funds into experimental programs.

At the meeting with the USAID representative in the Philippines, Leigh was frustrated by David's time-consuming approach. He wanted to get onto the business of documents and signatures.

'How long have you been in Manila?' David asked the representative. 'How have you found living here?'

David continued the conversation as if he had all day. Twenty minutes of warm and casual banter followed, moving from questions about the man's family and his job to discussion of the Philippines, the richness of its resources, the needs of its poor. Before long they were bouncing ideas off each other—the men had a visible rapport.

Soon the USAID assistant director was verbalising the need for investment into micro businesses among the poor of the Philippines. 'We need a locally owned organisation that will provide these loans to the poor,' he concluded. 'This is the kind of help people need here in the Philippines.'

David had used his gift of drawing out people's feelings and ideas, and had transferred ownership of the idea to the director without even selling it to him. Then he talked through the TSPI proposal to secure matching grants for the IIDI funding.

'How can I help?' the director offered warmly as they parted.

Before the end of that year Leigh arrived in Manila, planning to stay for three months—he would stay for a year. At first he stayed in the home of Mac and Rhoda Bradshaw; then he moved to the Army and Navy Club in Metro Manila for a year, as a guest of Dr Jumawan. It was the only luxury he enjoyed in the city. He refused to waste donor money on taxis or a car, and travelled by crowded jeepney for two, sometimes three, hours each day to a windowless hole-in-the-wall office out at Quezon City, close to many of the borrowers.

It was still comfortable compared with remote village life in Indonesia. He spent his days tramping down dirty alleys and squalid neighbourhoods to meet potential small business owners. He wrote funding submissions, sometimes with David by his side, and presented projects to the board. Leigh had been an excellent student of David's methods. His lesson in sensitivity had been the most important of all.

The first loans went out in February 1982 after the board agreed to create fifty jobs in the first year, then seventy five in each of the next two years. Nobody knew it then, but within ten years from a humble beginning TSPI would grow to make more than six thousand loans. Within the ten years after that, it would reach almost forty thousand loans (each generating more jobs).

Leigh soon needed secretarial help to administer and type reports on the clients. A board member suggested Noel Alcaide, a softly spoken industrial engineer who, at the age of twenty-two, was at a crunch point in his career. He had worked in the construction industry but questioned whether or not that was where he wanted to invest his time. While hopeless at typing—thirteen words per minute was his speed—he proved well suited to micro finance, and soon abandoned his secretarial role to work directly with the poor as Leigh's assistant.

Next, a man named Eliseo (Eli) Lademora was hired to take over from Leigh, who had been acting as executive director. On paper, Eli was overqualified. He came with an undergraduate degree in chemical engineering, a Masters in science and an MBA. In reality, he was ideal. He was kind-hearted, and found great satisfaction in the possibility of helping poor Filipinos find their feet. Leigh drove Eli at a furious pace, never failing in his belief that micro enterprise development would work in the Philippines. Eli was as measured and methodical as Leigh was enthusiastic.

The first loans were slow. The IIDI team in Washington wanted to keep a lid on administration costs. There were guidelines about project size, and the number of pesos per person employed that would be lent; these were adjusted and developed as the projects became real people with names and faces and families instead of numbers on paper. Loans went through a drawn-out process: every project proposal passed through the TSPI board for discussion about whether or not it should go to the US for approval. Then the applications were shipped to the US, stretching the process to months. Leigh soon saw that every project recommended to the US received funding, as they had no way of really knowing about the individuals from afar. He pushed to expedite the process by making decisions locally, and IIDI agreed to the new, more efficient arrangement. At the same time, by handing control to the Filipinos, the US venture capitalists cleared the way for future growth.

In a new country, in an urban setting, there were many lessons to be learned. For the first loans, it was trial and error. One of the very first loans went to a woman named Mrs Belen Marciano, who came to TSPI with the idea of setting up a chicken-raising business. TSPI loaned her 40,000 pesos (US$5063) to set up chicken enclosures and buy chicks. In 'contragrowing' chickens, the supplier delivered the day-old chicks to be raised for forty seven days, when they would be collected again. Mrs Marciano proudly presented her business plan to Leigh and Noel at TSPI, but no one picked up on the fact that the chicken houses on the Marciano's plot of land were not well-designed for the collection of the grown chickens. It took four times the anticipated time to load trucks with her five thousand birds. Then Mrs Marciano's chick supplier could not deliver as promised and she had no income to pay her employees. After running the business for two years, she found she could not repay her loan.

Although the chicken business was not going well, Mrs Marciano had gained the confidence she needed to run her own business. It was important to her that TSPI had trusted her with a loan in the first place and had not asked for collateral. Her next plan was to set up a catering business with a small payout from a previous job. She found herself catering for sixty five people, then one hundred and fifty people, then three hundred people for a Christmas party. She proudly repaid her loan. Soon she could buy her own catering equipment—cooking utensils, plates, glasses and cutlery—and could work with ever-larger numbers. Later, she could handle seven functions a day. Her crowning moment was catering for five hundred people when the Miss Universe pageant was held in Manila in 1994.

Despite the wealth of banking experience on the TSPI board, no one actually knew how to lend to the poor. It was an entirely different concept from regular banking and there were no role models. The first clients were scattered across a wide area, and there was not enough research into their ability to repay. The board soon came to the conclusion that it should concentrate on greater Manila first, where the cost of monitoring the clients would be lower, before looking to the provinces.

It was logical that larger loans would be cheaper to make—smaller loans involved the same transaction costs as larger ones. Suddenly, a group of poor Filipino market vendors found themselves with twenty-five thousand pesos each, more than US$3000, more money than they had ever seen. In some cases TSPI's only point of contact was a roadside stall, and when the government swept through the city shifting vendors off the footpaths, there was no way of finding the borrower.

Still, the clients were smart business operators, turning a big profit in the marketplace by buying wholesale from the grower. If they bought one kilogram of cabbage for one peso they could make a ten per cent profit by selling it to the middleman, who would sell it for ten per cent more. Just five turnovers in a day could yield a fifty per cent profit. The borrowers were unfazed by the TSPI interest rate, which at first was higher than the bank rate. They could never borrow from the banks anyway, and TSPI rates were considerably lower than those of neighbourhood moneylenders, their only other option. These loan sharks demanded up to twenty per cent each day in interest.

After a few months David challenged the board to make smaller loans, and more of them. 'But we're working to guidelines, and it is too expensive to make small loans,' was the response. David put his money behind the challenge. 'If I put four thousand dollars on the table we can make ten loans of four hundred dollars. What's now stopping us making small loans?' The board set out on a new learning curve to discover the best way of making many small loans. In reality, four hundred dollars was still a lot of money for a person who was accustomed to living on very little, and the loan amount would continue to shrink to meet the needs of the extremely poor, who were not accustomed to handling money and could be overwhelmed by large amounts.

Dr Adriano, a dentist who ran his practice from a tiny surgery at the back of a candy store down one of Manila's back alleys, was also among the first to receive a loan under the new program. He had one leg shorter than the other, and stood on a step-ladder to work on his patients, who sat in a precarious fold-up chair, constantly battered by the stench wafting up through the floorboards from the open sewer that ran underneath the building. Lines of blood had squirted up the walls and dried into a piece of abstract art. At least it distracted them from the dentist's implements—long-nosed pliers more suited to a mechanic's workshop than a dentist's surgery.

Before Dr Adriano's first loan, he could only clean teeth and make extractions if there were cavities. Fillings were too expensive for most of his patients and he could not afford the equipment he needed. 'I'll use the loan for a proper dentist's chair and some other equipment,' he promised Leigh. But before long he had defaulted on his loan repayments, even though his practice appeared to be going well.

Dr Adriano's wife was much younger than him. She was a beautiful woman, well used to calling the shots in the marriage. Though her husband had agreed to the loan, and had planned to make regular repayments, she thought otherwise. There were far more pressing family needs, in her view, and they soon swallowed up the money. Leigh dug a little deeper and found out that Dr Adriano was planning to leave for Saudi Arabia to work there as a dentist. He went to talk to Dr Adriano, and soon convinced him to stay and meet his obligations.

Now that he was staying, Dr Adriano informed his wife that not only would he be making his repayments, he would also be doing a refresher course in the latest dentistry techniques. He would soon be making more than enough to money to meet all the family's needs, he explained.

Much later Leigh met the Adrianos at the opening of the new TSPI office in the area. He was surprised to see the couple together and openly affectionate.

'The last year has been wonderful for our marriage,' Dr Adriano told Leigh. He had won back his wife's respect and affection by choosing to stay, to work hard and turn his dental practice around.

David's commitment to relationships came through mostly in his dealings with the board. He raised funding for board retreats in comfortable resorts away from the work, in places like Hong Kong and Bangkok, insisting that families be included. Always the entrepreneur, he developed a knack for finding newly opened or partially renovated resorts that offered absurdly low rates.

Not everyone could afford to bring family members, but David didn't allow lack of resources to be an obstacle. Often he used his own money to help, so strong was his conviction that the families needed refreshing as well.

He saw his work through a builder's eyes. You could build a tall building if the foundation was deep and secure. The retreats would cement the bonds between the board members, let them draw together with a common vision. His plan paid off for TSPI. Through the retreats, the board members became firm and committed friends, and when it came to making the tougher decisions, they understood each other's strengths and weaknesses. All this ultimately benefited the poor.

The idea of market-based aid had arrived in the Philippines. By the end of 1983, TSPI had exceeded all its early, conservative targets. The investment needed to create a job had shrunk considerably and would continue to come down as the lending methods became more sophisticated and efficient.

Early in 1984, IIDI hosted a conference in Sag Harbour, New York, that for the first time drew together those who worked in the field with the poor, plus donors and supporters. It was a time for airing differences, and a turning point in the history of the organisation. 'Affiliates', the organisations implementing the programs, now became 'partner agencies or partners'. Instead of decisions coming from Washington DC, authority was handed over to regional directors and the partners themselves. The program model now aimed to develop partners in other countries so that they could operate independently within three years, with IIDI providing support and on-site technical personnel, operating funds and loan capital, and leaving each partner with a loan fund of $300,000. At the same time, David continued raising other funds for the lending programs through Maranatha Trust.

Micro enterprise development (MED) was a new concept in the Philippines, and indeed worldwide. Over the years, David and others would refine what MED actually meant. The micro enterprises they worked with were small, income-generating businesses, many employing family members or others in the local community. The target group was typically too poor to get a loan from a commercial bank. With the small loans and training they received, these people could start new businesses or expand what they had; and they paid a market interest rate, thus allowing the programs to become self-funding.

Over the next decade, the term 'MED' came to include mentoring, and giving financial advice, marketing training and leadership development. The small business clients worked closely with trained loan officers who helped them with their businesses. From the start, the focus for the IIDI Maranatha programs was on the whole person, and not just financial improvement. The impact of increased income was immediate and often lasting, and invariably improved the family's ability to afford food, shelter, education and health care. Other equally important changes, such as the ability to offer community service, and personal development, soon followed.

It would be some time before the Philippines Central Bank would see MED as more than a curiosity. One important shift came with a visit from IIDI board member Rimmer de Vries, a towering two metre tall managing director and chief economist with the global financial firm JP Morgan. He had worked his way to the top of his field and now advised the US government on financial matters. Rimmer and David had formed a strong friendship, and frequently met in the US around IIDI board meetings, which were often held in the JP Morgan offices.

Rimmer's encounter with Dr Adriano and others in the markets of Valenzuela had confirmed his own commitment to the process of empowering the poor. A call to the Bank of the Philippine Islands secured a meeting between his friend, who happened to be the president of the bank, and Leigh, Jun Llenado and Ric Jumawan from TSPI.

The bank president listened to what the men had to say, but had only a short time before his next meeting. He glanced impatiently at his watch. 'What's the bottom line here? How much are you asking for?'

'We haven't come here for money. We want you to understand that we can all help the poor. There is no other agenda,' Leigh told him, looking him in the eye.

The banker pulled out his diary and said, 'I'll give you a day.' It was a day that opened up a new and lasting partnership between TSPI and the bank.

David came and went from Manila every few months, advising and challenging, but never imposing. No one really knew where he had been in the meantime, but over the years he often arrived with new ideas, encouraging the board and staff with stories of micro businesses in other countries, and bringing others with him to see first-hand what TSPI was doing. After three years it was time for the board to take full responsibility for the Philippines programs.

Leigh had lived in the Philippines for the first year, then moved his home base back to Sydney. He came to Manila for extended visits before leaving to follow David as he blazed a trail into other developing countries.

'We said, "It's all yours, you do it yourself." I think they were surprised, because westerners always come in with some sort of vision and agenda. We really just wanted to help them as business people working with the poor,' Leigh said.

By now David was travelling the world making new connections, acting as a bridge between the poor and the comfortable. He found he had pulling power for both the finance and the talented people who were excited by the work. Though he rejected the label of 'fundraiser', he would inevitably come up with the money needed for the loans, as well as for staff training, board retreats and new development programs. He was able interest people who might never have given the poor a second thought.

Despite the deprivation of his childhood—or perhaps because of it—he had the constitution of an ox. Lack of sleep and jetlag would not stand in his way. He might be weeks on the road, working in India, Pakistan, Sri Lanka, Indonesia and the Philippines on his way through from the US, Germany or the UK. At each stop he could spend sixteen hours a day in meetings, starting with six o'clock breakfast meetings for donors and ending late at night with a group of board members. He never seemed to tire because it hardly felt like work to him.

The stream of relationships that had flowed from Mac Bradshaw's early initiative, Partners in Mission (PIM), had also borne fruit. David's plans for setting up lending programs in India with his friend, Reverend Vinay Samuel, were well underway. They planned to start lending later in 1984. David had also been in discussion with Bishop Michael Nazir-Ali in Pakistan, and Sri Lanka had been raised as a possibility. This would become the pattern. David never asked, 'Where is the worst poverty?' He simply went where he was invited by someone who saw the need. This kind of 'organic' growth would later pose a challenge to management. By now PIM had been disbanded and rolled into another group called Infemit, an affiliation of mission theologians scattered around the world's poorest nations. Infemit's participants all had first-hand experience of the injustices of poverty, and most worked in isolation. It was a network of support and friendship. When its members met, they exchanged ideas and read each other's writing. They challenged each other in their work.

At first in these meetings David felt his academic inferiority keenly. He often sat quietly through hours of verbal tussling over a particular detail, only to be asked at the end, 'David, what do you think?' He was surprised that such highly educated and eminent people listened to his answers and took his views seriously. But they valued his perspective, which always came from experience, not theory.

David brought some of the missing puzzle pieces to the group. One was micro enterprise development, a practical way to bring economic relief to the poor and oppressed. Another was business nous. Through his relationship with the group, David learned a non-western view of partnership, and the firm biblical basis for helping the world's poor, beyond his own natural response.

One of Vinay's dreams was to set up a non-denominational facility where leaders of churches and church institutions in non-western countries could train and work towards research degrees. He wanted Christian leaders in the developing world to be able to study issues like poverty and religious pluralism, which were relevant to their work in Asia, Africa and Latin America, rather than matters that were of importance only to western cultures and societies. David came in with practical help in areas such as writing job descriptions, the nature of governance, and how to sustain and manage such an organisation. The Oxford Centre for Mission Studies (OCMS) was up and running in England in 1983, operating out of a disused, 19th century Gothic church, renovated for the purpose.

Another role David had never bargained for was that of lecturer. His experience of formal education had been dismal. He had not read widely, and was often too busy to read anything but proposals. Yet over the years he discovered that complex theories did not speak as loudly as raw experience. He started by making something happen, then worked back to the theory. Repeatedly in the years ahead he would be called on to lecture on micro enterprise development at the OCMS in Oxford and at Eastern University in Pennsylvania, among others institutions.

Between trips further afield, David made frequent visits to Tonga. Back in 1982, Cyclone Isaac had devastated the small Pacific Ocean island kingdom of Tonga with a ferocity only seen once every twenty years. The island's lightweight woven and thatched houses had no chance of withstanding its force, and hundreds of Tongans had been left homeless. After assessing the damage, the Australian Council of Churches, which had been helping out in Tonga for a number of years, asked David to look at building housing that might withstand another cyclone of that magnitude.

Tonga was a poor nation of less than one hundred thousand people, living on a subsistence diet of taro, sweet potato, fruit and fish. A grand occasion might be celebrated with a suckling pig cooked underground over hot coals. There was no wealthy government, little insurance money and scant personal wealth among the Tongans to fall back on. It would be too expensive to bring boatloads of timber and roofing iron from Australia.

David made his first visit to Tonga three months after Cyclone Isaac, relishing the challenge to develop housing that was affordable and strong, and that used local materials. After the first visit, he asked Garry Cairncross to help draft a simple design, and ended up with a small, oval hut, about six metres long by three metres wide, on a concrete slab. It looked much like the traditional Tongan *fale*, an open-sided, thatched-roof hut, but had a much stronger construction. It had slats under its eaves so that air could circulate freely and pressure inside could not build up. Best of all, it could be reduced to two or three modules that locals could build using coconut trees that had fallen in the cyclone.

By the time David left for Tonga a second time in 1983 to oversee the building of the first two huts, he had already simulated a cyclone in a wind tunnel to test their strength. He found that square, European buildings would collapse in a wind of eighty kilometres per hour, but the new design could withstand winds of up to one hundred and sixty kilometres per hour. At the end of this trip, during which he trained Tongan builders and helped in construction of the first huts, it had been hard to find a supervisor to take over. After he left progress had slowed to a standstill.

Months later, David returned to kick off the next stage of the project, the construction of one hundred huts. This time he would enlist some helpers. He called his friend Alex Wilson in New Zealand to discuss the project. He had known Alex since his early twenties through Carol's friend Sherryl. Alex knew what a wild-card David could be. Once, in Sydney, when Alex had admired the shirt David was wearing, David had pulled it off and insisted that Alex keep it. 'Here, if you like it you can have it,' he'd said. Alex learned to be careful about what he admired around David.

Alex now managed the Harbours Board in Auckland. He was a practical man, handy with a hammer and, like David, something of a jack-of-all-trades. When David explained how he was arranging to build cyclone-proof houses in Tonga, Alex not only agreed to join him, but offered to ship essential materials such as nuts and bolts from Auckland, which was half the distance of Sydney from Tonga.

Alex soon found himself with David in Tonga's capital, Nuku'alofa, paying a courtesy visit to the Tongan Prime Minister in his elegantly ramshackle residence. The men were met by two high-ranking Tongans who ushered them into a sitting room and motioned for them to sit on the only settee in the room, a dangerously threadbare piece of furniture with a rug over its loose springs. The Tongans then settled themselves onto the floor to wait for the Prime Minister. It was some time before he appeared, greeting them with a warm smile. The Australian churches had been good friends to the Tongan people, and those here doing their work were most welcome.

The men shook hands and the Prime Minister apologised profusely for keeping them waiting for such a long time. They had assumed that he had been engaged in meetings with staff or some issue related to running the country until they noticed his feet, which were clothed in a pair of knitted bed socks. Thinking he should explain, the Prime Minister sheepishly told them, 'I was reading the last chapter of a book that completely captured my imagination. I just couldn't put it down.'

The next day Alex was left with the unenviable job of unpacking two shipping containers, whose contents had to be divided into one hundred lots for the one hundred houses. Meanwhile, David left for meetings with church leaders in the Ha'apai group of islands with Neill Mawhinney, an accountant who had just joined Maranatha Trust. After the containers were sorted, Alex approached the only mill in Tonga to see if they could cut coconut trees for framing and floors.

The shipment from Auckland had included a small transportable mill so that coconut trees in the outlying islands could be cut for framing and floors once the hut modules were transported to the villages. The most useful piece of equipment the men had with them in Tonga was an innovation at the time—the tungsten tip saw blade, which could easily slice through the hard timber of the coconut tree. Before they started building, the team asked each villager to bring in four coconut trees to make the walls and slats of one hut.

Over the next few days David arranged to transport the houses, trained local workers to construct them, oversaw the building of the first few, and found a supervisor for the others. Then it was time for him to move on to the next project. Neill, who had found himself in Indonesia in the first week of his new job and Tonga soon after, was introduced to the local people and told by David, 'You can handle this now.' Neill soon discovered that this was David's way of stretching those around him into new areas. David knew when a person was up to the job. In Neill's case it worked. He became David's right hand man in projects of this type, filling a gap in David's way of operating. Donor institutions such as the ACC wanted higher levels of reporting than David proffered in his fast-paced, entrepreneurial approach to development, and Neill did the chasing up as David moved on.

Increasingly, requests for funding came to David through Maranatha Trust. 'The volume got so great that I decided I would only support things that I identified rather than things other people brought me. A few programs have been a complete rip-off. You can pick those that are intended to benefit individuals rather than a community,' he said. In one case, there was funding for a program to set up a referral system so the poorest people in the village could see a paramedic, then move up the line to a nurse, doctor and finally hospital for serious cases. 'There was funding for these out-patient clinics, and some of the doctors were using the money for their own practices. They used the funds to build the clinics and then just charged through their practice, so the poor got left out of the process again.'

Once David flew to the New Territories of Hong Kong to help out with a fish harvesting project. The ocean fish were doing well in the natural saltwater rock ponds the locals had built, but when it came time for the harvest it was impossible to coax the fish from their safe hiding places in the rocks. The obvious solution, to drain the ponds and reconstruct the walls so that the fish were more accessible, was going to be a large, expensive project.

When David arrived to assess the project his response was, 'How can we use what we already have here? There has to be a simple solution.' He went away and came back with drawings of a scheme to set up a system of bamboo pipes placed into the wall, connecting with the ocean outside the ponds. When opened up, the pipes were small blow-holes, and the jets of water from the surf outside would gently blast the fish away from the rough walls and into the nets.

He was always willing to share what he discovered, and often brought Priyadi or Leigh along with him as he travelled, so he could compare the work in Indonesia with that in other countries, and bring new technologies back to Indonesia. When invited, he flew to Papua New Guinea or Fiji to lend his expertise on building training facilities like Dhyana Pura. At other times he was in demand on projects where indigenous groups were looking at the commercial viability of their ventures: How can we promote our goods to the west? How can we find markets? How can we ensure that the quality will be of a high enough standard?

At times he had to be brutally honest and try to steer people away from being dependent on external markets. 'You would be best to focus your efforts on local consumption,' he told them. He had seen this before, a small, struggling community were geared up for international markets only to find that western tastes had already moved on and they were left, still poor, with unwanted stock.

David's frequent trips to Manila were peppered with interests outside the lending programs. If there was time, he would visit Mac and Rhoda Bradshaw, the American friends who had helped with his first connections in Manila. The Bradshaws lived in a big household of sixteen people, including their own and adopted children, and David often stayed with them on his visits to Manila.

Poverty and large families had bred their own issues in the Philippines. In the late 1970s Rhoda had started working with babies who had been abandoned in hospitals or government orphanages. At the time she was one of the few people caring for this forgotten and voiceless group. She employed a nurse who would seek out the babies who might not make it and bring them into a sick bay the Bradshaws had added to their home, where the babies could have individual attention. She then found homes where they would receive care and love.

At first, Cribs, as Rhoda named the new organisation, was staffed by expatriate volunteers, but over the years Rhoda drew more and more Filipinos into her project, with the aim of handing it over completely when she could.

Next she turned her attention to young girls between the ages of seven and thirteen who had been subjected to sexual abuse, and started a program called New Beginnings. Many of the girls were abused in their own homes by family members, so Rhoda set up a home where they could feel safe and receive counselling through the government's social services.

Then she wondered about ways to help women earn an income so that they could keep their children with them—rather than being compelled to abandon them—and even pay for their education without having to work long hours in factories. She started experimenting with a group of women who devised designs for handicrafts they could make at home. Some women started making 'Cabbage Patch'-style dolls they could sell in stalls and markets. Then Rhoda stumbled across *tripunto*, an intricate and beautiful style of quilting. Her group of women started by embroidering pillow cases and baby quilts, then expanded into full-sized bed quilts. Before long this evolved from a humble helping ministry into a large concern. The Bradshaws used some of the proceeds of the sale of their home in the US to start a company called Morning Star, which soon employed forty five full-time staff and trained three hundred women in sewing.

David and Carol first visited Rhoda's projects when she was finding foster homes for the babies. Later, David organised funding for a piece of land outside Manila, so the families could have their own homes. Carol was deeply moved by Rhoda's work with the children and longed to help. She became one of Rhoda's greatest supporters, and when the sewing project developed into nursery products and was renamed Heartline, Carol stepped in to find markets in Australia. She was sure Australians would love the products, and they did. She found people like the designer Kate Finn, whose imaginative designs of baby rugs, soft rattles and animals in pastels and small checks with ducks and flowers proved popular. Before long, Rhoda and her women were shipping boxes and boxes of baby products to Australia. In Sydney, Carol gathered a group of close friends and held home-based parties and sold Heartline products through church and charity outlets.

For Carol, it was never about the business: what she did was just a small part of the larger picture. Over the next five years, Heartline gave her many opportunities to bring attention to women living in poverty and to the solution David was working on. It demonstrated that every small action could make a difference in the life of another person, even when that person lived thousands of kilometres away.

10

Slaves and Scavengers

Reverend Vinay Samuel was an Indian national whose Cambridge education had given him a precise and clipped English accent. He delivered his ideas in rapid-fire speech, and moved easily between the contrasting worlds of the international intelligentsia and the slums of his native Bangalore in the south of India.

Although they were as different as could be, David and Vinay agreed in their thinking on poverty and suffering. They were kindred spirits, both entrepreneurial, and both responsive to need. Long before they met, Vinay had realised that he was steeped in middle-class western thought—he deliberately embarked on an exploration of his own Indian culture and his Christian faith within it. By the 1980s his work and opinions were being discussed in church circles around the globe.

Vinay's was a rebellion David could identify with. 'He was very vocal and very angry about the western church and the way it dealt with the church in the two-thirds world. I identified with Vinay in that he wasn't intimidated and took a very strong position about not being beholden to the west.'

Vinay had been to Washington and met Al Whittaker and the IIDI group several years before David made that connection, and he and his wife Colleen had already started down the path of community development work. David first visited Vinay and

Colleen in Bangalore in 1978, a year after they had been introduced by Mac Bradshaw, when Vinay was rector in the comfortable inner-city parish of St John's.

Although most of the parish members were from the city's well-to-do middle class, Vinay and Colleen also cared for the growing number of squatters in the area. They watched with concern as poor farmers and rural labourers flooded into Bangalore looking for work. They saw how the poor were often forced into selling themselves and their children into prostitution. Then there were the rag pickers, the young scavengers who had run away or been forced from their homes to live on the streets. There were now as many as twenty five thousand living off the waste of growing industry.

By 1982 the city had doubled in size. Bangalore was the fastest growing industrial city in Asia. Many wealthier families came from overcrowded Bombay to seek new business opportunities, and as land prices rose and land became scarcer, the poor were forced further out of town. One-fifth of Bangalore's population lived in slum areas without adequate health facilities or basic services. It was unsightly, and not at all in keeping with Bangalore's growing reputation as a corporate centre. The city council decided it was time to clean up. Bulldozers rolled into the urban slums one night in 1983 and, under cover of darkness, authorities loaded the squatters into trucks and drove them outside the city limits, only to unceremoniously dump them in an area called Lingarajapuram, a semi-rural district lacking in even the most basic amenities.

It outraged Vinay and Colleen. 'If they are going, we are going too.' They packed up their home and moved, with their four children, to Lingarajapuram, to live near the slum dwellers and run an offshoot of St John's. This marginalised group was now their priority.

One of the Samuels' earliest projects, while they were still in the city, was setting up a school for children aged between ten and fourteen years whose parents, earning less than two hundred rupees (US$20), could never afford to send their children to school. Most were illiterate, and looked forward only to a life of hard labour. At the school, the children caught up enough in one year to enter the mainstream schools. Within five years the school was teaching three hundred students.

At Lingarajapuram, Vinay and Colleen extended what they had started in the city, setting up facilities to support the social, health and spiritual needs of the people around them. Through the church they established an association named Divya Shanthi, meaning Divine Peace, and drew upon their wide network of friends, including David and the Maranatha Trust, for support in building a school, a children's home and a health clinic.

Vinay had already started his journey into holistic ministry when David came along with his strategies for microeconomic development. Even before the move into the Philippines, the men had discussed Bangalore as the next place to establish a lending partner agency. David had already approached his colleagues at IIDI and they had agreed to contribute to its start-up.

The Bridge Foundation (TBF) made its first loans in 1984. Paul Roby, an Anglo-Indian former squadron leader in the Indian Air Force, became the first executive director. Paul was unswerving in his integrity and commitment to the poor, laying a strong foundation for those who followed. In the first years, David and Leigh were in Lingarajapuram every other month to meet Vinay and Paul and to help establish TBF on solid footings.

Once they'd laid the groundwork together, Leigh stayed on to support, train and encourage Paul and the other staff. The earliest clients set up businesses in steel fabrication and poultry farming, with encouragement from two of the founding trustees of TBF, Jagdish Devadasan, who owned several large steel fabrication businesses, and David Lobo, who at the time owned the largest poultry operation in South India. A whole village was set up to raise day-old chickens to a marketable weight. The loans paid for the chicken pens. However, raising chickens proved to be risky, with tiny margins, so TBF funded the same villagers into a variety of other small businesses. Before long Vinay and Paul were documenting changes in the quality of life of those who received the loans. Anecdotes pointed to a dramatic improvement, and by asking the right questions and collecting data they could compare changes here with what was happening in the Philippines and add to the growing pool of knowledge about micro loans.

On one of his visits to Bangalore in 1984 David encountered the poorest group he had ever met. James Solomon, an employee of EFICOR, a local Christian relief and development agency—another of Vinay's initiatives—introduced David to the rag pickers. Some were as young as nine years old, homeless and scavenging in garbages, in gutters and the filthy laneways behind shops for any scraps of paper or plastic or metal they could find, then dragging as much as twenty five kilograms of stinking waste to a gathering point to be sorted and sold. In a good month, when the weather was clear, they might make three hundred and fifty rupees (US$30). During the monsoon, when the waste paper became wet and useless for recycling, life was even more fragile. The children went hungry unless they could find food scraps in hotel and restaurant bins. At night they sheltered in dirty drains or slept in the open without anything but newspaper for cover. They were often sick, without money for medical help, and had only each other.

As James observed the boys, he saw that there was a bond between them. Mostly they looked sad and unloved, but there were times when they laughed and joked together. He soon understood that the children were organised into working gangs. At the end of each day they carried their paper to a small retail paper shop, barely one and a half metres square, tucked into an alleyway in the slums. Here it was sorted, baled and collected by wholesalers who sent it to the paper mills. If they were lucky, they could get a fair price, but often their collections were underweighed and they had no avenue for complaint. To add to their woes, the local police exploited them, sometimes stealing their takings and arresting them on minor matters.

At first James found it almost impossible to befriend them. They were accustomed to being outcasts, despised outside their own group. The boys lived and worked together, but could not even trust each other. They stole food or takings from other scavengers when the chance arose. It took some time for James to coax them into conversation.

When he did, he asked one boy, Balraj, 'Why have you left home to join this gang?'

'At home I am not wanted. On the street I was lonely. Here, I am wanted,' was Balraj's reply.

Many were escaping alcoholic or violent parents. They were working under a system of almost bonded labour. They worked for leaders who might beat them if they tried to leave, but at the same time might care for them if they were sick, or bail them out when the police arrested them.

James took it upon himself to help them. He borrowed two and a half thousand rupees (US$225) and a small room from EFICOR to set up a paper collection point where the boys could be sure of a fair price and honest scales. The loan bought the baling box, a set of scales, one week of wages for two sorters, a kerosene stove, pots to make tea or coffee and some games for the boys. He worked after hours and in his holidays until the project started to make a profit. He set up literacy classes and started planning a hostel for the children to live in. The project soon attracted the attention of a local newspaper. He planned to take it further but could not do it on his own. By this time he had grown fond of the boys; he respected their resourcefulness, and they were learning to trust him.

The Bridge Foundation was considering whether it could support his project when Vinay invited David and Leigh to talk to James about the rag pickers. Soon after, the group stood by the tiny retail store where the rag pickers came each day with their assorted paper collection. The TBF board members and Leigh fired questions at James about the feasibility of the project while David stood quietly by. As he listened, David's well-tuned sense of injustice came to life. That children were involved only stirred him further in his resolve to act. They would find a way through.

It riled David that police and middle men exploited the penniless young boys, and that they were reduced to sleeping in drain pipes at night. Later, when they were back in the comfort of their hotel, David commented to Leigh, 'That would have to be the worst of depravity.'

David's response was practical indignation, rather than raw anger. 'Increasingly I accepted that there is injustice and inequality in the world, and the magnitude of the problem is so huge that getting upset about it is more of an emotional drain. A lot of people get emotional about it but don't do anything.'

With Paul Roby from TBF, James and Leigh, David hammered out the components of the project. The social welfare side included literacy classes, health care, a place for the boys to stay at night, and skills training for those ready to move out of scavenging. Each child would have an identity card with the project's phone number on it—this would mean that the police could not take action against the boys without first contacting the project workers.

Then there was the business side. This was the part that would ensure the program could benefit more than just one small group. If they set up a series of paper collection points, all running profitably, the surplus would be used to help more children. Eventually, the more enterprising of the rag pickers could run the project themselves, according to the plan. David and Leigh brought the commercial edge to the project: the mixture of welfare work and a commercial side could sustain it. Their other contribution was money. They wrote a large proposal that attracted donors from Australia, Europe and the UK.

James Solomon loved to see the bright faces of the young scavengers as they arrived at the project. Here the boys found acceptance and people interested in their welfare.

The plan was always to train the boys in skills that would prepare them for more rewarding jobs, so they could leave rag picking and eventually live away from the streets, in homes. It was a slow process, but gradually James' hours of building friendships with the boys started to pay off and the first of the boys left the scavenging life and started a paid job in carpentry. He was soon followed by another, and another.

Characteristically, David too had moved on to many other projects. His role—beyond working out the commercial side of the project—had been to ignite interest among others and bring in the money. These days he was never the one who stayed around to drive such projects. He simply blew on the flames. He felt no need to hang on and lead. His encouragement had spurred James on. But some years later, the project ran out of steam. David never viewed a project losing momentum as failure. Development was an uncertain and risky business where not every project would flourish and grow. If it helped a group of boys for a time it was worth the effort. He would remember the rag pickers project as one of his most rewarding.

David and Leigh had other work in India at this time. Far to the north, at Nagpur, in the central Indian state of Maharashtra, Rev. P Y Singh and an American, Ray Bergin, were talking to them about setting up loans programs to empower the poor in that city and the surrounding region. Out of that came the Community Development Society (CDS), another vehicle for creating jobs for many thousands through small loans. Later the Indian partners joined to form an association called All India Micro Enterprise Development (AIMED).

The poverty of the rag pickers had disturbed David but before long he encountered a community that was even worse off. The young Bishop of Raiwind in Pakistan, Michael Nazir-Ali, was another of Mac Bradshaw's original group who had discussed the possibility of micro enterprise development programs with David. Michael had a unique understanding of the cultural and religious context in which he conducted his work. He was born a Muslim, educated in a Catholic school in Karachi and then became an Anglican bishop. Much later, as it seemed the world was polarising along religious lines, he was an advocate for dialogue between faiths, a voice for greater understanding and tolerance.

Like Vinay, Michael met each day with death, sickness and suffering in the slums. His first posting the summer he arrived back in Pakistan, after studying in the privileged environs of both Oxford and Cambridge Universities, in the 1990s, was a poor parish in Karachi. An outbreak of cholera had swept through the community, killing many small children. The distraught parents could not even afford to buy the most basic of coffins in which to bury their children. Instead they visited the local store to plead for discarded fruit boxes.

Of all the desperately poor people he encountered in his daily work, it was the brick kiln workers who caused Michael the greatest anguish. They were the poorest and most marginalised of all Pakistanis, lower than the sweepers. There were thousands of brick kilns scattered around the Punjab region, and they employed unskilled farm labourers who had been forced off the land in hard times, and others equally desperate to survive.

The labourers took the jobs in the kilns, thinking that they could at least feed their families that way, and the kiln owners seemed kind enough when they agreed to pay a cash advance to cover the workers' outstanding debts. Little did they know that in joining the kiln they could be locking themselves and their children and grandchildren into bonded labour, a cruel cycle that could chain the family to the kiln for the next ten generations. They effectively became slaves to the kiln owners.

Michael was already ameliorating the poverty of the kiln workers by providing literacy programs, health care and clothing for cold winter days, but he wanted a more permanent solution. One time when they met outside Pakistan, Michael asked David what they could do about the brick kiln workers.

Before long David was in Pakistan pacing around the brick kilns himself, exploring an empty, pain-filled tableau. The heat hung hazily on the flat open plains, and the workers sweated as they reached into the pits in an endless cycle of digging and moulding and drying, without any chance of respite and without shade to protect them as they worked.

If the rain melted all the bricks lying out to dry, or a family member became sick from dysentery and could not meet the day's quota of twelve hundred bricks, the family fell deeper into debt. There was no way out. They relied on the kiln owner to supply tiny huts to house their large families and goats and chickens, all crowded into the one room, and for cash advances to stay alive through the monsoon.

Whole families of *pathairas*, the lowest caste of all, spent the entire day in 45°C heat digging mud and mixing it with water and straw to make the clay they formed into bricks, as they had done since ancient times. David saw an old man, the grandfather of the family, carried out into the sun on a stretcher so he could spend the day on his side, reaching into the mud to mould his share of the days' bricks. He had made bricks since he was six and would soon die making bricks. Beside him, his young grandchildren, barely old enough to walk, played in the same mud into which they later urinated and defecated.

'These people are worse off than the rag pickers in India,' he commented to Michael. At least the rag pickers had some sense of community and were out and about together each day. Here it was a mechanical action all day, every day. There was no spare energy for laughter or companionship.

'It was just this endless process of turning clay into bricks. There was no vibrancy about it, no joy in it, just death, this process of exchange of labour for survival—for food. For me, there was a darkness there. It epitomised futility. It is the worst I've seen in terms of hopelessness,' David later reflected.

One day as David and Michael walked through the kilns a desperate woman's scream cut through the air from the direction of the mud diggings. 'No!' she cried, in her native Punjabi. The men ran to the source of the cry, where a crowd had already gathered around the woman. She kneeled, cradling a lifeless baby girl who just minutes before had taken her last breath. They ran to her side, where her family was gathered around the small body, but there was nothing to be done. The pathairas knew they had no rights. Not even the right to healthy children.

'Let's bury her now,' the baby's father said, with resignation in his voice. They had no community, no wider family or friends to mourn her death or share their grief. They were isolated and alone. Bishop Michael prayed for the family, and then he and David left them to go sadly into the bushes to bury their daughter.

Within an hour the remaining family members were back at work. They had to keep making bricks or they would never reach their quota for the day and they would be deeper in debt. David later heard the mother had given birth to another baby a year later. She hoped it would survive as the family needed more hands to make bricks, just to keep going. Many others were in the same position, planning their children around the workforce needed to pay their debts.

'It upset me that there was no value to the life,' David said later. 'The baby really was just like coinage, just a transaction that had been lost and it had to be renegotiated, so life was brought down to an exchange of contracts. People's lives were the coinage.'

It was not David's only encounter with death in the kilns outside Lahore. On another visit with Garry Cairncross that took them as far west as Hyderabad, the men came across a baby girl lying limply in her mother's arms. 'What's wrong with her?' Garry asked, disturbed. 'She's probably going to die,' David replied, as he handed a couple of hundred rupees to the child's father, motioning to him to use it to take the ailing child to the hospital. He helped the distraught family into a taxi, but it was futile. The baby later died, but at least they had been given the unexpected option of treatment in a hospital.

Afterwards David explained to Garry, 'It's no good giving them one hundred dollars, because the money will be taken away from them.'

In the cool of a hotel room Bishop Michael and David sat for hours sifting through all the options to help the workers. One possibility was a friend of Michael's, Phillip Lall was a lecturer in management at university and knew the workers' plight well. The men worked their way through the kiln workers' needs: health services and education were vital.

But David's mind was racing in a different direction. What is the business solution to the problem? he mused. If they bought the workers out of their debts it would free some families, but how would they support themselves? Many only knew about making bricks and lacked the confidence to dream of doing anything else. 'We could build our own brick kiln and let the workers work their own way out of bondage. That will work long term,' he suggested. It was an exercise in self-determination. In David's initial funding proposal he wrote, 'Dignity, self-esteem and self-worth will slowly develop once the community is liberated from bondage.'

Over the years, Michael saw David answer need in many ways. 'David doesn't respond immediately sometimes, but he responds by doing things. If you live in an ideas world, you expect people to say, "That's a good idea", or "That's not a good idea", or "Have you thought about this?" He just listens. Then you find out later on that he has acted in some way on what he has heard.'

There was now work to be done in raising the money for the brick kiln; the men set out to research the cost and feasibility of the project. Both David and Leigh Coleman had been participating in IIDI's board meetings since 1983, and they both now made the journey to the US several times each year. At the next IIDI board meeting in 1986, David presented the brick kiln idea to his colleagues. The IIDI office had been relocated to Chicago from

Washington. Larry Reed, who joined IIDI in 1984, fresh out of student leadership at Wheaton College, was the only employee to make the move; he was soon joined by local employees.

At the time that David made his presentation on the kiln project, IIDI had just started a series of new programs in Latin America. The board baulked at trying to stretch resources in another direction, particularly when it was not strictly for micro enterprise. Emory Griffin, a newcomer to the board who taught communications at Wheaton College, was at the meeting, and after the board voted a resounding 'no' to David's request, Em approached David to apologise. 'I think to free people from that kind of indentured life is so great, but I don't think we have the money to do it now.'

'Oh, that's OK, I'm going to do it anyway. I'll find another way of funding it,' David replied, not the slightest bit upset at being turned down. Em admired his tenacity.

Back in Australia, the development committee of the Australian Council of Churches was interested in the Pakistan brick kiln proposal. The Archbishop of Melbourne, David Penman, who had lived and worked in Pakistan for twelve years, travelled with David to visit the kilns himself, and was moved by the workers' plight. Half way through 1986, David returned to Pakistan with Es Giddy, a filmmaker, to make a short documentary about the kilns. Filming the documentary proved to be risky. 'We're doing a story about bricks, so shouldn't we film some of this beautiful brick architecture in the old part of the city?' David had asked Es. They had then moved around the city of Peshawar filming the city's ancient, bustling market, and its majestic buildings, some made with five thousand-year-old bricks. They did not realise that one of the buildings they had chosen to film was a fort, strictly out of bounds for visitors, and soon they were surrounded by gesticulating policemen and soldiers asking them to stop, which they did.

The same day, Es had kept the camera rolling as a gory procession came down an ancient laneway—the men were members of an Islamic sect who flagellated with chains and sharp barbs until blood ran down their bodies. Again, the military made a move toward them. 'Quick, into this taxi,' David called to a reluctant Es, grasping his arm and pulling him in. The documentary was aired on the Australian Broadcasting Corporation (ABC) on Christmas Day 1986.

That year, the ACC's Christmas Bowl Appeal, combined with a contribution from a German benefactor, raised enough money to lease land for the brickworks, buy dozens of the workers out of bondage and buy land in a nearby village to subdivide for the workers' houses. The money allowed the group to build a clinic and provide each family with a milking goat. David and Michael then assembled a board, a group of business leaders, to oversee the project. So began a consuming project that took David to Pakistan a dozen times over several years.

Within the year the new brick kiln was operational, built on land leased for ten years. After that time the kiln would be exhausted of clay and it would be cleared for a farmer to start growing crops. Soon teams of kiln stokers and families of pathairas from other kilns in the district arrived at the new kiln. They had heard this was something new, but their expectations for a life outside drudgery were low. When David's group paid out the workers' debts at the old kiln, they became the new 'owners' of the kiln workers. David had played many roles, but never before had he 'owned' bonded workers.

At first it seemed to the workers that the new owners were just another master. They still worked just as hard. Then they started to understand a little more about the new owners' intentions. 'We are crediting you with ten per cent of all the bricks you produce each day,' the foreman told them. 'These bricks will be used to build your own houses on the land near the village.' It would take eighteen months to pay back all the debt, and by then each family would have enough bricks to build a small house. The new owners would supply roofing iron, a clean water supply and a nursery at the kiln so children no longer needed to play in the mud while their parents worked. They worked a little harder, and had reason to smile.

Despite all their research into ways of helping the kiln families, David and Michael had not reckoned on the ferocity of the backlash of other kiln owners, who for centuries had lived comfortably off the back-breaking work of those they exploited. They viewed it as a smear on their names to have these people attacking the system of bondage. Michael had also been a vocal opponent of the Islamicisation of the nation of Pakistan under General Muhammad Zia-al-Huq. He worried that Islamic Law would further erode the basic rights and freedoms of women; this stance created even more enemies for him among the ruling elite.

Soon Michael became the target of the kiln owners' ire. Groups of strangers once stopped his car on an empty road to intimidate him. In another incident he woke at night to find his house surrounded by seventeen kiln owners and their associates. Then his wife Valerie came under attack. Valerie was a refined and gracious Englishwoman Michael had met and married while he studied in Cambridge. She was gentle, caring, and absolutely devoted to Michael and his work. When David and Leigh arrived to visit that year, the kiln owners embarked on a smear campaign that saw posters of Valerie plastered to lamp posts; the posters claimed that she was intimately involved with the western visitors.

From there it became worse. Intimidation led to death threats, and although Michael had grown up in Pakistan and understood the cancer of corruption, it became too much when the threats turned to kidnapping Chammi and Ross, the Nazir-Alis' young boys. At the height of the dirty tricks Michael's back gave up and he was bedridden, immobile for days. It was then that David arrived.

There was something uncanny about David's timing, Michael had discovered. The same thing had happened when Chammi and Ross had been bitten by a rabid dog and had to be given a series of needles. David arrived in time to help Michael deliver the painful rabies shots into his sons' buttocks. At other times it seemed that just when Valerie was at her loneliest, David was there to lean on.

In England, the Archbishop of Canterbury, Lord Runcie, was concerned for Michael and his family. 'We think it would be safer for you and your family to come to England,' Lord Runcie told Michael. Reluctantly, Michael agreed to move back. Valerie and the boys were already in England, and Michael soon joined them, leaving with just a suitcase to avoid arousing any interest as he waited at the airport.

It was only natural that small business loans, David's main area of expertise, would follow the kiln project. David was drawn by the great need he saw and the challenge to make it work in an entirely different context from any work he had previously started. The Alfalah Development Institute kicked off in 1986, with Younis Farhat as executive director—this was not long before Michael had to flee for his life. Younis had already moved to the US with his family, but he returned to help poor communites in his homeland.

Pakistan was David's biggest development challenge yet. The country was littered with the bones of foreign aid groups who had tried to help and failed. It would only work if they could identify local people who would make the programs their own, and run them within the context of their own culture. David had had some hint of what lay ahead at an early breakfast meeting to screen prospective board members. When a thief was caught in the restaurant and dragged out publicly for a taste of local justice, David's companions, all local Christian businessmen, sprang to their feet and joined in the melée of kicking and beating that was the customary punishment. Stunned, David sat back and thought long and hard about how he could find leaders with whom to set up a solid lending organisation.

In another meeting, a prospective board member looked at David with a warm smile and made a comment to a colleague in Punjabi. The other man nodded in agreement. When David later asked the translator the meaning of the exchange, he was told they said, 'He is a bird in a gilded cage', an expression relating to the fact that they saw David as a soft target. In their eyes, he was a source of funding, a means to personal gain, and they now felt they had him captive.

He soon came to see why so many other altruistic endeavours had failed in Pakistan. 'It was really hard to work out how to help people with the knowledge that everyone was ripping the system off, wanting to line their pockets. That got a little depressing after a while because you were a foreigner trying to help, and the nationals rip their own people off.' Still, he and Leigh pushed on, and eventually they gathered a group who seemed committed to the poor. Pakistan would figure heavily in their travel schedules for the next few years.

The Live Aid fundraising concert of 13 July 1985, organised by singer Bob Geldof, riveted millions of people in every country to their television screens and exposed them to the tragic, starving faces of some of the six million famine-struck Ethiopians in need of food aid. Around the world, people watched their fellow humans suffer and were shocked into action by what they saw. Soon, millions of dollars had poured into non-government organisations who scrambled to receive the money. It revolutionised the charity sectors of countries like Australia, where many groups had only a post office box, and it forced governments to take development funding more seriously. A hurriedly prepared outline on a single page would no longer pass as a proposal for funding.

David's wide experience in the field was proving invaluable in his consulting work to the Australian Council of Churches, World Vision and large European donors. In 1985, he made a dozen trips— through Indonesia, India, the Philippines, Thailand, Singapore, and Pakistan, the US, Hong Kong—consulting on disaster relief and sustainable technology projects or working with new loan programs. He revelled in finding creative solutions to each problem he encountered. Development and micro enterprise were hand in hand.

Apart from travelling with Leigh, who in the early days of Alfalah accompanied David on all his Pakistan trips, David often brought friends and colleagues with him. Carol rarely came to the remote places, preferring to go where she could spend time with friends. David had already been mugged and robbed in Pakistan. In Bangladesh on a flood mitigation project his boat had been pirated. The bandits moved systematically among their captives, first working through the foreigners, who would provide the richest pickings, then striking at their compatriots—all the while firing their guns off every few minutes as a warning not to resist.

The move into Sri Lanka in January 1986, with a partner organisation named Jeeva Sanwardhanaya Ayathanaya (JSA), came soon after the long-running tensions between the Sinhalese majority and the Tamil minority erupted into violence. Sri Lanka was not at all like neighbouring India. Before the civil war the standard of living had been higher, with fewer of the hallmarks of abject poverty, such as open sewers, street dwellers, beggars and shanty towns.

The war in the mid 1980s brought with it social havoc. Tamil separatists from the north and anti-government insurgents in the south both declared war on the Sinhalese majority government. The government's response was to form squads to hunt out the warring groups. The brutal tactics of both sides put the city of Colombo on edge. People disappeared with alarming regularity; others were tortured, jailed without trial, sent to untraceable camps in the hills. The daily activities of city dwellers were over-shadowed by a fear that the next bomb to go off would be in their own neighbourhood or gathering place. There were roadblocks in and around the city, dead bodies left to rot, strict curfews after dark. The foreigners, both tourists and hardy journalists, had left and with them went the only livelihood for tens of thousands. The conflict had been too protracted, too complex. On the beaches, once crowded with wealthy families and visitors, the big resort hotels were deserted.

David and Leigh had too much at stake not to move ahead on Sri Lanka. Donors had put money up for lending programs and there were sustainable technology projects on the go. Even so, there were limits to the amount of peril they would place themselves in. David had worked on a project in Pakistan for a large German donor who also had a project up in Kandy, an area right in the middle of the rebel stronghold. For months, there had been silence from the field. 'We put a whole lot of money into a project in Kandy and we haven't heard from the people up there. Can you guys go up there to make contact with them and investigate what is happening?' the donor asked. It was a simple enough request, but in the middle of a civil war it was far too dangerous to drive there when no one could confirm who controlled the road. Despite the threat of random bombings right around them in Colombo, David and Leigh were quite comfortable operating out of a near-empty five-star hotel, almost the sole users of all its facilities, and were not inclined to drive into the unknown.

They decided that a helicopter would be the only way to reach Kandy and had started making enquiries around the helicopter rental companies when the military arrived at the hotel.

'Are you the two businessmen looking to hire a helicopter?' the soldier asked.

'Yes, we are,' David replied, not sure where the conversation was headed. Perhaps they were suspected of helping the rebels. Dissidents were being executed for less at the time.

'We need to go to Kandy to look at some aid programs,' he explained.

'Well, we have a helicopter right outside for you,' the soldier replied. 'We'll give you a good price. Come see.' On the street outside their hotel, with the rotor blade circling slowly, was a government-owned helicopter gunship, freshly withdrawn from the war, ready to take them to Kandy. It was hard for soldiers to make money in the war, but here they had two foreigners who would line their pockets.

'We'll take you up—come on,' the soldier beckoned.

'But what about the war?' Leigh asked.

'Don't worry about that, we're the government, we have the ammunition. How much money have you got?'

David and Leigh had to make a quick decision. 'If we go up in that gunship the rebels are going to fire missiles at it,' Leigh whispered behind his hand to David.

'Sorry, we've decided not to go north,' David announced to the soldier, who promptly stomped off to his gunship and back to the war.

11

The Walls Came Down

On the night of 22 February 1986 the people of Manila left their barrios and shacks in places like Quezon City, Tondo, Tatalon and Valenzuela and made a pilgrimage to Manila's heart. Radio Veritas broadcast calls to freedom from the church leader, Cardinal Sin, and from Agapito Aquino, brother of Benigno Aguino, the opposition leader who had been assassinated on 21 August 1983. The crowds pushed onto jeepneys and buses to congregate on Epifanio de los Santos Avenue, a spacious boulevarde in Metro Manila known as the EDSA. Within days the EDSA would become the site of liberation for the Filipino people.

First there were ten thousand, then one hundred thousand, then one million people chanting 'Cory, Cory, Cory' in support of Corazon Aquino, widow of Benigno and the presidential candidate who only the week before had rallied a million people and sparked a campaign of civil disobedience across the country. Now the roads to military camps were clogged with people demanding change.

'Cory, Cory, Cory,' they chanted, voices filled with hope and defiance. A column of tanks emerged, like bulldogs strutting their way along the EDSA in search of a target to sink their teeth into. They were after the rebels, but what they found were passionate, unarmed civilians, the poor and the middle classes, who had come

THE WALLS CAME DOWN

too far towards democracy to be cowed by force. Mac and Rhoda Bradshaw and their children came to support their Filipino friends as they now peacefully stood up against decades of corruption and exploitation.

The tanks rolled right up to the crowds, staring down black-clothed nuns and priests, hopeful women and children, who kneeled down before them. The soldiers would have to kill, and in large numbers, to reach the rebels. The world watched nervously on television—the situation could turn to mass murder—and collectively sighed with relief as the tanks backed off. The soldiers could not kill their own people. At home in Sydney David and Carol were glued to the news as the drama unfolded, knowing how the outcome of this event could affect their work.

On the Monday morning, 24 February, helicopter gunships hovered threateningly over the crowds, who remained in the streets, standing firm. The pilots lost their nerve and thundered away; later they joined forces with the protesters. By the next day Ferdinand Marcos was in exile and the People's Power movement had won. The nation was filled with the euphoria of victory, and it was all done without violence.

The Philippines was not the only nation to experience revolution around this time. Through the late 1980s and early 1990s the political and social landscape in other parts of the world was changing at an equally tumultuous rate. Like the Filipinos, the oppressed in many nations were finding a voice. Some less developed countries of the world were asserting themselves. They did not want economic, social or spiritual dependence on the wealthy west. They wanted empowerment and self-determination.

In the space of a few short years, there were challenges to barriers and dictatorships in East Germany, China and Africa. The Berlin Wall came down on 9 November 1989 as communism toppled in Eastern Europe. Suddenly millions behind the Iron Curtain were coming out from under the cloud of oppression. In China, students had stood their ground for democracy in June 1989 at Tiananmen Square, although the soldiers had not been as compassionate as those in Manila. In South Africa, the laws imposing apartheid were in the process of being repealed and the nation was on the cusp of its own social revolution.

The Philippines entered an era of optimism with its new government in 1986, but as the euphoria subsided, the issue of poverty remained. President Aquino's reign brought a renewal of social conscience, and renewed hope among the nation's thirty million poor for a better life. She called on private enterprise to help eradicate poverty and bring stability to the new democracy.

Aquino's plea was heard by the leaders of TSPI, who were talking through ways of reaching more poor people in the Philippines. In 1986, David joined the TSPI board in Manila for a meeting that would seal the fate of many thousands of poor in the Philippines. The revolution brought an urgency to TSPI's plans to expand throughout the country. The question in the board meetings was now, 'How soon can we roll out our micro lending programs?' Now empowering the poor was not only a matter of compassion; it was acknowledged as necessary to build the social fabric of the nation.

In five years TSPI had matured into a strong, independent institution, no longer solely reliant on foreign finance. David's hard work in building bonds through staff and board retreats had paid off and TSPI's people were close and committed to the poor. The board was confident that it could reach further afield, and conceived an ambitious plan to start independent partner organisations in the fifteen provinces of the Philippines, each with its own board of directors and focus on local needs, with a goal of being self-sustaining within six years.

David was more than happy to be a silent partner, particularly where the borrowers were concerned. 'I had fixed in my mind this concept that it was better for westerners to be behind the scenes so it was perceived that the funds were from local successful business people. Part of my theory was that if we could develop an environment where loan recipients thought it was their own people who were providing the capital they were more likely to pay it back because it wasn't seen as western charity.'

David's model in founding TSPI itself would be the blueprint for the new lenders. Eli Lademora made contact, mostly through church connections, with local business leaders keen to help the poor in their communities. TSPI encouraged diversity, allowing the new partners to work with their clients in the most appropriate way. The size and delivery of loans in urban areas, where there would be small-scale manufacturing and vending, would differ from what happened in rural areas, where many businesses inevitably related to agriculture.

TSPI's first recruit, Noel Alcaide, had flourished in the micro enterprise development field. 'I would very much like the job of executive director of the new partner,' he told Jun Llenado.

'But we have only a little money to start with. The wages will be less than you are earning now,' Jun told him.

'Never mind—I want to be the head rather than the tail. I'm willing to take a pay cut,' Noel replied, without hesitation.

The first new partner, Kabalikat Para Sa Maunlad Na Buhay Inc., known as KMBI, started early in 1986 in the Valenzuela municipality of Manila, an industrial part of the city often disturbed by strikes and unrest. Within the municipality of Valenzuela were both comfortable and severely depressed *baranguays*, or neighbourhoods; the wealthy and poor lived side by side. Noel set out to work at the lowest level of poverty. He wanted to reach into the warrens of Valenzuela, where the extent of suffering was hidden from the outside world. KMBI's mandate would be to go into the dirty alleys where large families crowded into single rooms, without the basic amenities of safe water, street lighting, or road access. Here street urchins ran wild, disease was rampant and early deaths were commonplace.

Next, TSPI set up a national office to deal with the new partners. It was a feast of acronyms, all meaning 'Bridge to Progress' in local dialects, all expressing the hope of relief to the nation's poor. Each would have its own identity, to fit its region and its needs.

In 1986 Taytay Sa Kauswagan Inc. (TSKI) was set up in the port city of IloIlo on the island of Panay, bringing loans to groups of women, small vendors, farmers and transport workers. Fishing families living in squalid huts by the Sulu Sea could improve their nets and fleets and at the same time their living quarters and diets. The next year, in the rural areas around Baguio in northern Luzon, Rangtay Sa Pagrang-ay Inc. (RSPI) set out to target women living below the poverty line who already had small enterprises but no way of building on their meagre income. The same year, Allay Sa Kaunlaran Sa Gitnang Luzon Inc. (ASKI) in Cabanatuan City, central Luzon, embarked on its loans to groups and individuals. Hagdan Sa Pag-uswag Foundation Inc. (HSPFI), on the southern island of Mindanao, and Talete King Panyulung Kapampangan Inc. (TPKI), in Pampanga, a province north of Manila, followed. Later there would also be DSPI (Daan Sa Pag-unlad Inc.), in Baatan, Luzon Island.

Soon there were seven new partners, like small birds, all squawking for the attention and support of their parent, TSPI. In choosing to go out into the provinces, TSPI had taken on a weighty financial burden. David's role was again highly entrepreneurial. He was committed to creating an environment where the character of each of the partners could grow, where the management could experiment with creative ideas and initiatives that were their own, not implanted from the west.

While Eli identified local leadership to run new programs, David developed the relationships. 'I would meet a person and explain the vision and develop a friendship with that person and then build a board with them. I was involved in board formation and crafting.' His closest friendships were often with the chairs of the organisations.

Harry Edwards, an Australian Member of Parliament who at the time chaired the overseas aid committee for the Maranatha Trust, was a tireless advocate for the work, throwing his political weight, time and contacts into the cause. He was able to break through walls in both Australia and the Philippines, as government officials and others in development circles at first struggled to accept micro enterprise development as a legitimate form of poverty alleviation. It would be another ten years before micro finance would be broadly accepted as a highly effective tool in the fight against poverty.

In 1985 Harry had introduced David to an Australian by the name of Bill Taylor, who was soon firmly behind the TSPI expansion process in the Philippines. At sixty years old, Bill was fifteen years older than David, a focused, driven person who had enjoyed a distinguished career at the formal end of overseas development. He had worked on economic development programs for the United Nations for twenty years, and had a deep academic knowledge of development that complemented David's hands-on approach.

By the time he and David met, Bill had retired from overseas service and set up an agri-tourism project called Sunshine Planta-tion—home of the Big Pineapple—at Nambour in Queensland and an eco-tourism venture in Hawaii. Bill travelled with David through Indonesia, and was convinced of the effectiveness of what he and his colleagues were doing. When he heard of TSPI's plan to reach out across the Philippines he was eager to help. He had made his fortune through his tourism ventures and was looking for a way to use it to help the poor. Along with IIDI and Maranatha, Bill poured hundreds of thousands of dollars into the expansion program.

As KMBI grew and Noel explored smaller loans and group lending, David arranged for him to visit Priyadi in Bali to study MBM's successful programs. It was part of his strategy to promote the cross-pollination of ideas and methods through exposure to others in the field. Under Priyadi, MBM had branched out into making ever smaller loans, with the average loan size now only sixty five thousand rupiah (US$40). Through the village system, the borrowers were organised into small groups, mainly of women. This method had started a small revo-lution in the communities. Once they had businesses and incomes, the women found they could turn their attention to savings as well as to repaying the loans. When they came together they often discussed family issues, building a strong sense of community.

Noel came away from Bali inspired. He saw how community-based groups could reach those battling at the lowest level of poverty. TSPI had generated many new jobs in poor areas by making loans to individual entrepreneurs who had expanded their small-scale manufacturing into bigger concerns. After Bali, Noel determined to take KMBI down the group lending path. Later he would build on Priyadi's tutorship, and his own experimentation over six years, by incorporating elements of the group loan pro-grams of ASA and Grameen from Bangladesh.

By now Priyadi and David had also gone on the expansion trail in Indonesia. Maranatha had already founded Duta Bina Buana (DBB), the vehicle they would use to expand across Indonesia through a series of lending partners and small rural banks. DBB became a centre that supported and provided training for the new lending partners. The new partners were in southern and central Sulawesi and Sumatra, following the path of poor Balinese trans-migrants. The success stories had continued at MBM, which now had offices at Sangsit in Bali's north, and Melaya to the west. A network of young loan managers, most with university degrees in business or agriculture, made and administered the loans. They were always prepared to lend their expertise to the problems of poor villagers.

Nyoman Sunartha, an enthusiastic loan manager, had walked alongside Pak Made Tegeg since he first received a one hundred thousand rupiah loan (US$110) in 1983 to fill a large order for his simple clay pots. At the time, annual sales of his pottery amounted to six hundred and thirty thousand rupiah (US$690) and the business supported seven families, all related to Pak Tegeg. The families shared a spartan house right off the main road through the village of Kapal, not far from the MBM office. The order to make clay tiles for a big hotel turned Tegeg's world on end. He quickly enlisted other local families to help him, creating a cottage industry within his community that soon employed one hundred people from twenty four families. The orders began to flow. Again and again he came back to Sunartha, and MBM would lend him the money for a new piece of equipment or materials. His single house grew into a compound and his family prospered.

Micro enterprise development now ate up the lions' share of David's time, much of it spent in Asia, where the programs were thriving. In its new home in Chicago, IIDI was looking around for a new chief executive to take over from Bud Hancock, who had followed Barry Harper for a short time in the job. The board started a search for the right candidate, and had narrowed it down to a handful of people when someone suggested David Bussau.

The presiding chairman, Al Whittaker, was assigned the task of talking to David about the role, and soon came back with what he thought was a postive response.

The board thanked the candidates who had already been interviewed and told them that a colleague, David Bussau, was taking the job. It was a full month before it became clear that David had not actually accepted the role. The Americans were puzzled. It seems that David's answer to Al—'I'll help you in any way you want'—had not included the chief executive role. There had been a colossal misunderstanding.

'No, I would never agree to spending a third of my time in the US,' David told the board. 'I couldn't possibly be the chief executive.' He was already away from home sixty per cent of the time and he felt his skills were better used on the ground. Besides, operating out of Maranatha Trust allowed him the autonomy he needed as an entrepreneur.

The previously preferred candidate, a lawyer by the name of Gordon Murphy, a man of robust personality, was not put off by being second choice to David.

'I'm interested in the job, but I'll need to meet David Bussau and visit the work in the Philippines before saying yes to it,' he said when offered the position.

By July 1986, Gordon and US board member Em Griffin were in Manila, slushing through the mud in the torrential rains of the monsoon season and visiting the leaking, tin-roofed businesses of small borrowers. Em had seen the programs in Latin America, but the more he heard about what the Australians had started in the Philippines, the more interested he had become. The previous year he had personally helped raise a large amount for the Philippines, and now he would see how it was used. He was thrilled to find that TSPI had delivered exactly the number of jobs it had promised with the money he and his friends had sent.

For hours, Gordon and David sat in coffee shops, talking about life, family, faith, philosophy, business, poverty and micro enterprise. There was so much to talk about, and no doubt that they were on the same wavelength. Both men were business-minded, entrepreneurial, and deeply committed to relationships. It was not a hard decision for Gordon to say 'yes' to the job of leading the US office.

'It was absolutely wonderful, because it meant I had the opportunity to get paid for spending time with David Bussau and Leigh Coleman,' Gordon said. 'David taught me in many ways how to be a good friend. A lot of friendship is just hanging out. Friendship doesn't need an agenda to call up and see what's going on in a person's life.'

175

In June 1987, when David was in Chicago for a board meeting, Em asked him to go ultralight flying. David had been once before with Em, and loved the sensation of swooping high above the golden mid western fields, buffeted by insects and cold wind. It was Em's 50th birthday and he intended to spend the day doing something he loved. David would later be joining a crowd to celebrate at the Griffin home. Again they drove beyond the suburban sprawl of Chicago and into the farming community of De Kalb where the plane was stored. It was late in the day, when the wind had died down enough to swoop and glide at sixty kilometres (thirty five miles) per hour without being tossed around. Em knew David was game for adventure, so he took it a little harder this time. At one hundred metres (three hundred feet) above the ground they skimmed the plains and soared over to skirt a small clear lake. David was strapped in behind Em with a grin as wide as his face when, with a small splutter, one of the engines stopped. It was an ultralight pilot's nightmare. A small machine lifting more than its weight with two large men, and with a twenty-four-litre (about five-gallon) fuel tank strapped to the back of the craft. One engine was not going to keep two men in the air.

Em steeled himself for an emergency landing, pointing the plane towards the ground to keep the flying speed up. He managed to get them down relatively smoothly, landing in a farmer's field, hitting the ground at a speed of sixty four kilometres (forty miles) per hour. It would have been fine if they could simply have run the plane along the ground as it slowed down, but when Em looked up he saw they were speeding towards a barbed wire fence—he and David would be like cheese in a grater if he could not slow it down. The brakes were not nearly strong enough to stop their careering pace, so he jammed on the rudder and pulled a ground loop that wrenched the plane around, breaking a wheel.

There had not been a sound from David, and now they sat in the field in silence with only the sound of crickets and the smell of stressed brakes.

'You know, until the wheels hit the ground, I thought we were just swooping,' David said after a few minutes. Then they ditched the plane and walked a couple of kilometres in silence to the nearest farmhouse.

Finally, Em spoke. 'Do you think you'd ever do that again?'

'You bet,' David replied.

Later, as Em reflected on the accident, he was horrified to think that he had might have maimed or killed David. 'I regarded David as the corporate treasure of the organisation and here I was, almost killing the guy that's making it all go.'

One Sunday in 1987, David and Carol met a young couple from New Zealand in church. David and Dianne Middleton lived in nearby Woollahra, and David was working on a one-year assignment with a stockbroking firm in the city. He and Di were expecting their first child, and like the Bussaus when they first arrived, had no close family for support in Australia.

They were happily drawn into the Bussau extended family and as the friendship developed and the baby's birth grew imminent, Carol made an offer they could not refuse.

'We've got a flat at our place—why don't you come and live with us?' Carol asked. They were soon settled into the small flat attached to the busy Bussau household, following in the footsteps of many others. The two Davids built their friendship on the squash court, where the younger David learned much about this man who could be both gentle and fearsome: it seemed the longer they played, the more energy he had, and the more his mental determination willed him to win. He was one of the most fiercely competitive people David Middleton had ever met.

Most days when he was in Australia, David Bussau cosseted himself in the unglamorous office in the shed at the bottom of the garden, connected by phone and telex at all hours with his colleagues around the world.

'What do you do all day down there in that garage of yours, Dave?' David Middleton asked. He was growing increasingly intrigued by David's comings and goings and the stories he brought back about MBM in Bali, the projects in India and Pakistan, the aftermath of disasters he encountered. David Bussau was more passionate about what he was doing than anyone he had ever met, and it was infectious.

As it turned out, David Middleton was clever with computers—David knew nothing about them. Most of his work was stored in his head. However, the lending programs were developing quickly and he needed to get systems and a database in order. It was time to leap into the modern world, and David Middleton was the one to help.

When David and Di's first child, Emma, arrived, the bond between the families grew stronger, particularly between the two women. Carol was often on hand to babysit if Di needed time to herself. Most nights the two families shared a meal. They had no idea how important the friendship would later become.

During the 1980s, David's overseas trips got longer, and the breaks at home got shorter. An average marriage might have crumpled under the pressure long before. David and Carol had come to an unspoken agreement: that they should release each other to explore the full range of their gifts and talents. Somehow, Carol kept abreast of David's movements through long phone calls and faxes to the Maranatha office. (By now the office had moved into an old house in Bondi Junction, just across the park from their home.) Others threw their hands in the air. 'Where is he this week, Carol?' her friends asked, wondering how the couple managed to stay close. 'I think he is going to the Philippines today,' Carol replied. She found it easier to think loosely about which country David might be in, rather than exactly where he was every day. From time to time she saw news of a plane crash on television and quickly checked it was not her husband's flight. She learned to overcome her fear of losing him. 'I just had to trust God.'

Some friends were indignant on her behalf, but she chose to remain positive about David's work. 'I don't resent him going, because I believe in the work,' Carol explained to them. Still, there were hard moments when Tasha and Rachel misbehaved and household appliances broke. One night, when the old house was under renovation and looked vacant in its shrouds of plastic, Carol awoke to hear giggling and banging. She sprang out of bed to see what the racket was all about. She climbed up a ladder linking the ground floor with the half-built upper floor, and found a group of teenagers she didn't even know—they had climbed into the roof space and were sitting up there having a drunken party.

'Come down here, right this minute,' she called in her best schoolmarm voice, trying to hide her fear, despite the pounding in her chest. 'Off you go. This is our home and we live here,' she told them as they backed down the stairs, suddenly sober and mumbling their apologies.

Leigh Coleman was away as much as David. His wife, Vera, was one of the few people who truly understood Carol, one of the few she could joke with and know it would not be taken as bitter resentment.

Carol only heard the bare bones of David's travel stories on his return. Leigh took much the same approach with Vera. The men came home punch drunk from weeks on the road, too emotionally drained from the pace and volume of activity to relive the weeks of serious, intense work.

Stories dribbled out over the weeks, when David might ask Carol, 'Did I tell you about our car being stoned as we drove through Nablus to inspect the new hospital?' Once David told her how, on a flight out of London to Hong Kong and Manila, the flight crew found the words 'this plane will explode when it reaches thirty three thousand feet' scrawled across the mirror in a washroom. Within twenty minutes the plane had deviated and landed at a military base in Germany, where passengers were pulled aside singly or in pairs and questioned at great length.

'Now, please write these words twice, once with each hand,' the security staff instructed, handing each passenger a felt-tip pen. They then went through the laborious task of fingerprinting and photographing each passenger, all the while employing the technique of stirring up anxiety among the passengers, hoping that someone might confess.

David was frustrated and impatient. The airline sent the passengers to a hotel for the night, and on to their destination the next day, with David arriving a day late for his appointments in Manila. Those nine scribbled words had cost the airline more than one million UK pounds, or US$ 1.5 million.

At dinner with the Colemans, David might tell a tale at Leigh's expense months after the event. 'Vera, did Leigh tell you about being mugged in Vietnam by a group of women?' He then amused them all with the story of how the women had surrounded Leigh, grabbed the front of his trousers and squeezed until he gave them his money.

There were other reasons for David's reticence to share his stories. He was not one to hang on to experiences for the sake of it, or to use them to entertain. More importantly, he did not want to create unnecessary anxiety in Carol's life. She had enough to think about with Tasha and Rachel.

For David, normality was the antidote to constant travel and the intellectual stimulation of his work. Back home in Sydney, he slipped easily into a simple daily life. He donned his old football shorts and terry towelling hat and headed for the garden. There were weeds to pull, petunias to plant, flower beds to fertilise. He fell into the role of father and husband and friend, and helping out at the local church, with as little fuss as possible. His relaxation from building institutions and projects was the old-fashioned building in which he had started. In his down time he made adjustments to his own house and helped friends with their building projects.

He unwound with the girls, who delighted in being around the house with their father. They heard nothing of his most dangerous escapades. Tasha was reaching the mid teen years, when fads and friends dictate what a girl needs. Rachel was not far behind. David gently set out to foster independence in them. From an early age they were handed a lump sum of pocket money and had to work out their own budgets. Now, when they needed extra pocket money, David suggested they set up a small business.

'What sort of business would you like to start?' he asked them.

'We could do cleaning. We could start with your offices at Bondi Junction,' Tasha suggested.

David took them to the Maranatha office and together they sat down to work out a business plan.

'What materials will you need? How many hours a week can you work?' he asked them. Before long their first venture, the 'MopaLot Cleaning Service' was underway. Though their enthusiasm waned as other interests took over, the business set a pattern of money management they would only later fully appreciate.

At least once a year Tasha and Rachel came along when David travelled, making new friends of many nationalities among the children of board members and program directors throughout Asia. The years spent as a family in Darwin and Indonesia had helped the girls understand, even at a young age, that their father was doing something outside the ordinary, something most fathers did not do, although it did not stop them missing him during the year.

Carol handled the loneliness by reaching out to others. If David's gift was for encouraging and building others, Carol's was for caring for those she found in need around her. She was able to build her life in Sydney around her interests. She had first started her pastoral work in the church in the mid 1970s.

Initially there was a budget for her pastoral role. She undertook training and found there was indeed a great need for an impartial ear and gentle guidance.

There was no end to the number of people who crossed her path. Some were lonely, in need of a patient listener and a good friend. Others suffered from serious mental illness and made greater demands on her time and emotional energy. There were times when Carol was out in the middle of the night searching for someone who had left home and not been seen. She came to know where to look for them. She took calls at all hours of the day and night, often rushing out to meet someone or bringing them into her home for a solid meal and a good night's sleep. She cared for a dozen or more people at any time.

When the budget later ran out, she continued her work unpaid for many years, until a team of counsellors came on board. Through those years, and for many years later, she visited retirement villages, taught scripture, kindergarten and remedial reading.

It did not surprise David that Carol's attention had moved in the direction of helping others, particularly those who suffered through mental illness. Who better to understand their fears and pain than someone who had been through it? At other times he felt slightly put out by the demands on her time outside their relationship. He well understood the irony of this reaction, given the vast amounts of time he spent away, and he never made a fuss.

It was now more than twelve years since David first made the decision to sell up and work in the development field. His pace had never really slowed. He still spent sixty per cent of the year travelling, much of that in Asia. The lending programs now extended to fourteen countries, offering loans of more than US$2 million in a year, and David was co-ordinating much of it. 'It was intellectually challenging, satisfying work,' his close friend Vinay recalls. 'He was dealing with some of the cleverest people in different parts of the world, trying to maintain common standards globally. It was building a global business and David was at the heart of it. There were no textbooks to go by.' Even if there had been textbooks on the specialised field of micro enterprise development, David would not have read them. He responded to what he observed for himself. He calmly handled the dangers and the complexities of the many cultures and personalities he met with as he travelled. He seemed to be unstoppable.

Yet events at home in Sydney would halt him in his tracks that year, 1988. For more than three years, since she was fifteen years old, Tasha had been in a relationship with a young musician called Wayne, a boy whose family life had been as turbulent as Tasha's was nurturing. Neither Carol nor David thought he was right for their daughter, but there was little they could do. This relationship was the topic that caused Carol most anguish when David travelled.

One Friday evening in August, Tasha called David, Carol and Rachel together. She was eighteen years old, and in her first year of a university degree in education. As the family gathered in the lounge room, Tasha grew more agitated and tears welled in her eyes. She'd dreaded this moment for days, and the warm smiles of her family made her feel worse. Finally, she told them, 'I'm pregnant.' There was a moment of stunned silence, then, without a question or word, David stood up, crossed the room and embraced his daughter. When Tasha, feeling unworthy of affection, tried to push her father away, he held her.

Meanwhile Carol sat quietly, shocked at the news, and unsure of what to say. Then she blurted out, 'I'm a bad mother. I should have seen something.' Tasha would not hear of it. 'Don't be ridiculous, it was nothing to do with you. It was something I did,' she told her mother. Tasha soon faded with emotional exhaustion, and her parents and Rachel settled her into bed with more hugs and kisses and the family prayed together. It would take some time for the news and its implications to sink in, for David to work through his anger at the young man and Carol to work through her feelings of guilt, but for now it was a huge relief for Tasha to have the news of her pregnancy out in the open.

The following Monday Carol quietly told her friends and colleagues. She felt a little awkward, and half-anticipated judgment. Instead, the news broke down barriers and opened the way for an outpouring of honesty and compassion as more than one person came to her privately to talk about long-held grief over their own youthful mistakes.

Soon after, the Bussaus' good friends, Vinay and Colleen Samuels, came to stay. In India, it was a disgrace for a single girl to become pregnant—such a girl would soon find herself in a home for girls or with distant relatives, to avoid bringing shame on the family. They observed with interest how David and Carol looked for ways to help Tasha. This experience had a significant impact on the Samuels' work at Divya Shanthi, where they already rescued female babies from infanticide, provided a refuge for unmarried mothers and helped restore the girls' relationships with their parents. 'David and Carol's experience was an important resource to help us communicate with these people,' Vinay says.

At a conference in Manila soon after, David had a meeting that pushed any lingering concern for his own family issues into perspective. David Stiller, a softly spoken Canadian businessman with wavy white hair and beard, came to Manila via West Africa, where he had talked at length to a struggling young artisan in the market. 'I could do well, if only I could afford the materials I need,' the artisan told him. When the Canadian related the comment to a friend in Manila, his friend replied, 'David Bussau is the person to talk to about small loans.' He resolved to meet this person, and sat waiting outside a conference room until David Bussau appeared and he could pull him aside. 'How are you?' David Stiller asked when the men met.

'I'm OK, but things are difficult for our family at the moment. My teenage daughter has become pregnant. I don't think the father is going to stick around,' David Bussau said, sighing heavily, as if they were old friends. It was rare for David to share his personal life outside his closest circle, let alone with a stranger, but for some reason he felt immediately comfortable with David Stiller.

David Stiller listened as David talked about his concern for Tasha and the responsibility of raising a child at such a young age, then clapped his hand on David's leg. 'Brother, you have a daughter who is healthy and you're gaining a grandchild. Be thankful,' he said, with an unexpected degree of passion. He was close to tears as he related his own story. 'My wife and I lost our dear daughter last year when she was eighteen years old. Look at what you are gaining.' David Bussau pulled himself up. 'You're right.' These words suddenly put everything into a new light. It was the beginning of an enduring bond between the two men.

Throughout Tasha's pregnancy Carol had a growing sense that the baby would be a great blessing in their lives. In January 1989, David and Carol held Tasha's hands and offered encouragement as she gave birth to a healthy girl, Jessica. Joy soon overwhelmed Carol's sadness that Tasha was not sharing this emotional moment with a partner. It was now clear Tasha's ex-boyfriend would not play an active fatherhood role.

Jessica's arrival at home in Randwick attracted a flood of attention. She slotted into David and Carol's lives somewhere between a third daughter and a grandchild, and they all pitched in, caring for Jessica while Tasha attended classes at university. Di and David Middleton still lived at the apartment within the house, and by now had a second child, Nicholas, just three months younger than Jessica. Carol and Di often strode out to Centennial Park across the road with Nick and Jessie in a twin stroller, looking like unlikely siblings, and Emma alongside.

In the US, IIDI had been through a labour of sorts itself. It was a time of clarifying the vision of the organisation. It had taken months of discussion, but now the decision was made. IIDI and Marantha Trust needed a new, more descriptive name, something other than an acronym, a name that would at least hint at the work they were doing and that was more suited to global ambitions. From the end of 1988, the micro enterprise development work of IIDI and Marantha Trust became known as Opportunity International, a name that reflected its core activity: bringing small business opportunities to the chronically poor. David held the position of global co-ordinator, and Leigh continued as Asian regional director. David still ran many activities and funding through Maranatha.

There was also change afoot in Manila, where TSPI was getting a new director. The executive director, Eli Lademora, left for full-time ministry, and after scouting for a replacement, the board found Benjie Montemayor, a feisty banker with a keen commercial eye. He knew little about non-government organisations or small business, and his family was at first unimpressed by his move from a comfortable city office to a dingy basement. But after many years in banking and government, Benjie was weary of creating more wealth for the wealthy. Many years before, working with landless farmers in Negros, he had learned valuable lessons about the dignity and empowerment of the poor. He now aggressively pursued the expansion program, seeing it as his chance to help meet some of what seemed to be an insatiable need. The work with TSPI, effectively banking to the poor, was as close to the cutting edge as it got, and he rarely missed the suits and board-rooms of conventional banking. Benjie was like a sponge around his new Australian mentors, travelling with David, and watching David intently as he raised money for the lending programs.

'The focus was to train executive directors, so I was being trained and exposed. David was able to make things happen and bring information from the outside world that we would not have been international enough to access.

'I saw Leigh Coleman and David Bussau as people who spent themselves so that other people could grow. They decreased so others could increase. They taught me what helping was all about,' Benjie says. David's response was to make himself available, to fly in whenever the local partners needed him, to arrive without his own agenda. He inevitably asked, 'What do you want to happen?' in meetings, rather than imposing himself on the Filipinos. There were times when he had spent hours preparing for a meeting, only to throw his papers away when he saw that it was not what the Filipinos wanted.

By now David Middleton occasionally travelled with David when he went to Indonesia and the Philippines. In June 1989 the men travelled to Bali and were staying at the Sanur Beach Hotel when David Middleton received an urgent message: 'Call Leigh Coleman in Sydney.'

He soon got through to Leigh, to hear shocking news. 'There's been an accident involving Di and the children. I'm afraid she's lost her mother, and both the baby and Emma are in hospital,' Leigh explained to him. 'We'll arrange for you to be on tonight's flight home.'

David watched his friend's face go pale. For once David Bussau was at a loss as to what to do. It was Carol who had the gift for comforting people. 'What can I do for you?' he asked.

'Well, you could pray,' David Middleton replied, feeling helpless and a long way from his family. It had been such a happy time in the family. Di's father had died many years before, and her mother had come to Sydney only weeks before, with her new fiancé, to remarry. They had planned to live close to the Middletons for a few months, to get to know the grandchildren.

That evening Priyadi and David Bussau bundled David Middleton over to the airport and onto a plane. It was pouring with rain, and the scent of frangipani hung heavily in the air.

'Bali is crying for you and your family,' Priyadi said as they parted.

It was only on arriving home that David Middleton learned the circumstances of the accident. Carol and Di had organised an outing to El Caballo Blanco, a show of Spanish dancing horses, on the outskirts of Sydney. Carol drove her car with Tasha and Rachel and Di's new father-in-law John, ahead of Di, who had her mother in the front and Nicholas and Emma in the back seat of her car. As Di waited to turn right into a side road, a truck came barrelling down the hill, unable to stop, and pushed the car into the path of oncoming traffic.

Carol and John had looked back in disbelief as they saw the smoking wreck at the side of the road. The front passenger side of the car, where Di's mother Val had been, was crushed. Di jumped out and ran to the passenger side just as Carol and John arrived.

'I don't know who to help,' Carol cried out, exasperated. Val was horrifically injured and trapped in the front of the car.

'I need you to be with my mother,' Di told her decisively, as she looked for her children in the back. At first she could not even see the baby, Nicholas. She found him wedged under the front seat—he had slipped out of his baby capsule and become stuck when the velcro holding the strap burst. Emma lay unconscious in the back. She had taken a tremendous knock from the side, and there was no telling what her injuries would be.

The ambulance soon rushed Di, Emma and Nicholas to hospital, while Carol stayed with Val, holding her hand as the rescue squad cut the car wreck from around her. John, Val's new husband, was in a state of shock.

'Val, stay with us. Don't go, Val. You have so much to live for. Think about John. And there's Emma and Nicholas, Di and David. We all want you to hang on.' For half an hour, through the sawing of metal and yelling of directions, Carol spoke quietly to Val, willing her and praying for her to live. It was not to be. Val died soon after arriving at the hospital.

At Westmead Hospital a doctor thoughtlessly told Di, 'Both the children are in intensive care. We're not expecting them to come through.' The X-rays showed that Nicholas had a fractured skull and seven broken ribs. Emma's injuries were even more serious. She would have brain damage, according to the X-ray.

The doctors then decided to airlift the children to another hospital, where they could have a CT scan and receive specialist care. Here a second set of X-rays confirmed the fractured skulls, but the CT machine had broken down—they were transferred to a third hospital.

David Middleton was now on his way home from Bali. Word of the accident had gone out around members of the Bali church and at the Church at the Marketplace in Bondi Junction. In both places friends were earnestly praying for the children.

At the third hospital, the children were again wheeled in for X-rays, and this time the doctors could not explain what had happened. The fracture in Nicholas' skull was now gone, though it was visible in the previous two X-rays. It was not the only thing to go his way. It had been cold, and he was dressed in layers of warm wool clothing, hand-knitted by his paternal grandmother. 'The wool may have saved him from going into shock and dying,' another doctor later told them.

Some time later Emma, who doctors said had suffered severe brain damage, opened her eyes, looked at the bright light above her, and then at her mother, and said, 'Light, Mum.' She, too, had made an inexplicable recovery. After five days in intensive care, she and Nicholas were on the way to a full recovery. A heart-broken John returned to New Zealand soon after the accident.

If the families began as good friends, the events of that day, and the months of grief that followed for Di, cemented the relationship. Only Carol could fully understand what Di had been through. Emma and Nicholas grew up knowing Carol as Nana B.

12

A Force for the Poor

Half a world away, the volatile nation of Pakistan now emerged as a hotspot. Lahore, the capital of Punjab Province, was a city of contrasts, with lush and elaborate gardens dating back to the times of Mughal rule, and slums as desperate as anywhere in the developing world. Working on micro enterprise development within the Pakistani context and culture was proving complex. Though the need was acute, it was not possible to make long-term plans or talk about sustainability here in the same way that it was in the Philippines.

Alfalah's executive director, Younis Farhat, was a strong, no-nonsense man who ran a good operation, going out himself to meet and collect the loan repayments of small business people in businesses like renting televisions, mechanic shops and making clothes. This way he understood the challenges they faced and the training he and his team might help with. Several years into the loans programs, Alfalah had started a large community development project in the Awami Colony, an isolated community of poor Pakistanis who had filtered in from country areas and could only afford to live in this crowded brick and cement tangle of housing on the desert. Outside the fertile greens of the city, the people of the Awami Colony lived in dry desolation.

David had worked with a team of researchers from Punjab University to look at the needs of the community and found funding for the project; Alfalah became manager of the programs, which included a pre-school program, adult literacy classes, a community health centre, vocational training for young girls, and small loans. One evening David and Leigh visited the community with Younis. 'You've got to come over and meet the families involved in the project,' he told them. They were sitting with the local leaders of the project when a woman came over to speak to Younis.

'The women would like to talk to us without the other men there,' Younis translated for the foreigners. It was a highly unusual request, even though these women were all part of a sewing group who had received training and small loans through the project. Then the women asked all the young people to leave as well.

'What is it you'd like to talk with us about?' Younis asked the women, now curious.

One woman, their leader, addressed them, 'There is no employment around here—the only work we can get is as gardeners and domestic workers in the homes of the rich people who live in the houses near here,' she explained. That did not surprise the men. The projects aimed to give the women another source of income, so that they had options.

'That is not really the problem,' she continued bravely. 'When we go to the homes of rich landlords we are raped. We can't tell our husbands or they will disown us, and if we tell the police, they will kill us. It is a man's word against ours. They will not believe that we have been raped.'

The women looked down, ashamed. It took many male witnesses to win a case of rape. The rapists were safe from justice in their own homes and the victims were without recourse. To make a complaint was to risk death.

The leader now explained why the group of women risked retribution to share their concerns with the foreigners. Anguish was etched into her face. She glanced over at the other women, drawing on their combined courage to keep going.

'It is our daughters. They are now teenagers and going into these homes to work. They are being raped too,' she told them.

David and Leigh were dismayed. Alfalah was already working on improving the economic state of the women in the colony through sewing projects, but they clearly had to do more. David and Leigh were in a delicate position, with little power to help with this sort of social change. Still, it gave them added incentive to work in the community.

'We will do what we can,' David offered, before leaving the women. Later, he and Leigh talked about the women. 'If only we could find outside employment for them,' Leigh mused.

As it turned out, they were working with Alfalah on an apprentice scheme in another part of Lahore. They decided to involve the Awami women in that scheme. Small business owners receiving loans were required to take in apprentices from the Awami Colony, with wages covered for them. Now at least some of the women would not have to work as domestic staff and endure the abuse.

It looked as if Alfalah might emerge as a rare development success story in the nation. Yet within five years it was plagued with the same problems faced by other aid and development groups in Pakistan. Bank transfers of donor money could be withheld for months pending a 'commission' payment. Christian communities were often among the poorest, and although Alfalah worked with both Christian and Muslim clients, businesses owned by Christians were targeted by extremists, who convinced suppliers not to deal with them.

It was the money David and Leigh attracted on behalf of the poor and brought into the country that caused the real problems. Opportunity International was a major provider of funds, as were the Maranatha Trust and David's circle of philanthropic friends. Soon the work caught the attention of other big donors, and then of government aid agencies.

The troubles began in earnest when one donor switched its support from another development group to Alfalah. Before long the shunned group attempted to close down Alfalah's operations with accusations of western spying and false accounting. Success had drawn jealousy from every quarter, and the welfare of the poor seemed to be lowest on the list of priorities. Even some members of the local church were upset that money had come into the country and was to be directed towards the poor rather than into their own pockets.

These antagonists then set out to bring the organisation down by hiring a professional blackmailer to start filing charges against the board and management of Alfalah so that they would be distracted by a series of time-consuming court cases. It was the Nazir-Alis' experience all over again. Younis Farhat became the subject of death threats, mobs started demonstrating outside the office, and armed guards were placed at the office gates.

One day two truckloads of armed men surrounded the office and fired at it to intimidate the staff. Later, in the middle of the night, the leader of the group arrived at Younis' home and knocked at the door. 'They're going to kill you if they don't get the money. I know who they are and how they plan to do it. I can help you,' the man told Younis.

Younis soon worked out that the man was in fact one of the troublemakers, and was looking for payment to prevent the attacks. He grabbed the man by his shirt, dragged him out onto the street and gave him a swift kick to help him on his way. 'You go and get those guys and bring them here. We'll have this out right now, tonight.' The man scuttled away and did not return.

For that night Younis had won, but it did not get any easier for him. Eventually the threats took their toll. Alfalah lost a million rupees in loan repayments while the staff were so busy with court cases and uncertainty that they could not collect the debts. Later, when the threats became more serious, Younis left the country, leaving his younger brother Yousef in charge.

In 1990, David and Leigh were taking a now familiar route, from a round of meetings in India to another round of meetings with board and staff and clients in Lahore, Pakistan. When the meetings in India ended a day early it seemed logical to keep moving forward. At times they both felt the strain of their travel schedule, so a relaxed day would be good for them.

By now, after ten visits, and having observed the dirty tactics that drove his friend Michael from the country, along with having been robbed in an elevator by three men threatening him with a baton, David thought there was nothing left in Pakistan to surprise him. He was soon to find otherwise. When he and Leigh arrived in Lahore from Bangalore they were met by an agitated board member who told them, 'You can't stay here. It is not safe for you. You'll have to go to the hotel tonight and we'll get you out on the flight tomorrow.' This man had been tipped off by a friend from the local intelligence agency.

'What's the problem?' David asked, trying to make sense of his words.

'Look at this,' the man said as he shoved a newspaper under David's nose. There, right on the front page under a large banner, were his and Leigh's faces. He could not read the script, but he suspected the story was not positive.

'They have laid charges against you for anti-state activities,' the board member told him. 'It is in five other papers. We tried to warn you not to come but could not find you.'

'Who laid the charges?' David asked. He should have known he would not be immune to blackmail and trumped-up charges. Spies had been intercepting faxes from David's Sydney office, and they soon informed the press of the charges laid by his adversaries. They even published David's flight times so mobs could be at his hotel, shouting in rage at the foreigners, who were now branded criminals.

When the story made it into the newspapers, David was already judged guilty in the readers' eyes, whether or not he could prove his innocence. In any case, these were serious charges. If upheld, they would at best mean jail without a trial, and at worst, the death penalty.

Poor political relations between Pakistan and India made it almost impossible to communicate back and forth. While this had worked against them as the Alfalah office tried to warn the men off, it now worked in their favour. The military police assigned to apprehend David and Leigh did not know that they had changed their flights and were already in the country.

The one night David and Leigh spent in Lahore on that visit was a long one. As expected, agents monitored their every move, but the two men never actually knew who their silent escorts were. They nervously waited the night out in their adjoining hotel rooms, dozing and then springing to attention with each nocturnal creak and shuffle they heard. They prayed that the footsteps they heard in the corridor would not be military police. The next morning they woke unharmed, but exhausted. They quickly gathered their bags, then slipped out of their rooms and into a waiting car and headed for the airport. 'I don't fancy a stay in a Pakistani jail,' Leigh commented.

In the departure lounge of the airport, a basic room filled with smoking, chattering nationals, the two men waited as calmly as they could, blending into a big group of travellers. Meanwhile, the military police stood vigilantly in the arrivals hall just a few metres away, their weapons in clear view. They scoured the faces of new arrivals, on the alert for two Australian men aged fifty and forty, arriving from India. By the time the last of the stragglers came through the gate and the soldiers realised their quarry was not among them, David and Leigh were taxiing up the runway, on their way to freedom.

That was David's last visit to Pakistan. The charges now prevented him from returning. He would have been pleased to see the last of the country had it not been for the burden of Pakistan's poor. He carried with him the pitiful face of a dying child, the blank faces of the kiln workers, the pleading looks of desperate mothers. The kiln project lasted for a decade. The school and health clinic proved to be a valuable step up for the workers and their children. For that time, David estimates that forty families were liberated from bondage each year.

He was not ready to give up on Alfalah, and still thought it could work. Alfalah had been in operation for five years, had never succumbed to paying bribes, and had helped many people into small businesses.

'Opportunity International never paid anyone off. We refused to. Once you slip into that, everybody expects it. If you don't do it they exert more pressure. It is just part of the game of bribery and corruption,' David later explained.

In time the charges were all dropped by a judge and the instigators were exposed.

That same year, 1990, Carol took on a more demanding pastoral role as assistant to the Uniting Church chaplain, Len Cliff, at the Prince of Wales and Prince Henry hospitals, not far from the Bussaus' home. It was a job she would hold for the next twelve years.

This could be gruelling work. She had no idea what to expect when she walked through the front doors of the hospital. Often she simply talked with patients, some of whom were in hospital for a short stay, and welcomed a friendly face for a chat to pass the time. Others she met were terminally ill and felt comfort in the touch of a hand and a prayer. Hardest were the sick children, who saw an adult and assumed it was another person coming to poke or prod them. Friendship with the lonely and sick came naturally to Carol. In the hospital environment intimacy flowed; she could cut across the usual pleasantries and talk deeply about the patient's illness and the fears and anxieties they so often carried alone. Her training allowed her to be sensitive to each patient's spiritual and emotional needs, to bring God's love to them, at times with barely a word.

One day, Joan, a dear friend from church, arrived at the hospital, critically ill, and Carol made her way down to her ward. Her friend lay back on her bed, unable to respond other than with a slight flutter of recognition. Carol could see she was low, ready to slip away, and felt a weight of responsibility. 'Whatever I say to her now will be the last words she will ever hear,' she thought. She gently picked up Joan's hand, letting her own warmth flow into her friend's cool fingers. With her other hand she lightly stroked Joan's face and leaned over to be close to her. She wanted to be sure Joan left this world knowing she was loved and honoured.

'I love you. We all love you and thank you for all you've done. Your life has been a great blessing to many other people,' Carol said quietly, feeling humbled and inadequate.

She then opened her Bible to read from Psalms, 'Go and receive the inheritance the Lord has prepared for you.' At that moment, Joan died with her friend Carol holding her hand.

An important date in David's diary was 29 October 1990. He had made sure he was in Sydney on that date as it was Tasha's twenty-first birthday, and he had promised he would be home. Carol and Tasha had been planning her birthday party for weeks.

On the night of the party sixty of Tasha's school and university mates and a large group of family friends gathered in the back garden of the Bussaus' home for a barbeque. Jessie was two years old now, dressed in her best party clothes, delighted at being the centre of attention of so many grown-ups. When Tasha stood up on a step to say a few words of thanks to her guests, David by her side, Jessie stayed with her aunt and grandmother, keenly watching.

Tasha launched into her speech. 'I'd like to thank you all for being here tonight . . .' she started. Her father had rested his arm across her neck as she spoke. This was not unusual—the Bussaus were a close, tactile family. As she began to speak again, David's hand was now on her neck and his grip was tightening.

'What is he doing?' she wondered. She looked around and saw the mischievous grin on his face. She still had no idea what was happening. Then she turned to the audience and noticed a group of friends, led by Di Middleton, descending upon her. When David's hand held her neck so that she could not move, she realised what was happening. This was a pie fight. Tasha had made the mistake of telling Di and others she would love to have a pie fight, and here it was, custard pies flying from every direction, landing on her face and head and shoulders until they dripped down her body. Hardly a dignified coming-of-age, but then she should not have expected the ordinary from her family and friends.

By 1991, Opportunity International could claim a twenty-year track record of self-help for would-be entrepreneurs, going back to IIDI's first work in Latin America in 1971. There were now twenty eight partners in fifteen countries. More than fifteen thousand new jobs came into being that year alone through Opportunity loans, with the Asian region still leading the pace.

Through the 1980s the Latin American regional office had expanded into Costa Rica, Peru, the Dominican Republic, Guatemala, Jamaica and El Salvador, in addition to Colombia and Honduras. A Nicaraguan partner was now starting up. Micro enterprise development was becoming a force in poverty alleviation. Opportunity International alone had created more than sixty one thousand new jobs since 1978. The businesses were diverse, from making furniture and ceramics to processing and selling food, making clothes and shoes and raising animals.

Others in the development world were now convinced that stimulating the capacity of micro entrepreneurs was a most effective weapon against poverty. In its 1991 Development Report, employees of the World Bank wrote, 'Good government policies, institutions and investments are vital. But the key to rapid development is the entrepreneur.'

Still, Opportunity saw that there was one big gap in the work to be addressed, and that was Africa. The images of poverty, suffering, and starvation on television often came from this part of the world. The US and other western economies had powered through the 1980s and their middle classes had never known such personal wealth. At the same time the African economies had gone the other way: African nations were poorer, hungrier and in more conflict than they'd been in in the decades before, despite the richness of the continent's natural resources. The largest concentration of the world's poorest nations were now on the African continent.

Late in 1990, the large group of Opportunity International decision-makers, including Al Whittaker, Em Griffin, David Hardin (who had mustered many supporters to help), Dick Hoefs (a partner with a large global accounting firm), David and Leigh, came together for a momentous meeting, held in a glass-walled hotel conference room high above the urban sprawl near Chicago's O'Hare Airport. It was an appropriate venue for taking an expansive view—there were planes landing and departing each minute, and the board looked out to sky and clouds. 'Do we go to Africa?' was the question they pondered. The topic of working in Africa was raised in the early afternoon and was still being discussed as the sun set behind the clouds.

It was risky, and people warned that making small loans would never meld with the culture of African nations. 'You'll lose every penny,' was the advice passed on from others who had tried to work there. There was also the issue of taking on too much. Why go into the unknown and court failure when there was so much to be done in Asia and Latin America? As the afternoon discussion boiled on, a realisation gently swept the room and the answer to the question became clear.

'If we are serious about poverty alleviation, how can we not work in Africa?' asked Dave Hardin, who chaired the meeting. He then, one by one, asked for the opinion of each person at the table. They would put it to the vote. Each person had to search their own heart. When it came to David Bussau, there was no question about it. 'I can probably help with some contacts there,' he responded. Overwhelmingly, they said, 'Let's go', and even those who voted against it now added their support. It was a watershed moment.

Over the following decade the same dilemma would arise in relation to other places, such as East Timor and China, where both the need and the obstacles to success were great. At the end of the day, helping to meet the needs of the poor was the only compassionate response.

At the time, Larry Reed, who had joined Opportunity from graduate school and was now the vice-president of programs, had no idea what the implications of this meeting would be for himself and his family. But he had an unmistakable feeling that it was the right move. For him it felt like a holy moment. It was soon apparent that he was the obvious choice to go to Africa. He had worked within Opportunity from IIDI days and was already working closely with those on the ground. Larry was a quiet, intellectual man, the son of missionaries, born in Tangier, Morocco. His childhood had exposed him to varied practices of faith and he grew up in the knowledge that most of the world did not have the advantages he had had. He was a person who could be sensitive and responsive to the ways of the culture he found himself in. His wife Sandy was game for the challenge, and his children Aaron, Rachel and Anna were aged nine, seven and four—it seemed like a good time for them to experience life outside American culture.

When David and Leigh first started working in Asia, they had the luxury of time. They had spent weeks, months, even years making sure partners' foundations were deep. Now there was a momentum behind the work and an urgency to the expansion. David had a friend in Zimbabwe from his PIM network, Phineas Dube, and he soon set out to explore local contacts who could work with the poor. He knew people in Zimbabwe who would be interested. Among them was Eddie Cross, who was already moving in the same direction. He understood the need for self-empowerment and had set up a business in Harare just to employ the chronically poor.

It was an interesting time to start lending programs in Zimbabwe. Ten years earlier Robert Mugabe had been elected prime minister after decades of white rule. By 1990 Mr Mugabe had been elevated to the position of executive president after his Zanu-PF party won the presidential election. He was yet to show his true despotic colours and Zimbabwe was politically stable in comparison to nations further north that were still wracked by civil war and political strife.

Larry knew micro enterprise development inside out, but much of his experience was in Latin America. Once the decision was made to go into Africa, he and David took time out on a visit to programs in Jamaica to work through some of the vital aspects of starting a loan program. Instead of the cursory advice he had given Leigh in Jakarta—to be sensitive—David set out to prepare Larry as best he could for the task ahead in Africa. Twelve years on, he recognised the need to pass on his field and personal experience.

The mentoring continued once Larry was on the ground in Zimbabwe. On David's frequent visits to Harare he helped prepare Larry for expansion through the African region, talking about cultural sensitivities, and how to live with what the west might see as contradictions. He showed him how to attract the right people to leadership, then nurture them and help them grow into the role so that they would take over themselves. Larry's job would be successful when he himself could move on.

It took some months to find the right people for the new lending organisation, people who were comfortable with large amounts of money and willing to sacrifice higher-paid jobs in downtown Harare to work in poor neighbourhoods. They came with MBAs, gave up careers in formal banking, were prepared to stay in Zimbabwe, while more prestigious jobs beckoned from South Africa, and to be paid far less than an international corporation might pay them. Most felt the work as a calling, a way to use their skills for the poor, a practical way to serve God.

The new partner was named Zambuko Trust, *zambuko* from the Shona word for 'bridge'. Zambuko started lending in 1992, the first loans going to borrowers who had run businesses for six months or more. The loans were under three hundred dollars, so the borrowers would not be over-extended, and it weeded out the small business people who might have access to banks.

Before any loans were made, Zambuko staff, led by Evans Maphenduka, the first executive director, explained the lending procedures and responsibilities to a group of potential borrowers. They had heard that there were loans going, and overcoming their embarrassment at their shabby clothes and dirty children, they streamed into the Zambuko office to hear more about this unexpected opportunity.

They were told there would be a training program covering marketing, managing staff, simple accounting and inventory control. 'If your business is growing and you have a good repayment record, Zambuko will support your growth with increasing loans, until you can go to the formal bank.' It was a tremendous incentive to work hard and run a good business.

Larry Reed had no illusions about his task. This would be the biggest challenge he had faced to date. Zimbabwe had once been one of the most prosperous of African nations, the food bowl of the continent, but the economy was deteriorating rapidly. Now almost two million people were unemployed—forty per cent of the adult population—and a severe drought was forcing many rural workers off farmlands and into the urban shanties. The job market in such an economy could absorb less than ten per cent of young people leaving school, so there were children on the streets hustling for money, begging for food, extracting Zimbabwe dollars to mind cars. Theft, both petty and serious, was on the rise. The children of unemployed parents were disadvantaged before they even tried to get out into the world.

In circumstances that over the next decade would plummet from bad to tragic, the small and micro business sector gave a modicum of hope to poor Zimbabweans. This sector was the most resilient in tough times. It provided employment for sixty per cent of the working population and only one per cent had ever received credit. Even when big business failed, the informal sector kept going, through shoddy market stalls, traders going across the border to South Africa to exchange goods, women weaving in their huts.

Word about business loans soon spread through the poor neighbourhoods of Harare and further afield. The devastating drought brought an opportunity to help farmers as well as those struggling in urban areas. In the Domboshawa Valley the crops had failed, the streams were drying up, and hunger would soon set in. One family, the Munyawiris, was among the early borrowers. They spent their small loan on pumps to irrigate their land, to buy seed and fertiliser, and so made it through the drought.

Parishioners at the Glad Tidings Church were among those invited to apply for small loans. The church, with David's connections and ministers actively looking for ways to help people, was the obvious place to start. But Larry had to be careful not to create 'credit Christians' who would join a church or express a faith in order to obtain a loan. He was quick to explain that loan decisions were based on the viability of the business and the character of the loan applicant. Zambuko, like all of Opportunity's partners, was serving all poor, regardless of religion, race or gender.

One church member, Terezia Mbasera, a sixty year old with a broad toothless smile, was among the first to find her way down to the office of Zambuko in 1992. She had educated her five children by selling twig brooms for twenty five cents each. She was a canny woman who knew she could do more, and she dreamed of a bigger, less back breaking business.

Terezia's heart almost skipped a beat when she heard of someone making loans to women like herself, who had nothing material to offer as collateral. As soon as she had worked out exactly what she wanted she was down at the Zambuko Trust office, asking for a loan of US$650 to purchase a small shop and buy her stock in bulk. Before that she sold soft drinks in the neighbourhood, one crate at a time.

Her path out of poverty was not without incident. After the first loan had been made she was three months late in making her next repayment, an action that disqualified her for further loans. It was a huge dilemma for the newly hired loan officers, who wanted to see new clients thrive but were also only just establishing a loan portfolio and could not afford to be imprudent.

Mama Mbasera was not about to let go of her ambitions. One day she marched right into the office. 'Give me another loan and I will make sure I meet my repayments,' she demanded. She was a compelling figure. Despite all the rules, Zambuko relented, and true to her word, the next loan was paid back within the month.

There was no stopping Terezia Mbasera from that point. With the next series of loans she expanded her small grocery business, opened a beauty salon and a barber shop, set up a second grocery shop and bought a truck, after winning the contract for wholesale drink distribution in the area. She managed a large woodpile, a core business in a poor neighbourhood where most cooking was still over wood fires, and set up a pool room so local children had somewhere to congregate and play.

She was constantly on the look-out for business ideas. The next need she identified was the funeral business, so she started manufacturing and selling coffins and providing basic funeral services. A further loan allowed her to buy a truck to transport the coffins, as well as to start a sock distributing business.

With each business expansion, Terezia hired more employees, created more jobs in the area and helped change the prospects for many families. A decade later she employed over thirty people. Though she was now prosperous by neighbourhood standards, she would never leave her dusty slum. Her house expanded and she could afford the comforts of a television and a refrigerator. That was all she wanted. By now she was the matriarch of the neighbourhood, personally taking young people down to the Zambuko offices, inspiring them to run with their own simple ideas for businesses or passing on her own. 'We need a photographer for weddings in the neighbourhood. That could be your business,' she advised one young person.

Terezia's resourcefulness raised the prospects for many around her. She was so successful, she started asking Zambuko to receive her savings, preferring to stick by the micro lender, rather than save in a commercial bank, which had shunned her when she was poor. The greatest reward of her new prosperity was being able to give freely when women came to her, saying, 'We can't afford shoes for our children' or 'We can't put them through school.' There was even more joy when those same women, with small businesses of their own, could buy shoes themselves for their children.

Within twelve months, Larry Reed and his team at Zambuko Trust needed no further encouragement to know that micro finance could work in Africa. Terezia Mbasera was not the only borrower to shine. There were hundreds of others. Early clients in tailoring, transport, and food production had also been able to build substantial businesses. Zambuko was one of the Opportunity network's fastest growing partners, and would later become a model for other micro lenders on the continent.

Part of Larry's brief was to expand throughout Africa. The next question was, if it worked in Zimbabwe, could it work in South Africa? Government and private contacts were urging him to make the move. David was working with him on contacts and ideas.

In 1991, when Larry and Sandy Reed moved to Zimbabwe, South Africa was in transition. President F. W. De Klerk had only the year before lifted a ban on the African National Congress, and in the same year he released its leader, Nelson Mandela, after Mandela had served twenty seven years in jail. Apartheid laws were finally repealed after more than forty years, and the first democratic election was in the pipeline.

South Africa was a nation with a bounty of mineral resources, but the black majority of the population had not shared in the wealth. Under the apartheid system, many had been isolated, divided into townships where they lived under a regime of beatings, rapes and murders. The township of Soweto, a complex community separated from Johannesburg by wastelands of mine debris and desolate hills, came to symbolise the oppression of the time. Fifty per cent of its inhabitants were unemployed, there was hunger, and housing and schools were inadequate. On television, the world saw images of riots and lynchings and burning tyres around necks.

In 1992, David came to visit Larry in Harare and the two travelled to Johannesburg to meet with Caesar Molabatsi, a well regarded church and social leader in South Africa. They presented a new and exciting idea. They would bring funding and resources that could help people in Soweto build new businesses and thus gain economic control over their lives. It would be run for South Africans, by South Africans. The idea was well received. Economic empowerment of black South Africans was vital if the new nation were to succeed.

The partner was named IZIBUKO, later known as the Strategic Economic Enterprise Foundation, or SEED, an acronym that embodied the goal of bringing a seed of hope to a despairing people who had for so long been stripped of their rights and dignity. The Australian government's aid body, AusAid, came in with vital funding.

There were significant risks in going into the new, post-apartheid nation. For decades South Africa had been governed through violence and deprivation; this culture could not be turned off like a light switch with the handing over of leadership. David was to experience violence several times. One Sunday morning as he left a church in Soweto with Caesar Molabatsi and the rest of the congregation, smiling and talking, a car drove slowly by, showering bullets in their direction. Though no one was killed, it sent the crowd scuttling behind parked cars and back into the church for shelter. It was a reminder of the difficult path ahead.

On a later visit to Johannesburg with Larry, in 1994, knife-wielding youths accosted the two men, pushing Larry to the ground and robbing him with a blade to his throat. He came away clearly shaken. He was living and working on a razor's edge, and had a young family to consider.

David was also concerned, but he soon put the incident behind him. When he arrived back in Australia he failed to tell even one of his closest associates, Neill Mawhinney, about it: Neill only heard about it from Larry. Muggings had been such a regular feature of David's travel that he almost expected it. In Harare he had been robbed in broad daylight in the crowded central market opposite the ritzy Meikles hotel by two men with a broken bottle.

He was well past heroics. He had learned to keep a small amount of money in a back pocket and his credit cards and other cash tucked into an inside front pocket. His expensive-looking watch was invariably a cheap fake.

Before that, he had been robbed of his wallet and watch in Kenya, bailed up in a storeroom for several hours in Thailand, and robbed three times in the Philippines. He worked largely in countries where people had very little and every westerner was assumed to be rich. He understood why desperate people saw him as an easy target.

'I try not to let those events shape me. I don't live on them; they are just part of the work,' David said. 'I still think it's part of the conditioning of my childhood. I was brought up to live with the unexpected and to expect the unexpected. Not that I'm invulnerable, but I guess today is a new day. That was yesterday.'

From the beginning there were obstacles in South Africa that the programs people of Opportunity had never encountered, starting with the most basic of questions: 'Could anyone establish a strong credit culture in the new political climate?' Residents in parts of Soweto, where the program would be based, were at the time conducting a campaign of boycotts against the government, refusing to pay their electricity and water rates.

The social structure of Soweto was also in flux. After apartheid fell, the laws on racial integration were changed and many of Soweto's wealthier families moved into more comfortable neighbourhoods outside Soweto. The poor had no option but to stay, and their economic prospects shrivelled even further as more successful business people packed up and left.

Still, an air of anticipation accompanied the first loans at the end of 1993, and encouraging stories soon emerged. Many of those who took advantage of the small loans appeared to blossom overnight. Suddenly, they could see through their poverty to the future which looked better than ever before. The first South African loan recipient, William Mokou, was a skilled carpenter, bricklayer and electrician with seven children to support. He had lost his job the previous year and now, working alone, was struggling to win any of the large contracts that he needed if he was to be able to support his family. Two of William's children had had to leave school because there was no money for tuition. The family had started to slide into deeper poverty when the new partner opened its doors in Soweto. William received a loan of US$1493, which gave him the capital to win the larger contracts. He could then hire four employees. Before long he was ready for his next loan.

After living in isolation in Indonesia, David understood the pressure under which Larry laboured, and sought to lift his spirit in different ways. On one visit in 1993 David called Larry just before he was leaving for Sydney Airport to ask what he might bring for the Reed children. Knowing David would not have time to shop, Larry told him, 'Anything you can find at the airport,

David. A T-shirt, book or cuddly toy or something like that would be great.' When David arrived the next day it was like Christmas. He had collected each one of the items Larry had listed for each of the children.

It was inevitable that the flow of ever-increasing amounts of government and private money to the organisation would bring closer scrutiny. Opportunity International was making some large claims about low default rates, increases in the income of clients, growth and recycling of funds and the peripheral benefits of loans. Higher accountability standards were something David welcomed—even invited—as the organisation spread across the globe.

In 1992 a report by Richard Bond and David Hulme, from the University of Manchester, put the claims to the test. The men visited MBM in Bali, JSA in Sri Lanka and TBL in Bangalore, and concluded that 'the parts of the network which were visited are well managed and deliver their services in an efficient and cost-effective way . . . Default rates are low and job creation is in the order of one formal job per project supported, with total beneficiaries some ten to fifteen per project.'

The findings supported what David already knew from many years of working in poor countries: that poor entrepreneurs were more creditworthy than many westerners. Ninety two per cent of all the borrowers repaid their loans. Their small businesses were a ticket out of poverty and the majority would not risk their future by defaulting. But the heart of Opportunity went deeper than issues such as efficiency and repayment rates. The most important question was always: 'What was happening in the lives of the clients?'

13

Nature's Fury

For five years, from 1987 to 1991, David worked closely and fruitfully with Gordon Murphy, the head of Opportunity International US. They had built a deep friendship as they roughed it in flea-ridden hotels in isolated rural regions of India or the Philippines, and sweated it out playing tennis or racquet ball in the US. 'He had an accepting nature and shared the issues I was concerned with,' David recalls.

Before leaving the business world, Gordon had worked as a lawyer in a bank making housing loans. He was usually the bank's representative in property sales, negotiating with agents and buyers. In the process, he had at times taken a finder's fee in addition to the agent's commission, a common practice at the time. However, the practice was in fact a felony, and Gordon's past caught up with him. In 1991 he was sentenced to one year in jail.

'It was wrong. I should have known,' Gordon told David at the time. Gordon regretfully resigned his chief executive position. David was concerned. 'How can we support you?' he asked Gordon.

David, with his own childhood delinquencies, saw no shame in making a mistake and paying the price. Afterwards he commented: 'I believed in the guy, whether he went to prison or not, whether he committed a felony or not.' There would no longer be a business relationship between the two men, but he could support Gordon through friendship. 'He increased his affirmation of our friendship and went out of his way to write to me and communicate through my wife with me and that is a special thing about our friendship,' Gordon remembers.

A businessman by the name of Eric Thurman was hired to replace Gordon Murphy. Eric was a man of strong intellect who could think big, make split-second decisions and pull resources together in a hurry. He envisaged large amounts of money coming from US business people as the idea of micro finance caught on. Eric's mission was large-scale poverty alleviation. Already, there was a growing support group who raised funds for the programs. One board member in particular, David Hardin, had no reservations about drawing his wide and influential network of friends into Opportunity International as donors. He brought millions of dollars into Opportunity's programs, including a multimillion dollar bequest from his own estate when he died in 1994.

There were some similarities between David Bussau and Eric Thurman: each had 'sacrificed' a successful career to work in the developing world, and each came with considerable talent and a deep passion for helping the poor. However, the differences in their styles, some purely cultural—more aggressive American versus laid-back Antipodean—soon became an issue. Eric focused on results in his quest to work with the poor. David's emphasis was on relationships and supporting those working in the field. Both were valid. Later, the organisation would find a balance between these two views.

At this time, David still ran Maranatha Foundation as well as doing all his work with Opportunity International. He had built a broad network of foundations and philanthropists in western countries and increasingly found himself in the corridors of power. He met with government aid bodies in the US, the UK, Europe and Australia.

The travel was relentless, and meant days locked into meetings in hotel rooms and office blocks. One trip might take eight weeks and cover every continent of the globe. His circuit included the Philippines four times in 1991. The year before it had been six times to the Philippines, Thailand and the UK (seven times each), the US (four times), Zimbabwe (three times), Indonesia, Sri Lanka, New Zealand (twice each) and Jamaica, Costa Rica, France, Pakistan and Canada. Yet he would not allow loneliness into his range of emotions. 'I think in the Boys' Homes you learned to cope with loneliness. You ended up dealing with your own world.' He still had memories of other boys' loneliness. He recalled seeing boys sitting in corners, totally overwhelmed by the isolation of being disconnected from their parents and families. David saw loneliness as a form of self-pity.

Some time before, Benjie Montemayor had made a significant connection for David with Ruth Callanta, a professor at the Asian Institute of Management and a consultant to one of largest companies in the Philippines, the San Miguel Corporation. Already she had run the biggest foundation in the country, Philippines Business for Social Progress, helped World Vision find its way in the Philippines, and represented the Philippines on the World Council of Philanthropy. Although still young, she had led a life of activism around poverty, starting at high school, when she volunteered for the Philippine Advisory on National Minorities. This had involved living in subhuman conditions in the mountains with the tribal minority, the Aeta people, who were being robbed of their land and livelihood. As a university student she had narrowly escaped prison after joining the underground movement against the Marcos regime.

She was perplexed by the inequities of her homeland. 'Why are there so many very poor in a country of so many resources, so many people hungry when there are so many fish, and why in a country with so much land are so many people without homes?'

At the Asian Institute of Management she aimed to help young people see the possibilities for tackling the poverty around them. She poured herself into the cause, only to find that at the end of the course most of her young students took up high-paid jobs and forgot about the poor.

Benjie Montemayor arranged for her to meet David at his hotel in the Makati business district of Manila when he was next passing through. On the day of the meeting it poured with rain, and Manila's smoke-spewing traffic was gridlocked. Ruth sat in her car on a freeway, resigned to crawling along, while David sat at his hotel, waiting. David's latest idea was to set up what he would call the Asian Resource Centre (ARC) in Manila for the new lending agencies that were fanning out across the region. It would be a place where executive directors and other leaders from the Philippines, Pakistan, India and Sri Lanka could come for support. Here, managers would learn about industry trends and best practice, the most effective way to train loan officers for their task, how to manage growth and how to relate to boards of directors. It would lift some of the training load from TSPI, the founding partner in the Philippines, and give the new partners autonomy.

When Ruth's car finally made it to the hotel she feared she would find a fuming, impatient man. She had heard he was a busy person. Instead, she found a kind smile, as though she were minutes rather than hours late.

David was not quite so sure what he was getting into. Ruth was a diminutive firebrand, one and a half metres tall, loquacious, with a loud but engaging manner. When Ruth returned his smile, her face shone. She talked with an urgency and passion about her country and its struggles. David thought she could well be the person they were looking for to head the Asian Resource Centre.

When Mt Pinatubo in the Philippines erupted on 15 June 1991, David was not far away. Less than a year before, on 16 July 1990, hundreds of people were killed when an earthquake hit the city of Baguio, north of Manila. Two staff members, Noli Canilas, the executive director of the Baguio partner TPKI and Grace Fabella, an accountant with TSPI, were meeting with USAID and others on the top floor of an upmarket hotel when the earthquake brought the whole building down. They died, along with a number of participants in the meeting that day and in the confusion that followed. Two others from the Opportunity partners escaped, one of them spending two days under rubble. It was weeks before the recovery could start. Hundreds of Opportunity clients lost their businesses.

Now, Mt Pinatubo again brought grief to the nation. In the lead-up to the Pinatubo eruption there were weeks of warnings from seismologists who had been watching the volcano gently spew clouds of volcanic ash and gas before unleashing its full force into the sky with such violence that it rained down ash on continents thousands of miles away. In Central Luzon, villages in the provinces of Zambales, Pampanga, and Tarlac surrounding the mountain were devastated.

There was warning enough to shift the indigenous mountain dwellers, the Aeta people, before avalanches of scalding mud swept their houses away, but what could they do now that they were down safely on the plains? Away from their tribal villages, built into the steep sides of the mountain, and the fertile land they had hunted and foraged on long before the Malays and Europeans came to their island, they were lost.

The Aeta were a proud people who had never lived alongside lowland communities before. The Catholic Church and disaster aid groups were quickly on the scene to set up tents and serve meals. The government had three hundred and fifty thousand homeless families to deal with and could ill afford to give special attention to this small group of five thousand. With so many mouths to feed, the rations of sardines and dried fish were inadequate. The camps were dirty and crowded and disease was inevitable. In the evacuation centres in Zambales province the Aeta were unable to cope with plastic tents and the crowds of suffering lowland evacuees.

The Aeta women kept busy cooking and caring for children. The men, stripped of their livelihood and dignity, idled, at a loss to understand why Pinatubo's wrath should be visited so forcefully upon their heads. 'Our sins are not so great for us to suffer so mightily. There is no place to go. We can only hope that the mountain will soon take us back,' Bitukan, an Aeta leader lamented. But the flow of lava had denuded the mountain of the vegetation and animals more efficiently than the deforestation process of recent years, and there was nothing to go back to. Their simple homes—indeed their whole way of life—had been swept away. The men fretted, afraid that militia men would loot the roofing materials from any houses left on the mountain. Away from their homelands they would surely die.

When Ruth Callanta heard of the plight of the Aetas she was soon on the phone to David. 'David, can you come with me to meet with the Aetas near Pinatubo? They are homeless.' Within days of Mt Pinatubo erupting David and Ruth made the four hour drive north from Manila to Central Luzon, to be joined by Nestor Estoban, who now ran TPKI. The sight they encountered was beyond belief. Before them was an ocean of lahar, a clay-like mixture of mud and water and hot volcanic ash, stretching out for kilometres from the mountain. Where homes and villages had stood, now just the tips of roofs protruded to point to their location. What had been a vibrant green landscape of banana plantations and rice and other crops was now desolate.

David had trained himself to keep his responses hidden; it was a frustration to many around him that he seemed never to react spontaneously. Behind the calm, though, he was deeply affected. He was not thinking about the eruption and its devastation; he was thinking of years ahead, of people living a better life than mere survival. He stayed a while, talking with the refugees, finding how they had fared, mulling over the long-term solutions. There would be months of consultation before any progress became visible.

Back in the Sydney office he challenged his colleagues, Leigh Coleman and James Allardice, who had joined Maranatha in 1990, to find a sustainable response, though he had already formed his own view. He soon came back to Ruth and Nestor with a plan. 'If we buy a piece of land below the line of the lahar we could resettle these families into villages and set up some industries that will give them a livelihood.' With a builder's precision he worked on the detail of materials and design, cost and timing.

Nicholas Colloff, who ran the Opportunity Trust in the UK knew of a Swiss foundation, Pro Victimus, that supported post-disaster housing projects, and before long David was pleading the Filipinos' case in Switzerland.

With a plan and funding in place, James Allardice was assigned to manage the TKPI Pro Victimus resettlement scheme. James had never worked in conditions like these. A thick layer of lava ash covered every surface and insinuated its way into each mouthful of food he ate, into his clothing and into his computer. Many families spent three years in tent cities in such hardship before finding a permanent home.

The team found a large tract of land near San Fernando. Water, power and roads had to be installed before the task of building could begin. Flat, arable land was by definition now some distance from the stark Mt Pinatubo. For many Aeta, it was further from the mountain than they could bear, and they started to drift back to scratch out a diminished subsistence life closer to where their homes had been.

The project was broadened to include the neediest among other groups from villages nearby, many of them from the Maimpis and Pilar Tent Cities in San Fernando.

Housing was a departure for the local lending partner, TPKI, but it was not long before Nestor and his loan staff could use their micro-enterprise training. TPKI helped set up a concrete block-making business to supply the building blocks for the new homes, drawing in a large number of unemployed. It took one bucket of lahar to make a building block and there was an endless supply of lahar for the many blocks needed to build the houses. TPKI also made loans for construction tools to make the blocks. Then each person received a loan to build their house and another to start a small business that would eventually help them repay the loan and allow them to own their own home and business.

Displaced villagers were eager to return to their homes to salvage what they could. One man quickly picked up on the need for shovels to dig through the mud and lava, approaching a loan officer with his idea. With many willing buyers, he soon had a thriving business. Before long, the partners were approached by retailers who wanted to open small stores, by crafts people who could make furniture for the new houses, by welders, street food vendors, farmers wanting to raise ducks, and drivers who could provide jeepney transport to the growing community. There were even borrowers making trinkets from lava for the tourist industry.

Sometimes it seemed to David that every one step forward meant two steps back. In Manila, the Asian Resource Centre had not attracted enough support to be viable and was closed down. It was several years ahead of its time.

In the meantime, in February 1991, TSPI and the new partners filled the support vacuum locally by joining together to form the Alliance of Philippines Partners in Enterprise Development (APPEND) and invited Maranatha to be part of the new venture.

Ruth Callanta, the Asian Resource Centre chief executive, only heard the news of the resource centre's demise on a visit to Sydney to outline her strategy for it. She went home confused and disappointed, with the impression that David did not trust her. She had found David hard to work with, someone who listened but would not hammer out the issues with her in an up-front manner. She could never read his thoughts and obviously didn't know where she stood. She treated him as a peer, and at the time there were few women around David in that category. Now she had twelve employees to think about. She knew the technical staff could find jobs, but what of those like Eugene, the janitor, who may not have other options?

Ruth soon bounced back, with a proposal for a new micro enterprise development partner she called the Centre for Community Transformation (CCT). She approached David again, looking for donor funds, and discovered another side to him. David was attracted to the idea of CCT, but more than that, he wanted to encourage Ruth.

'Come and talk to some of the women CCT is working with,' she said inviting him on a visit to Manila. Out of the acrimony of the closure of the Asian Resource Centre came a partnership that would prove far more fruitful than either imagined.

Ruth had already started making small loans in the dense, urban slum of Tondo, where one hundred and twenty thousand people, or more, lived crammed into little more than two square kilometres. David first visited the area in the early 1980s, and it had not improved much in the intervening years. Here, across the Pasig River from the expensive waterfront hotels, embassies, government buildings and open spaces of the famous Rizal Park in Metro Manila, lay the worst of human degradation.

The area of Tondo included Parola, a walled city by Manila's docklands, an abandoned expanse that many years before, when the rural poor first came to the city, had filled up with makeshift shacks, lining alleys just three feet wide, covered with holey tarpaulins. Outside the walls, other squatters had camped along the railway lines—and their children played on the lines. In Tondo, electricity was tapped from the main wires hanging overhead which was very dangerous, and often there were fires. Treatable diseases such as tuberculosis were rampant. Sections of Tondo's homes were frequently washed away with the Pasig River floods, only to be replaced with more makeshift dwellings when the water receded.

Ruth and David entered the muddy warrens of Parola through a gate off the docklands. It was a place neither David nor Ruth could enter alone, without someone to guide them out again. Loan staff at CCT had already overcome many hurdles, including finding a way around the armed warlords who controlled the comings and goings of those within the walled city, and convincing Parola's inhabitants that they were there to help.

'It could just as easily have been me living here, in this squalor,' David often reflected to himself as he met clients. He had thought about the issue of rights. 'Having a right is like demanding that we deserve it. I just don't have a sense that I deserve to have more than a person down in Tondo. It is part of the humbling process. It is just through God's grace that I am staying in a nice hotel when there are people living like this,' he maintained. He still firmly believed that the poor had the right to a much better life, and that access to the means to build that life—small amounts of capital—should be a basic human right.

'See, David, these women have been to the central markets this morning and they will sell their produce here,' Ruth said as they wandered down an alleyway lined with stalls of food and household goods. 'Six of them are now our clients,' Ruth told him. She smiled and hugged a tiny, reed-thin woman with sad brown eyes, introducing her to David as Gloria.

Gloria spent nights at her 'stall' in the central market, a mat with a few vegetables laid out on it. Behind the row of women selling vegetables were railway tracks on which her children laid out newspapers and slept for the night before she woke them for the bus ride home. During the day she sold vegetables from a table in the alley where she lived. As they continued walking Ruth told him, 'Gloria has tuberculosis and so do four of her six children. Her husband ran away. We're praying for someone to pay for her medication.' Not long afterwards, a generous Australian came forward to help.

Ruth's work took a more holistic bent than some others. It included health issues such as sanitation and child immunisation, education and training in computer skills for the children of clients, job creation and economic improvements, and spiritual and personal development.

Over the years David became ambivalent about making visits to the homes and businesses of clients, even when they smiled and welcomed him. It was not for lack of compassion; it was more that he worried that visits to poor clients were voyeuristic, that he was somehow taking advantage of their desperation. 'Often I'd feel embarrassed by being a westerner going into a slum and seeing the level of poverty existing alongside western affluence, seeing the poor in a terrible environment that was not of their choice.'

He could help Gloria and others like her in Manila by affirming and encouraging Ruth, who was on the ground, and delivering the finances she needed for her work. He pulled in Opportunity US, money from his own Maranatha Trust, a large German donor and Tear Fund from New Zealand, who would become one of Ruth's most loyal supporters.

Over the years, Vinay and Colleen Samuel had remained in David and Carol's closest circle of friends. As the Samuels prepared to celebrate the fifteen year anniversary of the establishment of Divya Shanthi, the children's home near Bangalore, it seemed natural for the Bussaus to be with them, and Vinay invited David to share the story of his childhood with the children.

The children were still going about their daily chores of sweeping and dusting as David and Carol made their way to an open building that doubled as a dining and study room. Some recognised David from earlier visits. Others just knew of him from Vinay, who had told them that David had somehow helped in the building of the home. 'Uncle David, Uncle David,' some called, with cheeky smiles. A ring of jubilant faces surrounded the couple. David greeted the children with a squeeze of a shoulder or a handshake. He cupped one young girl into a strong arm and carried her along.

Each child in the home had a story to tell. They all came from the edges of society. Some were left at the home by poor parents or grandparents, whose only alternatives to ensure their child's survival were bonded labour or prostitution. Some came as sick or abandoned babies, others were unwanted offspring of Anglo-Indian liaisons, or AIDs-infected children of prostitutes. Many of the girls in the home had escaped certain death, shunned because they were girls in a society that valued only boys. Vinay and Colleen's hearts could accommodate them all. They knew how dangerous it was for children growing up near a red-light district in a poor area. Many years before, a thirteen-year-old girl had come to Colleen pleading, 'Please let me stay here with you. My father has not been paid this week and he will give me to the landlord.' She was one of the first children they raised.

The children settled crosslegged on the concrete floor and Vinay addressed them. 'Please welcome Uncle David, whom I have told you about,' he said in Kannada, the local dialect of the Karnataka area. The children clapped politely and waited for David to speak from the front of the room. Instead, David moved over to the group and parked himself on the floor in their midst, as though it were the most natural thing for an adult to do.

'You know, I grew up without parents too,' he told them. 'The first thing I remember about my life is walking up a long, long driveway to a huge house. I was just a small boy and I was carrying a big bag which had everything I owned in it. And that wasn't much.'

David's words were met with silence. The flies buzzed around the small bodies on the floor and no one moved to shoo them for fear of missing his next sentence. 'At times I felt lonely, and that no one loved me, but I always knew God loved me.' It took a few moments for this to sink in.

He continued, 'I had to decide what I wanted to do in my life. You can't depend on others to make it work. You will be the ones to make a difference in your own lives.' They were intrigued, watching his every move, every smile, and every expression. These words came from someone who had been on the same journey as them. This quiet man could really understand them. It gave power to the words. 'You know, in some ways the years in the boys' home were my making. We had to work hard too, doing all sorts of jobs around the place. It helped me work hard and become independent when I went out into the world,' he said encouragingly.

'But I still don't want to see children go through what I went through as a child,' he said in a low voice. 'Now the work we are doing helps parents with work, so that they can buy food and clothes and pay for an education.' Then his tone became almost conspiratorial. 'What are your dreams and hopes?' he asked, looking at the keen, young faces surrounding him. They were shy, and it was hard for them to think of such things. Until Vinay and Colleen took them in, most had never thought beyond daily survival.

After a few moments of silence, one bright young boy piped up, 'I want to finish school and go to university.' The others remained quiet. David sensed their lack of hope and moved on decisively. 'You know it is up to you whether you climb out of the orphan mentality or not. You don't have to be victims. The decision is yours,' he concluded.

The visit was a turning point for David. Not until Vinay asked him to share his own childhood with the children at Divya Shanthi, and he had sensed the encouragement within the room, even among the adults, had he considered its relevance to those outside his own family.

14

The Poorest Among Poor

By 1991, almost half of Opportunity International's loan recipients around the world were women. Over the next decade the proportion of women clients would continue to grow until it reached eighty five per cent. It was not hard to see why. Worldwide, a higher proportion of women than men were living in poverty. In poorer countries it was often the women who fought hardest to keep their children, to clothe and feed them, to put them through school. The poor women to whom Opportunity gave loans could be found at the simple market stalls in the poor neighbourhoods of Manila, they were the women quietly sewing in Nagpur, or making trinkets for tourists in Denpasar, or selling fried chicken by the roadside in Bulawayo.

The growing focus on providing loans to women prompted an initiative from the US called the Women's Opportunity Fund, an entity first conceived as a way of raising money from women, for women. Linda Vander Weele, an Opportunity US board member at the time, was asked to pursue the idea. Soon after, she and her husband Ken moved to Costa Rica and she handed the project on to her good friend and fellow board member Jill Dailey Smith, who gathered other concerned American women in the Chicago area to the cause. They brought a women's perspective to the work of Opportunity, and were more interested in addressing issues relating to poor women than in simply being a fundraising arm of Opportunity US.

They were as concerned with the social and spiritual state of poor women as with their economic struggles and financial efficiency. 'Dignity', 'empowerment' and 'self-confidence' were the words used in relation to improvements in quality of life for women in developing countries. They pulled together the funding for a pilot project in El Salvador, a new direction for the organisation. The Women's Opportunity Fund aimed to reach down to the lowest strata of poverty, to a place where women could not see beyond the next meal they would feed their family.

Susy Cheston came on board as field director of the pilot program in El Salvador at the beginning of 1992. She arrived in war-torn El Salvador excited yet apprehensive about her role. Her background was in public broadcasting and the arts, although she had briefly sampled micro enterprise in Costa Rica in 1991 as a voluntary intern for the US-based micro finance organisation, ACCION. Her passion made up for her inexperience. 'When I discovered micro finance it made immediate sense to me because it was creating dignity rather than dependency. It was sustainable. It was not a far-off group of development experts making decisions about what should happen for a woman and her family, but putting that decision-making power and personal development into her own hands. I have never felt that clear sense of call before or since. It was as if the heavens opened up and God said, "Go, my daughter! This is what you are supposed to do." And all of my skills, my gifts, my experiences, the yearnings of my heart, everything was coming together in this one call to move to El Salvador.'

Before the move, David Befus, Opportunity International's Latin American regional director, handed Susy a half-page description of a new concept of 'business incubation' for very poor women. The existing model employed with all the Latin American partners, meant that entrepreneurs with existing businesses and a track record received substantial loans to expand and employ others in the community.

In El Salvador, Susy tried hard to make the model work, but every day there was another obstacle in her way. She contracted cholera, felt socially isolated and found few people with an interest in helping poor women. She could not reach the women she wanted to help. Then she heard about a community of squatters: twenty five women, five men and fifty children living on the hillside at La Paz, high above the capital, San Salvador. She set out for La Paz, arriving in her beaten-up car to find a small group of women gathered in a dirt-floored shack made from rusted scrap metal and cardboard. They were all single women, with children to support, and were living in fear of the violent crime so common in the area. To protect themselves, they had banded together as the 'Committee of Single Women for Dignity and Progress'. Susy's job that day was to introduce them to the idea of small loans.

'The existing model required a sense of hope and a sense of future that the very poor women I was trying to reach did not have,' says Susy. 'They needed to look at today and the income they were bringing in that day to feed their families.' The risks of taking out a large loan petrified the women.

She could make the model work with a different target group, those who might be literate, not quite as poor, who could take a view beyond their family's next meal, or she could find her own way through. She chose to jettison the usual model and started asking, 'What's working? What can we do? How can we make this work?' She knew a man named John Hatch who had created a concept called Village Banking, working with the poorest in the community, making the tiniest of loans. The program was growing at an astounding rate. John would later become a major figure in micro finance through FINCA. Susy took what she learned from John about making loans to poor women and developed her own ideas around the community-building, social and spiritual aspects that were so close to her heart.

Rosa Maria Rivera stood out among the La Paz women. Some had been squatting for five years since an earthquake destroyed their homes. They had lost all hope. It showed in their sad, dull eyes. But Susy noticed that Rosa, though no better off than the others, still had a liveliness about her. She and her four children shared two old single beds at night, and she struggled each day to provide the most basic diet of rice, tortillas and beans. She laboured on a construction gang several days a week under a scheme which would eventually allow her to have her own home, and made brown paper bags to sell to market vendors on the other days.

Rosa didn't just nurture a sense of hope; Susy soon found that she was a natural and effective leader. Rosa taught Susy how the informal economy around her operated and, as trust steadily grew between Susy and the women, they worked together on a loan program that would fit in with their uncertain daily lives. They had turned down Susy's offer of larger loans for a specialised business, saying 'We're afraid. We don't want to let you down.'

Susy found the women were more comfortable with smaller, short-term loans that they could use to diversify their businesses. This would protect them from the instability of local markets. They all had ideas for other small businesses they could start. Rosa used her loan to buy brown paper in bulk, and expanded into selling plastic water and sugar containers, immediately doubling her daily income from two dollars to four.

At first the Opportunity US board wondered about the sense of fifty to one hundred dollar loans. It was focused on larger, individual loans which board members believed would create more jobs through growing businesses. The Opportunity International board voted to risk it and gave the Women's Opportunity Fund the go-ahead to experiment under the Opportunity name, pledging to help with funding and technical know-how.

In October 1992 David made a loop around the Latin American partners. This time it was only Costa Rica, Nicaragua and El Salvador. A few months before, in February, he had skimmed through these and other countries, spending barely a day in each place. In Nicaragua he was drawn into relief work after a tidal wave displaced tens of thousands.

David was the first person from the Opportunity organisation to visit Susy in El Salvador. In the months leading up to the visit David had expressed his concern that Opportunity International expatriate staff might not be getting the support they needed in the field. At one Latin American regional meeting he pushed his point home: 'What about Julie in Nicaragua? No one has been to visit her yet.' The group froze. Julie in Nicaragua. How could they have forgotten her? It took a few moments for them to realise that there was no Julie in Nicaragua. 'Could you be talking about Susy in El Salvador?' someone ventured, before they all burst out laughing. At least his underlying concerns had been valid. Although there was an Opportunity International partner, CORDESAL, in the country, at the time Susy was cut off from others working in the region, fumbling along on her own.

Soon after he flew in from Nicaragua, Susy took David out to Rosa's ramshackle corrugated metal hut in the squatters' village. Here, a group of the La Paz women sat in a small circle ready to meet him. Susy herself felt a little nervous. She hardly knew David but expected he was visiting to assess the effectiveness of her work. She thought it might be awkward, his questioning and her interpreting in Spanish.

It was a profound moment for Susy—her first chance to share what she had been doing in isolation all these months—and these women were dear to her. By now the women had come together in what would later be known as a 'banco de confianza,' or trust bank. They didn't know it then, but the trust bank would become the model for the next generation of micro finance. It provided the means to supply loan capital to hundreds of thousands of poor people. Each woman in the La Paz group had received a loan, guaranteed by the others in the group. It had required a new level of solidarity among them. Rosa's life was already tangibly changed. She had moved to a bigger shack where she could work inside when it rained, she could now offer her children fish or chicken once a week, and she could afford fruit and vegetables. She could also afford to send her children, now healthier, to school for both morning and afternoon sessions, instead of just one session each day.

There were other, non material changes, too. Rosa had been able to express her leadership skills by organising women in her mother's neighborhood into trust banks as well. She volunteered as trainer, organiser and informal loan officer of that group, and was the elected president of her own lending group. Not long before, the solidarity of her trust bank had been tested when one day Rosa was hit by a speeding police car as she walked along beside the road. Her friends from the trust bank brought her food from the markets, cared for her children and looked after her business for the three weeks she lay bed-ridden.

David surprised Susy by simply sitting down among the women and asking a few questions. 'I thought he would want to probe, kick tyres, do what he could to find out what was really going on. There was none of that. It was all very low key, comfortable. There he was, just casually sitting and being with these women, and I remember how impressive that was to me.'

David was equally impressed with what he saw. 'I really identified with Susy's spirituality and her commitment to serve the poor.' He knew instinctively that helping Susy and the Women's Opportunity Foundation in its vision would benefit many. Personally, he still believed in the original concept of creating many new jobs through larger entrepreneurs, but Susy's work met another area of desperate need and he would support her in that. He soon arranged with donors to provide the money needed to take WOF to the next stage—from a struggling pilot program into a full-blown lender. Most importantly, at a personal level he sent thoughtful gifts of books and calendars to let Susy know she was not alone in the field.

In August 1993 the Opportunity partners came together in Thailand for their first global conference, a meeting that brought field workers, supporters, friends and family from every continent. It was an event stage-managed by David right down to the ice sculpture of a dove on the buffet table. He invited speakers who might stimulate and provoke discussion, and subsidised workers from the field who might not otherwise have made it.

The relationships built through these events bonded the network. David made no apologies for the luxurious surrounds of the conference venue, so different from the clients' circumstances. To him, this was a chance to recharge the enthusiasm of a dedicated group of workers. He encouraged families to come, spending months negotiating a cheap rate at a hotel with child-friendly facilities. Beyond his immediate family he had built a diverse, affectionate extended family within the Opportunity network. His own family, Carol, Rachel, Tasha and Jessica, came with him. Between meetings and sessions, and countless passing conversations, David found spare time to splash around with Jessica in the vast, palm-lined swimming pool, seemingly without a care in the world.

Susy and others were bemused by this side of David, the warm and accessible granddad, a man clearly treasuring the fact that Carol and the girls were there. In their work, most had only seen David as the energetic leader, focused on his work, and driven to travel the world for weeks at a time.

Among the group at the conference were Denis and Joy Perry, a New Zealand couple who had been introduced to Carol and David the year before in Christchurch by their mutual friends, David and Di Middleton. Denis was well aware of the effectiveness of small loans. He ran a small foundation in Christchurch called Kingdom Resources which offered interest-free loans to New Zealanders who struggled with poverty and debt. Denis had a more conventional business background than David. He had held a number of executive roles in the reinsurance industry before leaving to run the foundation. The Perrys came to Thailand to learn more about how Opportunity worked with the poor and to connect with the people at the heart of the work.

Susy Cheston met others in her field for the first time at the conference. She was surprised and slightly intimidated, as the new girl on the block, to hear that David had put her on the conference agenda as spokesperson for the Women's Opportunity Fund, sharing her work in El Salvador with three hundred other practitioners and supporters in the network. The conference and the subsequent visits to other partners threw Susy's world wide open. In the course of a few days she discovered that she was not alone in her experimentation with groups. Noel Alcaide at KMBI in Manila, Benjie Montemayor at TSPI in Manila, Priyadi at DBB in Bali, and The Bridge Foundation in India were all now turning their focus to loans for groups of women.

The conference spurred her on to refine and develop trust banks. For Susy, the most intriguing aspect of the conference had been David himself. She had seen his leadership in the field but at the conference he had been reluctant to go on stage, had refused to take a visible role, and instead pushed others into the limelight. He was not presenting himself as the visible charismatic leader of this huge group, as she had expected he would.

He impressed her. 'There were hundreds of people there and everybody revered him but he was doing everything he could to downplay himself; instead of being in front or taking that leader-ship role in a visible way, he was usually at the back of the room.'

Afterwards, Susy joined Leigh and Vera Coleman and another couple from the conference on a train ride from Bangkok to Chiang Mai, to join an elephant trek. In the hours they whiled away on the old train, Susy tried to get to the bottom of David's leadership style. 'What is it about David? He just doesn't seem to fit the profile of a major leader. I can't work him out at all,' she asked the Colemans.

It was Vera who replied. 'Well you have to understand David's role. He is able to comfort the afflicted and to afflict the comfort-able.' It was an explanation that Susy came back to many times, when David's behaviour ranged from gentle compassion for the broken and suffering, to being a prickly thorn in the side of those with power. Many times, she observed him at board meetings in the US, where staff might join the board over a meal, and smiled to see him seek out the least influential person or someone sitting alone.

Three months later Susy was back in Asia, this time in Manila for a field exposure program, or 'boot camp', with thirty other new board members, executive directors and staff from around the world. Among the group were David Stiller, whom David had already visited several times in Toronto to raise support for the programs, and Carol Stigger, a writer and communications expert who had joined the US office in Chicago three weeks before.

For two weeks they were put through training that would test their mettle and strengthen their commitment. For part of boot camp the participants lived in the homes of client families, watch-ing how they went about their day. The client hosts offered what they could, sometimes giving up a bed to their guest and sleeping on the floor. They could not hope to disguise the discomfort of their poverty, the rats that watched from a beam above the bed or the cockroaches that crawled into the bedding at night. It was a process aimed to break down preconceptions about the poor. The participants saw how a widowed woman could support a family on very little, how proud she was when the food her children ate and the clothes they wore came from her own labour. There could be no starker illustration of the gap between rich and poor nations on one hand, and the similarity of hopes and dreams on the other. David and Leigh both hovered in the background, stepping into training sessions when needed.

Susy was hosted by KMBI, the partner in Valenzuela, in Metro Manila. To her delight, Susy found KMBI's model of group lending had many similarities to the Village Banking model she had been working on. They were all moving in the same direction, towards a hybrid that would integrate the spiritual and social empowerment aspects Susy had been experimenting with.

'What we were after was something that was more community grassroots oriented, really developing the leadership of the clients. Our goal was that the clients would actually be trained to run the trust bank meeting and the loan officer would sit in the back of the room and almost be invisible,' says Susy. Only after the meeting would the loan officer sit with the leader and coach them in how to run the next meeting. 'We wanted to make sure that the client leaders within the group were the ones that were on top of loan repayments and managing all of that. We were doing that partly because of the financial efficiencies of it but also because we really believed in developing the leadership and the self-esteem of the clients.'

By the end of 1993 it was confirmed that Younis Farhat would not return to Pakistan. In his absence the Alfalah programs in Lahore had suffered from a lack of strong leadership. A retired military officer, Major Aftab Suri, was hired to step in and set things right, but it was an untenable situation. Major Suri had no clear mandate from the board and the staff refused to cooperate with him. A staff member organised a mass resignation of the entire staff and took the four wheel drive vehicles used for collecting loans away for 'repairs', so that loan officers could not collect repayments. Without repayments, the ability of Alfalah to help the poor came under question.

David could no longer visit, but along with James and Leigh, he poured hours into long-distance management. James and Leigh visited as frequently as possible given the global span of their workload.

By now the Alfalah board itself was flaunting its corruption, using loan funds to buy vehicles and build houses for family members. Against all advice, Leigh chose to return to Lahore in 1994. Alfalah had made loans for almost ten years without bowing to cultural pressure to pay bribes to survive, and it riled Leigh that corruption from within was now robbing the poor.

Even David cautioned Leigh to put this one down to experience. 'It's just too dangerous. You've seen what happened to Michael and Younis. We may just have to let this one go,' he told Leigh.

'I'm not going to let one rogue group destroy the reputation of our work everywhere else,' Leigh replied. He felt responsible to the donors. He sensed that David could understand why he felt compelled to go, but that it would have been irresponsible of him to actually send Leigh.

As corruption within the organisation surfaced, Opportunity found communication from Lahore shutting down. If Leigh was going to successfully bring out the donors' money, he needed access to all the financial records, yet Major Suri, the man hired to set things straight, was also being shut out. Leigh and Major Suri hatched a scheme to retrieve the donors' cash, which was kept in bearer bonds at the local bank. While Leigh sat in a meeting room demanding the resignations of the entire board, Major Suri arranged a 'takeover' of all the financial records down at the office, using a truckload of military personnel to secure the building. Leigh quickly fled the country, hoping the donor money he had come for would follow him electronically. He was relieved when it arrived soon after.

In his most foolhardy decision ever, Leigh made a final visit to Lahore later that year, intending to tie up loose ends and claim the last of the assets. He knew it was dangerous.

'Don't let anyone near my room,' he directed hotel staff as he left in the morning.

Sure enough, when he returned at the end of the day, turned the key in the lock and walked into the darkened room, he was not alone. Six angry men, all former staff members, surrounded him.

'Why did you try to destroy us? You called us corrupt and now we have lost our good name.'

'I didn't set out to do you any harm, but I couldn't sit by and watch the work destroyed by corruption,' Leigh tried to explain.

It only heightened their anger. They argued for what felt to Leigh like hours. As the anger swelled, only one of the men appeared capable of hearing what Leigh was saying, so he appealed to this one person. 'You know I meant you no harm,' Leigh said, careful not to lose eye contact with him for a second. His strategy worked.

'C'mon, let's go,' the man directed the others, and finally they left Leigh alone and unharmed. He vowed to be on the next plane out of Pakistan. A couple of days before this, alone in a hotel room, he had almost died of cholera. The hotel owner eventually called a doctor to the hallucinating guest and Leigh was rehydrated. Now he finally decided that salvaging Opportunity International's reputation in Pakistan was not worth his life.

David and Leigh knew Pakistan had been a risky venture, but its ten year lifespan had helped a large number of people. That made it worthwhile.

Through all of this, David was Leigh's only confidant. The roles of the two men were so intertwined that they rarely travelled apart. They were the first to admit to having almost a sense of ownership of the work; they felt personally responsible for its success or failure. Episodes like Alfalah illustrated the difficulty and pitfalls of operating a global, culturally diverse entity.

By 1993, hundreds of organisations were involved in micro enterprise development, and its delivery was so sophisticated that universities offered graduate programs in the study of it. Charities that had focused on disaster relief or conventional development such as water and infrastructure projects now scrambled to provide micro loans to the poor. Opportunity International was still one of the few to aim for global reach. This stage marked a change of direction for David and Leigh. There were too many programs for them to work as closely as they had for the last fifteen years. Around this time, David veered off towards the leadership side, and Leigh worked as Asian regional director with managers in the field.

The Maranatha Trust, which David and Carol had started in Australia in the 1970s as a way for them to personally help the poor, was attracting larger donations and Australian government funding. It now became apparent that a family trust was not the best vehicle for receiving major funding. Moves were afoot to formalise the relationship between Maranatha and Opportunity International so that there was one unified entity for donors to deal with.

'We were pushed and strained and stretched as staff, and so was David. David was constantly being challenged to look at what he was doing and where he was taking the organisation,' says James Allardice. Yet David had no grand plan for the direction Maranatha would take or for what Opportunity International might look like in the future. Though he recognised a need for guidelines and policies, he knew he would be stifled if rules and regulations were imposed upon him personally. Now David's fluid and entrepreneurial style was becoming a disadvantage for him.

Proposals and reports needed detail, and staying accountable meant installing state-of-the-art information technology. The stakes were higher, the level of technical expertise needed for accounting and reporting had risen, and Maranatha was outgrowing its capacity. It was time to move up a few notches in professionalism.

It was also apparent that if this global network was to reach its full potential, it would have to be knitted together more closely. In December 1993, the micro enterprise development work of Maranatha Foundation became Opportunity Foundation Ltd. Soon after, David started assembling an Australian board of directors, starting with businessmen Peter King and Terry Winters, both of whom had run publicly listed companies, and Harry Edwards, who had chaired the Maranatha overseas aid committee. Another CEO, Brooks Wilson, followed soon after. In 1996, Opportunity Foundation became Opportunity International Australia. Under the new structure, Maranatha Foundation became Maranatha Trust once again. It would continue as a source of funding for projects and David's numerous other interests, but the loan programs would all come under the Opportunity International name.

In 1993, Carol's mother Phyllis had moved into the Bussau household in Sydney. After years of living alone in Auckland, watched over by Carol's friend Sherryl and others, and visiting Australia year after year, she had set herself a milestone. 'If I'm still alive at eighty, I'll move to Australia,' she told her family. Sure enough, as she neared eighty in June 1993 she was still fit and strong and showing no sign of slowing down. She put her house on the market, packed up her things, locked the front door and went to stay with a neighbour until Carol came over from Sydney to collect her.

Towards the end of this year Rachel phoned David in Thailand with some happy news. For the past eight months she had been dating a young man named Richard Ford, and the relationship had moved along quickly. 'Dad, we're going to get married. We're thinking about January.'

The reply that came back was unexpected. 'But how do you know I'm going to be in the country? I have my whole year planned.'

Rachel was stunned.

'I'm sorry, it's just taken me by surprise,' David then offered.

Rachel's relationship with Richard had flourished as David travelled the world. It was irrelevant to her that David had only met Richard a couple of times. This was the harsh reality of his long absences. When the girls were young and missed him, their pining manifested itself in their behaviour towards Carol, usually around two weeks after he left. Now, it was evident that he had missed out on things. The travel had spiralled along with his network of friends and colleagues. It was self-perpetuating and even addictive.

Now David knew how far things had come, he made a point of getting to know his future son-in-law and made sure he would be in the country on 22 January 1994 to walk down the aisle with his younger daughter.

David prepared a speech for the reception, which he tucked into his inside jacket pocket. When it came time for speeches he stood up and reached into his pocket for the piece of paper. No sign of it. 'It was here,' he thought, before looking down to see a mischievous smirk on Leigh's face at the table in front of him.

Leigh could smell victory. 'How's he going to get out of this?' he thought as he watched David hesitate. He would have to ad lib, and he was not the most comfortable speaker at the best of times. Then, with just the slightest theatrical pause, David reached into his back pocket, pulled out a piece of paper and proceeded to unfold a spare copy of his speech. He had not taken any chances. He grinned at Leigh, who shook his head and laughed.

It was a big year for weddings in the Bussau household. Two years earlier, at the age of twenty two, Tasha had met a young man named Adam Florence, a twenty-year-old Qantas engineer.

David and Carol were thrilled to welcome both Adam and Richard as sons into their family. As Tasha and Adam's wedding drew near, Tasha sensed her father letting go. For so long he had been her close friend, and a mix between grandfather and father to Jessica. He was protective of them both. Now he deliberately invited Adam into their conversations, slowly stepping out of the role he had played and letting Adam in. By the time of the wedding, on 3 December 1994, there was no sadness at letting go, just a sense of completion, a happy feeling that Tasha and five-year-old Jessie were their own family now.

Late in the following year, David's work with the boards of Opportunity partners took him to the former Soviet states of Eastern Europe. Ken and Linda Vander Weele, from the US, had forged into the region in 1993, soon after the USSR fell, establishing programs in Bulgaria, Russia and Romania in quick succession. The euphoria of the early days after communism had soon faded as government-owned factories closed down, leaving a vast economic vacuum and millions of people without work or an income. It was an environment ripe for small enterprises that could soak up the unemployed, many of whom were well educated and highly skilled.

Opportunity's programs in Russia had started in Nizhni Novgorod, a city of a million and a half people and known for almost the last sixty years as Gorky. Of all the major cities in Russia, Nizhni Novgorod was the least influenced by the west, and the one with the longest history of commerce and trading. When the Soviet Union came asunder and democracy swept in, the city became a hothouse for free market initiatives.

In David's three week swoop around thirteen countries at the end of 1995 he passed through South Africa and Zimbabwe, touched down for meetings in the UK, France, Germany and

Austria and then landed in Russia for board training. He brought with him the history of Opportunity, the understanding that these new partners were connected to something bigger. He encouraged the early board members as they broke new ground. One of them, a woman inspired by the work of Mother Teresa, had pioneered private charitable activity in the city. Others were young business people and finance experts whose experience had been in highly regulated Soviet institutions. Indidvidual enterprise, which had been inhibited for decades, was coming to life. The first clients were budding entrepreneurs and groups of single mothers.

On that visit, Stacie Schrader, the executive director of Opportunity Russia, had organised a board retreat where David would come to train the board members of the newly-formed partner, Vosmozhnost. Until five years before, the city of Nizhni Novgorod had effectively been closed off from the world, and even now, the easiest access was by overnight train from Moscow. David found himself in a four-bed sleeper carriage with three sullen-looking Russians and no means of communication. He could not even determine where he was from station to station as the train passed signs written only in Cyrillic script, and there was no English speaker in sight. The aisle outside his carriage was crowded with people, some standing and others crouching in corners.

An hour into the journey, as the train snaked its way across a vast landscape that in a month's time would most likely be dusted in snow, David started to feel a little nervous about his travelling companions. Their faces had remained expressionless through his efforts to bring some warmth to the chilly atmosphere by smiling and nodding at them. The three of them sat, arms crossed, looking through him. Disturbing thoughts crossed his mind. He could be robbed and thrown from the train, into the empty forests that flashed by. He did not even have the Russian word for 'help' to fall back on. Would anyone ever know who he was or where to find him? Again, he tried to look friendly, as unthreatening and innocuous as possible. His battered black briefcase was not fancy or expensive by any means, but he knew it might look so here. He decided to stay awake all night, and pulled out his notes for the retreat. He could at least make good use of the time. He could feel the stares of his travel companions, willing him to sleep, but there was no way he would give in. He tried to look nonchalant, as if all travellers chose to read all night instead of resting.

Finally, he had to use the bathroom and pushed his way out the door, clutching his briefcase, past the bodies in the aisle to the other end of the carriage. When he returned to his sleeper car his suitcase had been ransacked. The men had broken into it, stolen the clothes they wanted and then sat straightfaced as if nothing had happened. For once, David was too petrified to act. It was an injustice he would have to let ride. He pulled a book from his briefcase and read until dawn, when he knew he must be near his destination.

'Is this Nizhny Novgorod?' he called out to a conductor on the platform, who confirmed that he had finally arrived with a terse nod. With a faint grin of relief, David hastily gathered his bags and scuttled off the train.

At the retreat, Stacie asked David to teach the board how to design policies for the organisation, a skill that had been all but lost in a society where most decisions were handled by government officials. David led the group through a process that allowed them to make their own decisions. It would be the same in other Eastern European emerging democracies such as Poland and Bulgaria, where his role would be to encourage people who had no experience of self-governance because they had lived their whole lives under a centralised economy.

Here, David's notion of ownership of the program and local empowerment proved to be culturally difficult. Through an external translator, the board told him, 'Why don't you just give us the rule book? We don't want to own it; we want the rules.' Even worse, after two days of David helping the group work through the concept of policy and the principles upon which it rested, he wondered why the faces staring back at him looked either blank or confused.

He discovered that the translator had used the word 'politics' instead of 'policies'— and most likely had no idea himself what a policy was—David never knew precisely what the translator had communicated to the board of directors. Language proved to be a huge challenge in other ways. The words 'stewardship' and 'integrity' were vital to David's teaching on board governance, but it proved difficult to translate these words into Russian. 'Even the word "poor" was a challenge, as the Russians were reluctant to use the word "poor" to describe their own people,' says Stacie.

Overseeing programs in such challenging conditions was a monumental task. Stacie was isolated, working in a country in transition, in a difficult language. David was impressed by her courage. She could hold her own among the groups, knowing when to be firm, but also sensitive to the new circumstances the local people found themselves in. As he had done with Larry Reed in Africa and Susy Cheston in El Salvador, he stepped into a role that was very supportive of her.

'David provided enormous personal support to me with seemingly simple gestures like faxing a birthday wish or Easter card. It was surprisingly important to me to be remembered when I was so far out on my own. David's quiet encouragement and insight were a great gift.'

The train journey was not to be the last of David's adventures on that trip. After Russia, he had also swung by the Macedonian partner, Moznosti, in Skopje for board training with the executive director, Nicolas Colloff, who had moved from Opportunity Trust, UK. As he prepared to leave Skopje, a dense fog was descending on the city and he arrived at the airport to find his plane to Germany grounded.

'You'll be here for five days once that fog lands,' the woman at the ticket counter advised him in broken English. In a split second he decided to get a seat on any plane leaving Skopje.

'A flight to Ljubljana in Slovenia is leaving in twenty minutes. We have seats available.'

'I'll take one,' David replied. He was so relieved to be in the air he had not thought through his actions. As his small plane shot down the runway and into the air he started feeling uneasy. He had never heard of the place he was now flying to, he had not a word of the language, and he would in all likelihood be stranded there without a visa. He wondered whether getting completely lost was a risk he should have taken. Not one to waste his time, he filled the four hours in transit in Slovenia talking about micro enterprise development to local business people he met at the airport. 'Slovenia is ripe for Opportunity's programs,' the men urged him. He could not promise them anything. He finally made it to his final destination, Stuttgart, through Munich and Frankfurt, on three separate airlines.

It seemed that wherever he went he found a need for micro enterprise development. Though their political and social circumstances were vastly different from those of Latin Americans, Africans and Asians, and their economy lacked the informal sector of the other regions, David found that the Eastern Europeans shared the same drive for self-improvement.

15

The Social Entrepreneur

When David had extended himself beyond the business world, he had realised his entrepreneurial gifts. He could bring excellent people together to make things happen, he could move quickly and spontaneously, always prepared to go for it without counting the cost, while maintaining his optimism and confidence that he could make anything work. The entrepreneur in him was driven to create, to find new challenges to conquer before moving on. He knew he was most satisfied when starting new ventures.

Long ago he had progressed from building businesses to building solutions to social problems, applying the same principles and business approach to any problem he came across. As a builder, he brought together carpenters, bricklayers, architects. Now, it was individuals, grant-making foundations and poor entrepreneurs. For almost two decades, the risks he had taken were on behalf of the poor, the problems he sought to solve were around the issue of poverty and its side-effects.

David also understood the cost of being an entrepreneur. He realised that he could be a maverick, out alone on a limb, always preferring to lead, mostly from behind, and that he could not slip easily into being a team player. At times it could be a lonely life. Until 1993, when he met an American by the name of Bob Buford, David had known very few people with a similar drive.

When he met Bob, David also discovered that someone had put a name to what he was doing. It was called social entrepreneurship.

Bob Buford had come through the business world at the big end of town. He owned a cable television company, Buford Television Inc. The company had been started by his mother who had picked up on the need for a television station in the small town of Tyler, Texas. Bob predicted that cable television would become big in the US, and the gamble paid off. He rode the cable television wave from its earliest days, building his company into a major communications player. By the time he stepped out in 1999 the company was worth several billion dollars.

At the age of thirty five Bob started to wonder, just as David had, why he should keep amassing wealth. 'How much is enough?' he also asked himself. Like David, Bob was quiet and unassuming, not comfortable with big-noting himself or stealing the limelight. He quietly set out to use his substantial wealth in a significant way. He wrote about his experience in a book published in 1994 called *Halftime: Changing Your Game Plan from Success to Significance*, in which he talked about reaching the midpoint in his life, essentially a mid-life crisis, and consciously deciding what he would do with the second half of his life, rather than being swept along in the same job and career path.

Unlike David, he decided to focus on work in his own country. He soon established a meeting of major Christian foundations in the US that became a force in philanthropy. He then set up Leadership Network, with the aim of bringing an entrepreneurial spark to church communities.

From his earliest days in business, Bob had admired the Austrian-born economist Peter Drucker, who now lived in California. He eagerly studied Drucker's views on management, innovation and organisation, as a lead for his own business. By 1995, when he was eighty-six, Peter Drucker had published more than thirty books and was one of the most influential business management thinkers in the world. He was a man well known for his gift of 'crystal balling,' of accurately picking future trends in economies and society. He saw social entrepreneurs becoming the mainstay of social welfare as governments lessened their contribution to the social sector. True to form, Peter Drucker was well ahead of the wave. Within five years, social entrepreneurship would be a movement with its own momentum. He called it the most significant development in the past hundred years.

Peter Drucker was both mentor and friend to Bob and, in the mid 1990s, still possessing the mental acuity of a young man, he was collaborating with Bob on a social entrepreneurs' project. The men set out to explore the phenomenon of successful business people who turn their attention, skills and finances to social issues. Social entrepreneurship was more hands-on than the straight-out philanthropic giving that was already so deeply ingrained into American society. These people differed from donors or philanthropists, in that each sought connection with the people their activities aimed to help. In identifying what made an entrepreneur successful in the first place, and the catalysts that made them turn around and use those skills in the social sector, Peter and Bob hoped to find ways to foster and support social entrepreneurs.

In June 1996, with no idea of what to expect, David joined a small meeting of social entrepreneurs organised by Bob and Peter in California. He had done well in business but knew he was not in the same league financially as most of these big players. Would it be a roomful of large egos or competitive tycoons? He was certainly not sure he would fit in, but if Bob wanted him there, he would come.

He need not have been concerned. He found a modest group of people, all, apart from himself and one Japanese man who owned a large bakery chain, American, and all working quietly, without broadcasting their achievements or seeking recognition. Ken Blanchard, an innovative manager who had written the business management bestseller *The One-Minute Manager* (as well as many other books), was also there. David found that he was not the only person there from the micro lending field, though no one had been at it longer. One participant was bringing computer technology to the disenfranchised. All of them had worked hard for their wealth before choosing to part with it creatively. It led David to wonder whether those who took risks to build their wealth were more likely to be generous and creative with it, and if inherited wealth had the potential to paralyse the creativity of the wealthy. He would never really know.

The group spent their time together talking with Peter Drucker and each other about their ideas and work. The similarities between the men came through clearly in the individual interviews they gave to Constance Rossum, a professor working on the project, before the meeting. Though their childhood experiences ranged from delightful to dysfunctional, the social entrepreneurs were all self-reliant and none saw themselves as victims. All were good, helpful people, and some, but not all, had strong religious faith. They had all worked at a variety of jobs from as early as seven years old and all had financial security and a sense of order in their business and personal lives that allowed them parallel careers. They all created activities out of gaps, fulfilling a need in society where government and regulators had failed, or where others were doing an inadequate job.

Peter encouraged and influenced the social entrepreneurs, leaving David with some vital lessons. 'He taught me how to think further into the future and how to focus on people who are thinking outside the box, people who are perceptive about political and economic trends and how they will influence the world.' Those few days were a rare time of reflection for David. On the same month-long trip, he was passing through eight other countries. He was soon on a flight to Central America and another project.

Of all the social entrepreneurs Bob Buford had met, none had had as wide an impact as David. 'David is a quiet arsonist, a fire-starter. He starts the fire, blows on it a bit to get it going, and then goes on to light another fire somewhere else. Most people use all their energy maintaining the fire.'

David's fire-starting was clearly at work in Asia, which, under the direction of Leigh Coleman, was the fastest-growing region for Opportunity International. More than half of the one hundred thousand annual loans that year were in the Philippines, Indonesia and India. There were plans for a scale-up in the numbers of clients, starting with a pilot program in the Philippines, and management predicted that within five years Opportunity partners could be making one million loans each year.

It had taken twenty-two years for the number of loans given in one year to grow to fifty thousand, and just three years to jump to one hundred thousand per year (in 1996). There were now

top: Gloria Navales, a trust bank member living in Tondo, Manila, pictured with two of her five children. By day she mans this scantly-stocked vegetable stall at the front of her home and by night she sells vegetables at the markets. Though still poor, her life has improved and she gains strength from the support of other trust bank members.

bottom: David goes back to his bakery roots with a client in East Timor.

top: Hundreds of Opportunity's clients live along these railway tracks through Tondo. It is not uncommon for fire or flood to sweep their homes away.

bottom: David meeting a client in Sulawesi. David's visits to the field encouraged poor communities to better their circumstances.

top: Mrs Terezia Mbasera a former Entrepreneur of the Year in Zimbabwe and one of Opportunity International's most successful borrowers. From a desperately poor past, she now runs a dozen small businesses and is a matriarch and substantial employer in her neighbourhood. She encourages many of those around with small business ideas.

left to right: Larry Reed started at Opportunity International as a university graduate and is now chief executive officer of a network making more than 700 000 loans each year. David was Larry's mentor when Larry opened the micro lending operations in Africa. **David Stiller**, a close friend and colleague of David's since the 1980s, now chairs the Opportunity International Network board. **Al Whittaker**, co-founder of Opportunity International, headed the organisation IIDI, which first made loans in Latin America in 1971. Al's contacts and corporate expertise brought institutional shape as David's work in the field grew.

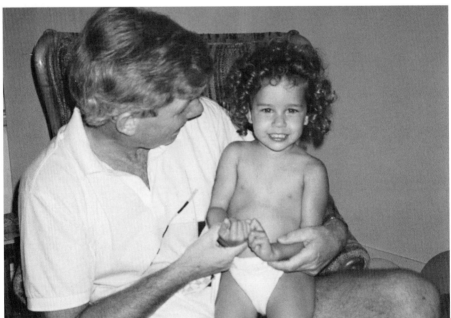

top left: Ruth Callanta, executive director of CCT in Manila, who asked David to help after Mount Pinatubo erupted in the Philippines.

top right: Ibu Gusti, an 80-plus year old client in Sulawesi, Indonesia, in 1997. She came to the Opportunity International partner's office to make a deposit. She was saving money to pay for her own funeral and feared she would be robbed of her savings if left in her home.

above: Susy Cheston was the first executive director of the Women's Opportunity Fund, which developed the highly effective group lending or 'trust bank' model to reach greater numbers of poor women. She and David worked closely together.

opposite bottom: Tasha's daughter Jessie, to whom David was father, grandfather and friend in the early years.

top: David meeting with the women of a trust bank in Dili, East Timor.

bottom: Denis Perry (right), a New Zealander hand-picked by David to take over as CEO of Opportunity International Australia, and Simon Lynch who was in charge of Indonesian operations. They are in central Sulawesi visiting a client's store.

top: Rachel, Tasha, David and Carol at the Australian Entrepreneur of the Year Awards. David was the first social entrepreneur ever to be chosen to represent Australia at the Ernst&Young World Entrepreneur of the Year Awards.

bottom: David and Carol in Monaco for the World Entrepreneur of the Year Award in May 2004.

David with four of his five grandchildren: Bronte, Ethan, David, Lisa (left to right), and Joshua (front). David's family is his greatest joy.

fifty-seven partners in twenty-seven countries. The implementers were at the coalface: the loan officers, management and support staff worked with those who received the loans. In addition, there were four support partners offering fundraising and technical expertise. In the first five years of the 1990s alone, Opportunity International started more than twenty-five new partners. The Australian arm was now fully integrated into the global entity.

It was not yet fully apparent but David, the entrepreneur, whose creativity and spirit suffused Opportunity, was on a collision course. Growing larger meant developing a more disciplined structure, increased accountability, more rigid lines of reporting. People needed a more corporate environment, yet being caged into a tight structure was anathema to an entrepreneur like David. Right or wrong, he made decisions quickly, not always thinking of the consequences.

Meanwhile, the tug between David and the US chief executive, Eric Thurman, grew stronger. Both were entrepreneurs, and accustomed to leading. There was a basic philosophical gap between the men. Eric worked towards his vision to see the poor receive loans in large numbers. David grew increasingly passionate and vocal in his defence of the rights of the individual organisations working with the poor to determine their own future. However, in the end it was disagreement with the US board about the role of CEO versus the board, rather than a clash of wills with David, that brought Eric's resignation. He was later replaced by Charles Dokmo, who came from a field position in development.

The Opportunity global conference some months before, in September 1995, had drawn hundreds to a mountain resort in the Genting Highlands outside Kuala Lumpur, Malaysia. Again, it was a mixed crowd of staff, management and boards, wealthy donors and those who simply supported the work, gathered from twenty or more countries, all committed to using their skills and education, time and money to help poor people. Here they could learn from each other, encourage each other in the work and perhaps even find new ways to support it. Between the larger global gatherings there had been smaller country-wide and regional conferences. In the Philippines, partners came together each year for a 'summer camp'. In addition, the Asian regional conference usually brought in participants from the other regions, so knowledge and experience could flow freely.

Behind the scenes, over coffee, in quiet alcoves, at supper late at night, discussions were taking place that would mark the beginning of the next phase of Opportunity's development. David had been engaged in informal conversations with managers for a couple of years over the most effective and fairest way to formally link all the components of Opportunity International into one global body.

This became the main topic of the conference. How do we tie these partners together, put a firmer structure around an organisation with such diverse cultures and needs? It would not be an easy task, when each partner had grown around the needs of its own region and culture. The global gathering brought together every party with a stake in the future of that organisation.

Working out the details would be a long and expensive process, one that needed to be done properly and in a way that would not use money that had been raised to help the poor. Soon after the conference, the chairmen of the US, UK and Australian Opportunity support partners, Dick Hoefs, Michael Feilden and Harry Edwards, met to formally start the process. David spoke with one of his network of foundations in the US and secured funding for exploring the best approach to building a global network. Jim Duncan, an American businessman and newly appointed member of the US board, put his hand up to organise the Network Design Council, a group of leaders from both the supporting countries and those running the programs. The Network Design Council included David and Australian board member Peter King, Larry Reed, Stacie Schrader and Susy Cheston from the US, Kwabena Darko from Ghana, Priyadi Reksasiswaya from Indonesia and Noel Alcaide from the Philippines. For the next two years the group met every few months in different countries to thrash out the issues of a global network.

And thrash they did. From the American viewpoint it was a huge concession and highly risky to even enter into a process that could see a weakening of their influence while they were still delivering a large proportion of the funding. Future fundraising depended on careful use of donor money, and for this to happen, there had to be some control over that use. While David agreed with the prudent use of donor money he also worked to ensure that partners in the poorer countries would not lose their voice in the process.

The Americans were the most financially generous nation in the world, giving US$125 billion in 1996 alone. Yet a concentration of financial support bothered David. He reasoned that if Opportunity International was to be a genuinely global concern, the funding net should be thrown wider. In his disaster relief work David had found the Europeans to be liberal and open in their funding. He set out on a new mission: to widen the fundraising base by expanding the number of support partners in wealthier nations.

As had happened in the US, networks opened up to David through a number of sources. Already, in establishing the Opportunity Trust in the UK, Vinay had set up meetings and Australian friends rounded up their business contacts in London. In Germany, David worked with Karl Schock, a wealthy industrialist he had met at the Oxford Centre for Missionary Studies, OCMS, to set up Opportunity International Deutschland in 1996. Germany had always been a rich source of funding as its government still extracted a church tax, and the money collected often found its way into programs in the developing world. However, its was Karl Schock's own money, through his foundation, that brought Oportunity International Deutschland into being.

In Canada, David Stiller had tried a couple of times to pull together a solid board of supporters to raise funds, and in 1998 he succeeded. The Canadian had been a loyal friend for many years, had been known to fly across an ocean to meet David in need, and David would do the same for him. He had zeroed in on Asia and Eastern Europe many times as a trouble shooter of programs, at David Bussau's request. The two men had shared the most candid conversations possible, to the point where Evelyn Stiller asked 'How can you call yourselves friends and be so sharp in conversations?'

'That's because we are very good friends. Never for a minute does his eye reflect disapproval of me or rejection,' David Stiller had replied.

There had always been strong support from Australia, and it continued to grow as Opportunity International Australia expanded. David was also working with people in New Zealand, France and Sweden to raise support. Now Opportunity International had the backing of a group of committed heavy hitters from developed nations who would raise funds and operate as advocates for the poor among the comfortable.

Over the years, David had increasingly found himself in the company of the wealthy and powerful. The decision he had made early in life, that he would not be intimidated by anyone, now came into play. He saw everyone as equal in God's eyes and treated them as such.

'Personally, I don't separate the poor from the non-poor. My commitment is not just to the poor. I can feel just as much despair for a politician as I can for someone begging on the street, someone who is struggling with their role in life, their values, their standards. So I don't see a lot of difference between the poor and the affluent when it comes to walking alongside people. If I go into a slum I have no problem hugging the kids, but I equally have no problem doing the same thing around politicians or royalty. Obviously, with that comes respect for everybody, whether you are poor, or whether you are affluent. Everyone is dealing with the same human issues, it is just played out in a different arena.'

The more he moved in the circles of the wealthy and the ultra-wealthy in the US and Europe, the more he saw how isolated and lonely it could be at that end of the spectrum. The more time he spent with millionaires and billionaires, the more compassion he felt for their situation. His gift for friendship let the wealthy, often hounded for their money, relax around him and know that he was interested in them simply as people, not moneyed people. 'He can be a friend to anybody, a billionaire or a pauper and treat them with same sense of dignity that every human being needs. He has been a wonderful ambassador of the non-western world's capacity to deal with their own situations. And able to overcome the cynicism of western donors who have had their fingers burned,' is how Vinay Samuel phrased it.

Some sensed a permanency and integrity about his offer of friendship. In coming without a fundraising agenda, he often helped the heads of foundations and philanthropists understand the enterprise solutions to poverty he had spent most of his adult life working on. Once they understood how effective it was, they often wanted to invest.

Through the mid 1990s, Opportunity International was held together by a management team light-heartedly named POSMM, Perpetual Opportunity Senior Management Meetings, a group of ten to twenty regional directors and the senior program people who met several times a year on different continents. In the early days, Susy Cheston was often the only woman at these meetings.

David was very influential, primarily through close, one-on-one relationships. His hallmark was the parting question in meetings he attended. Just when it seemed agreement had been reached and it was time to move on to the next point or close the meeting, he invariably asked a seemingly innocent question that threw the entire discussion into disarray. It was a technique that could be both helpful and destructive.

'But I was just asking a question,' he would reply when challenged.

To some, particularly in the US, it was a disturbing way of doing business that frustrated the linear pattern of meetings. 'In the American culture you have got to take responsibility for your contribution and then say what you think,' explained Em Griffin.

Yet it was not without a purpose. It was David's way of flushing out the most heartfelt concerns, to find out if the weaker parties were honestly in agreement or just bowing to the powerful. He pulled people out of their hiding spots. It was his way of protecting those he saw as having less power.

'David had this uncanny sense of knowing when people were really not in agreement. He was willing to pause a bit and let people rest on things and then come back and reconstruct a dialogue all over again, just to make sure that there was a legitimate meeting of minds and hearts,' said Dennis Ripley, who joined Opportunity International in the US as a vice-president of programs in the early 1990s and had often travelled with David.

Since their first meeting, David had pegged Denis Perry, whom he had met through David Middleton, as the man who could take the Maranatha Foundation in Australia forward. Denis had been on the periphery for a couple of years now, coming to conferences from New Zealand, meeting with Benjie and Ruth and Priyadi and others in the field, growing more and more convinced that he and his wife Joy should make the move to Australia.

Denis finally came to Sydney as chief operating officer in January 1996, two years after the offer was first made and soon after the micro enterprise work of Maranatha officially came under the Opportunity International banner. It was not hard for David to make way for Denis in Sydney and step aside from the day-to-day operations in Australia. An absent entrepreneur was by definition not a good manager of people. His global role continued to take him out of Sydney for at least six months of the year, and he had a strong sense that it was time for fresh blood in Australia, for new ideas and insight. By 1998 Denis had taken over David's role as chief executive of Opportunity International Australia, freeing David to do what he was best at, being a social entrepreneur.

The new structure of the Opportunity International Network was officially unveiled at the October 1997 global conference, held at the Founder's Inn near Virginia Beach in the US. Larry Reed was announced as the first chief executive of the network. Kwabena Darko from Ghana would be its first chairman. Darko's was a profound appointment, symbolic of the hundreds of thousands of clients who were at that moment on a journey out of abject poverty. Back in the 1970s, when Darko was a poor farmer living near the town of Kumasi, he met the American missionary, Paris Reidhead. Paris was the man who had inspired Al Whittaker and others to run with IIDI.

'I'd like to have a chicken farm one day,' he'd told Paris.

'Let's see what we can do to help you,' Paris had replied. He then arranged for Darko to visit the US to study how chicken farming was done in that country. Meanwhile, Paris had been travelling around the country, convincing American business-people that they should commit to helping people like Darko build small businesses—and had made the connection with Al Whittaker. Darko was overwhelmed by the large-scale farms in the US. He told Paris, 'I only have a tiny plot of land. I couldn't keep this many chickens.' Paris urged him to think bigger, and arranged funding for Darko's new chicken farm near Kumasi.

Twenty-seven years later Darko was one of the most successful businesspeople in the country, producing fifty per cent of Ghana's day old chicks. In 1992 he narrowly missed out on winning the Presidency of Ghana. Then he had been chairman of Opportunity's Ghanaian partner, the Sinapi Aba Trust, which started in 1994. Within five years Sinapi Aba had made eleven thousand loans to poor entrepreneurs like himself.

It was a proud moment for Darko when he stood before the seven hundred conference delegates as inaugural chairman of the Opportunity International Network. His first official task was to offer a vote of thanks to honour David for the years of work he had contributed to Opportunity. For David it was an embarrassing moment he had been unable to duck. He awkwardly accepted a plaque from Darko and slipped away.

The new structure was designed around the expectation that David would take an active role. Some even assumed that David would become leader of the new network, but despite taking a leading role for twenty years, he now made it clear that he did not see himself as the person for the job. He knew instinctively that as a founder—and an entrepreneur—he was not the best person to take the network forward. His heart lay in starting programs, in developing and nurturing people. So he chose not to sit on the network board at all. 'I wanted to give a new team a go,' he admitted.

Those close to him were accustomed to his contradictions, the paradoxes that he felt no need to explain. He was an impressive leader, but did not see himself as such. He was a man who had raised tens of millions of dollars on behalf of the poor and marginalised, often without actually even asking for it, while strenuously refusing to be called a fundraiser. He could be supportive and nurturing on a personal level, yet demanding as a boss, with no tolerance for those he employed who could not complete a job properly.

These paradoxes worked mostly in David's favour. The complexities in his character allowed him to manage the range of cultures and pressures of his global work, but also created a sense of mystery around him. Yet the downside, that he was unpredictable and hard to read, could leave colleagues feeling confused in their dealings with him. The same strength of character that allowed him to stand up to and for people sometimes also made it hard for him to back down.

He'd already struggled with the expectations put on him as a leader. In one anguished management meeting, the participants had pressed David to take the lead. 'But David, you're our leader. We need you to be our leader,' Susy Cheston had confronted him.

'When did I ever agree to be your leader? I have never said I would be your leader,' he answered defensively, almost in tears. 'I would rather be your friend.'

In subtle, subconscious ways, the remnants of David's childhood often crept into his adult life. He equated forceful leadership with domination, with one person exerting their power and control over others, and it pained him. Yet his sensitivity to domination was the very thing that had allowed him to be so effective. The style of leadership he was most comfortable with was servant leadership: leading by his own example. 'My leadership style is to walk beside people and facilitate their development. In many cases, I have the ideas, but it is only by placing good people around me, then empowering them to do a job, that an idea can be implemented.' He referred to it as growing fruit on other people's trees—the term borrowed from his friend Bob Buford. He was there to give, not to receive. At the same time, he was aware that with his hand on so many different projects, he received the plaudits for the work of whole teams.

Yet there were times when he was clearly the leader, and very much in control. James Allardice once received a stern rebuke when he questioned the direction David was taking him in. 'Look, sometimes you have to recognise that in the jungle there are those sitting at the top of the trees surveying the landscape, and others down in the undergrowth slashing away. There's got to be a trust between the people who are doing the work and the people who have got the vision,' David told him. But at other times David sometimes claimed that he had no vision, just a sense of destiny and skill as an opportunist.

Perhaps his greatest gift was drawing people out. 'He has the ability to see more in people than they see in themselves,' was how Bob Buford put it.

In 1997, David and Priyadi set out on a trip to visit programs in Sulawesi and Bali as part of a group of twelve which included Susy Cheston, David Stiller, Alexis Beggs, a twenty two year old university graduate from Chicago (in Sydney to help David establish a governance resource centre) Simon Lynch, who was starting as Leigh's assistant in Asia, and Denis Perry, who would soon be chief executive in Australia. Tasha, who had been teaching Indonesian in Sydney, went along as well, to hone her language skills. It became a mentoring odyssey. In visits to each community David thrust Denis into the limelight to address local leaders. Without saying it, he was telling those in the field, 'Here is my successor, I want you to accept him as you accept me.' Denis was bemused by this aspect of the journey. He knew he could not step into David's shoes. It was not possible to appoint someone to take over relationships that had grown over a decade or more.

In the village of Sumbersari in central Sulawesi, the partner David and Priyadi established some years before, Titian Budi Luhur (TBL), had just set up a rural bank in the community, and within six months had already made loans totalling US$150,000. With Priyadi's encouragement, TBL's work was creative and holistic, setting out to meet other community needs, as well as providing money. TBL had financed a health and community centre, whose programs included immunising children, and set up a food co-operative. It had brought telephones to the area and adopted Atholl Murray's rice storage techniques, which David had worked on with Atholl, so that rice farmers could earn a higher return on their produce by storing it, and selling it only when prices were high.

Most recently, the TBL bank had started taking savings as well as making loans, an important leap forward for the village. As the group of travellers sat in the rural bank complex having breakfast at 7.30 one Saturday morning, an old Balinese woman named Gusti Biyang Sayu came shuffling in, clutching a small plastic bag in her withered hands. She was eighty-five years old and over many months had saved six hundred thousand rupiah (almost A$300). She now wanted to bank her latest savings—but it was early, and the bank was not open yet.

Pak Rai Mertha, the head of TBL, knew Ibu Gusti well and greeted her as she explained her need to bank her money. Then

David jumped to his feet and joined in the conversation with the old woman.

'That looks like a lot of money. How did you save that much?' he asked her, looking at the roll of rupiah she had pulled from the bag.

'I saved it by making brooms from the coconut husks I collect in my village,' she replied.

'What will you spend your savings on?'

'I'm saving for my funeral. I know it will be safe here. If I keep it at home I will be robbed and I will not have a funeral,' Ibu Gusti answered. Within minutes Pak Rai had called a cashier, who safely banked Ibu Gusti's savings, and she joined the visitors for breakfast. It was becoming clear that being able to save was almost as valuable as loans to the poor.

The last stop for David's group on that trip was the village of Songan, built on dry, sandy terrain near Lake Batur in Bali. Each day busloads of tourists came to Kintamani, high on the caldera rim, to survey the view across the lake and the sweeping volcanic cones of the still-active Mt Batur and Mt Agung in the distance. No one but the hard-core walkers who ventured down onto the black and jagged lava beds would ever know of the struggles of the people of Songan.

Priyadi's quest to find the ten poorest villages on the island had led him into the Songan community in 1990. He had gathered the people together to explain his proposal, and afterwards forty villagers came forward and formed a self-help group called Kelompok Tani Wana Giri, The Mountain Forest Farmer Group.

Their leader was a peanut farmer named Pak Jero Gede Ardana. Before Priyadi came to the village for the partner, DBB, Pak Ardana worked as hard as the farmers on lusher parts of Bali but for much less income. He left his single-room lean-to each day dressed in a tattered sarong, old T-shirt and thongs. All day he worked with other villagers, planting, pulling, hoeing, harvesting. There was no escaping it, unless he was prepared to follow others who worked as day labourers in the capital, Denpasar. He was barely getting by, and he accepted his fate. One day there would be another flood in the valley, or the mountain could erupt again and they would all have to move.

The first loan to the group was 1.6 million rupiah (US$920) to be paid back within four months. It was enough for them to buy fertiliser to grow tomatoes. Soon after, they added the new crops of onions, beans, cassava, and other vegetables. The impact of the loan was immediate. 'Now, after a harvest I have money to buy more rice and clothes for my children, and to save for their future,' Pak Ardana proudly told the visitors. After four months, the farmers reported a twenty per cent increase in their income and they had created twenty new jobs within their community.

More loans quickly followed, each one allowing the farmers to enrich their soil, grow new crops, and fertilise the crops they had. They added garlic and chillis and melons to the crops they could grow with the more advanced farming methods Priyadi's team taught them. Within five years the loans had reached almost thirteen million rupiah (US$7000) and they were still able to repay the money on time, with interest. At the same time they became organised as a co-operative.

Priyadi's team had taught them the fundamentals of business such as how to keep a cash book, and how to run a group meeting. He worked on increasing productivity using marketing. Soon the lucrative tourist market opened up to them. They could supply organic vegetables to the big international hotels down at Nusa Dua and Sanur.

As his income grew, Pak Ardana's first investment was in better food for his family. He now had a surplus to trade with a farmer in another village for chicken, and with more protein came improved health. Then he thought about shelter. The group bought bricks and replaced their tiny straw huts with two-roomed houses. Pak Ardana now stored his tools and fertiliser where he had once lived. He had started saving through a group savings plan. This was a satisfying breakthrough. There had never been enough before, and now he had a surplus. He thought of how the group might be able to buy a vehicle to deliver their produce to the hotels fresh each morning and save themselves a three hour bus ride. With a mobile phone it would be easier to take orders.

Globally, there were layers of poverty, and no one-size-fits-all solution. By now Opportunity had refined its lending methods to reach the poor at different levels. Though shockingly poor to start with, the Songan people were by no means the poorest. The rural labouring poor, those on the brink of destitution, were worse off—for them, a US$50 loan could pull them out of the crevasse. Below them were the ultra poor, those without any assets and with little chance of earning an income. This group included the beggars, the scavengers on rubbish dumps, the discarded people of developing societies—Opportunity now targeted these people for its trust bank program.

The entrepreneurial poor, like Terezia Mbasera in Harare lived below the poverty line, but had the drive to build larger businesses that would employ many others. Between the Terezias and the Songan labourers were the self-employed poor, who took smaller loans and could meet only their own needs.

At all levels, the poor were always the most vulnerable to inevitable economic crises and natural disasters. The poorer nations around the Equator experienced more than their fair share of cyclones, mudslides, typhoons, famines and political instability, and had less ability to bounce back. The US office was to deal with yet another tragedy the following year, 1998, when the impact of Hurricane Mitch killed thousands through land-slides in Nicaragua and Honduras. Opportunity clients were among the dead and the displaced.

David had seen and heard a thousand stories of dramatic change in the lives of hardworking micro entrepreneurs over the years. There were always amazing tales from the field, of people like Esmeralda Castanos in Honduras, a woman who became president of her trust bank, and turned a tiny store, called a pulpería, into a large supermarket and restaurant. Her success gave her confidence and pride, and a voice in her community. In 2001 she successfully ran for mayor of the small town of San Mateus, population five thousand.

There were literally thousands like Esmeralda among Oppor-tunity's clients. The success stories pushed David to work harder for the poor—he was driven as much by the non-material change he saw around him as by the material improvements. 'I'm not interested in sending the poor to their graves with just a little more cash in their hands,' David commonly told people, a view which came from his own experience of poverty, material gain and the intangibles of his own spiritual life. The last thing David had ever wanted to do was to help create a class of prosperous people who would then turn around and exploit the poor. He saw raw capitalism, without constraints or values, as dangerous. If husbands still beat their wives, and neighbours still fought, what had changed? The evidence of change was when those who had been poor felt prosperous enough to help neighbours who were in distress and need. He had seen it in Manila, when a fire swept through one small section of Tatalon, destroying the homes of dozens of struggling families. Members of the trust bank brought the families into their homes and fed them while the families rebuilt their huts.

David was interested in the whole person. He often funded activities through Maranatha Trust that were outside the lending guidelines of Opportunity—a staff member visiting a sick relative in another province, or school fees for a loan officer's child, for instance. Along with material gain, David wanted to bring hope and a sense of purpose to the clients. It was the basis of his sense of Christian mission. His passion often came down to the children. He wanted to see the restoration of marriages torn apart by poverty, families reunited where before parents could not afford to keep their children, children in school and hopeful for future careers instead of begging on the streets, and parents proud of owning businesses that could support their children.

The question David now asked was: could the organisation grow at that rate and still concentrate on individual relationships and improvements in quality of life? He did not want the loans to become just financial transactions. It was a topic he and Benjie Montemayor spent hours discussing. The dialogue continued by email and phone when they were in different countries. 'It is the loan officers who will keep the close relationships with the clients,' Benjie said.

The Asian economic crisis of 1997 hit Indonesia with monstrous force. The Asian 'tiger' economies had soared through the 1990s, bringing unprecedented prosperity to the middle classes, also to some of the poor. Now the lives of many of these people were in ruins. In the two years from 1996 to 1998, unemployment in Indonesia rose from an estimated five million to twenty million, with President Habibie announcing in 1998 that close to eighty million Indonesians now lived below the poverty line of US 55 cents per day. Those living on one dollar each day were not considered poor in the crisis. In these years, the educated and skilled were reduced to working as labourers if they could find employment at all, labourers lost their jobs and returned empty-handed to their villages, families ate once a day, and the hungry poor commandeered any free land they could find to grow edible plants.

While other small and medium businesses failed, the micro sector soared. Selling vegetables in the market kept whole families alive. Dian Bhuana Lestari (Dinari), one of three Opportunity partners in Bali, found itself scrambling to keep up with the demands of unemployed Balinese and Javanese migrants. Nyoman Irianto Wibawa, known as Alit, was one of the recruits to whom Priyadi had passed on the lessons he learned from David so many years before. He had chosen Alit from university to run the partner in Sumatra, and later to start another operation in Bali, named Dinari. It would run alongside the existing Balinese partner Duta Bina Bhuana (DBB), making mostly group loans to women in urban areas, while DBB focused on the rural poor. One other Bali partner, WKP, was working in different parts of Denpasar. Competition was never a problem. There was an abundance of poor people who needed small loans.

In the midst of the crisis, Opportunity launched a new partner, Dian Mandiri (Diman), in the Tangerang industrial area of Jakarta, where more than thirty per cent of the two and half million population lived in poverty. As it had been so often in recent times, David's role in Diman was board development, to inspire the leadership in their efforts to help poor Indonesians. Diman became one of the fastest growing and most successful of the recent start-ups. It quickly reached several thousand poor clients, three quarters of them women, through group loans, with loans averaging just US$75. Within eight years Diman aimed to be able to make loans to eleven thousand poor businesspeople each year.

In contrast to Indonesia, the economy of the Philippines stood up reasonably well through the economic crisis, partly due to some hard economic measures introduced by President Fidel Ramos during his term in office. Interest rates had soared and the commercial banks had tightened up on higher-risk loans, but the hilippines' economy was stronger than the economies of its neighbours. For a time, Opportunity partners prudently put expansion on hold.

Leigh heard much of what was happening on the ground, often reporting it back to the support partners, to encourage their continued involvement. He was frequently humbled and burdened by the sacrifices of those working closest to the clients. In August 1997, on his return from a trip to the Philippines, he reported that two new project officers from the partner TSKI in northern Luzon had died only the weekend before in a motorbike accident while returning from the field. At HSPFI, in Mindanao, staff were robbed at gunpoint. They were carrying US$6000, to be dispersed to poor clients that day. Soon after, in two separate incidents, project officers of one TSPI branch in Manila were also held up. In the first robbery, a staff member was shot in the chest, and survived, and in the second the gun was fired but malfunctioned.

Opportunity partners in every country had their own stories to tell of staff being robbed of loan funds or mugged as they went about their jobs in the least hospitable parts of cities.

'As we raise funds, and support and encourage our partners and their work, let's consider with sober humility that most of the work is done by partner agency staff in very sacrificial circumstances,' Leigh wrote. 'Their lives are on the line and they may even have to lay them down in keeping this work and ministry to the poor alive.' At the same time, Opportunity International was putting in place some practical measures—such as a no cash policy—to deal with this reality.

The work in Soweto had grown in an entirely different direction from that of the Zambuko Trust in its northern neighbour, Zimbabwe. Zambuko was riding high on a visit from Hillary Clinton, US First Lady, on her way through the country on 22 March 1997. In Soweto, however, many found it hard to be positive about the future. The South Africans of Soweto were still dealing with the aftermath of decades of oppression. Clients of SEED in

South Africa lacked the sense of excitement about future prospects that was so evident in the clients of newer partners in Ghana and Zambia.

In South Africa the SEED Foundation project had been running long enough for others involved to start to see cracks. It was hard to know what to do. The board and senior management were not going to accept advice from western nations. 'We obviously weren't part of apartheid, but as westerners we were put in the same basket,' said David. Despite all his years of experience, it was impossible to get the board to gel at that particular time.

Emissaries sent from Australia to South Africa to oversee the investment faced a brick wall. The five year program drew to a close after three years, with great sadness and more valuable lessons learned about governance and working in a new context. At around this time, a move into Thailand that had also shown great promise succumbed to corruption within the staff. Malaysia and Sri Lanka also teetered.

These were the clearest signals yet of the need for change. As international co-ordinator, David had to accept some of the responsibility and look closely at his own free-wheeling approach. For the partners to be effective, they needed stronger governance. It was obvious that local education and empowerment on their own would not be enough. The donor environment had changed, with government and the private sector both now baying for higher accountability standards and increased involvement. David had fought hard for local empowerment through the implementing partners, but he was also aware that decentralisation was not working well as Opportunity was adding many more partners to the network. Monitoring systems, training and leadership would all have to be upgraded to keep apace with the programs.

David knew most board members around the world, and was the natural leader of the initiative. Governance had not been a central issue for the non-profit sector to date, but within Opportunity there was recognition that new disciplines and standards needed to be in place if the partners were to achieve their vision. Over the next three years, David and his assistant, Alexis, crisscrossed Asia, Africa, Eastern Europe and South America, talking with boards, strengthening them in preparation for growth, and documenting everything David had learned on the subject of board governance over twenty years.

In 1996, Rocky Burt, born Rochelle Bussau, now living on a farm near the small town of Lake Taupo on New Zealand's North Island, picked up a copy of *Readers' Digest* magazine, and there, in full colour, was a story about David Bussau. For thirty years she had wondered where her much-loved adopted older brother was and what he was doing with his life. She felt proud that he had made something of himself.

Rocky treasured the time they had shared as children. She kept every small gift David had given her—the small pencil advertising his fish and chips business at Caroline Bay, books, small toys—in a special box with all her other valuables.

Some time later, Rocky wrote to David, not knowing whether or not he would reply. She was in good health at the time, after successful surgery three years earlier for breast cancer. But when doctors found a growth in her lymph system late in 1997, and she started chemotherapy again, her husband Ken called David, who with his busy schedule had not yet replied to Rocky's letter, and with some urgency introduced himself. 'David, you don't know me, but I'm married to your little sister Rocky. We've had word she is quite sick with cancer, but she'd love to see you again. Are you coming to New Zealand soon?'

David was surprised by this contact with Rocky. He was not one to reflect on past events. One Christmas a woman called, saying she was his older sister. His reply was curt and final. 'I don't see much point in pursuing that part of my life,' he told her.

With Rocky it was different. He had affectionate memories of her, and he told Ken he would be happy to see her again on his next trip to Auckland, which was in April of 1998, to address a meeting.

Rocky had been through her latest bout of chemotherapy only a couple of days earlier, and was still suffering headaches and tiredness, but she rallied at the thought of seeing David. There were all those conversations she had wanted to have for over thirty years: how sad she was not to be at his wedding; how hard it was when her mother died of diabetes in 1970, when she was just eighteen; how much joy she had found in raising her son Ari and daughter Rebecca; how painful it was to be dying just as her own daughter was reaching eighteen. Her father Lyn, who had remarried after Vera died, had died late in the 1980s of a heart attack. Rocky had enjoyed a good relationship with him after her mother was gone, she told him. She had finished high school and teacher's training college in Hamilton before both she and her father took up teaching positions in the small town of Bennydale.

In the end, there was no time to say all the things she had stored up. They had just half an hour in an Auckland car park, before rushing off to their other commitments. For Rocky it was a poignant meeting. 'David was the most important person in Rocky's life as a child, and she was heartbroken when the family "bust-up" happened and they lost contact,' Ken later said. 'She had been incredibly proud of him. Even as a boy he had always gone out of his way to help people around him, and Rocky wasn't at all surprised he had become such a marvellous adult. It was very significant to her that she saw him again.' Less than two weeks after the meeting with David in Auckland, Rocky died from an undetected brain tumour.

At home, David mentioned the meeting but gave little detail about it. Life moved quickly, and David had never really talked about the family he had lived with after Sedgley, though Carol had known Rocky. His own children were unaware of his earliest past. He had related only the high points of orphanage life to the girls. Tasha and Rachel thought the early morning nude swimming, gymnastics and games all sounded fun.

David's hands were full with his own growing family. Bronte was born to Rachel and Richard in July 1997, and was followed by a son, Ethan, in April 1999. Tasha and Adam had produced Joshua, a little brother for Jessie, in May 1998. Their third child, Lisa, arrived in December 2000.

Every week, the girls descended on their parents' house with their families on Saturday or Sunday—often on both days. In the meantime, David kept tinkering at home during his down time, eventually pulling down the old garage from which he had first started his development work in 1979, and adding a large entertaining area that could accommodate the extended family and their many friends.

It was hard for David to say no to his oldest granddaughter, Jessie. She had completely won his heart over the years. Once, when he was leaving for a long trip, she asked, 'Grandad, why don't you bring the poor people home with you to your house? Then you wouldn't have to be away so often.'

He could only smile at her innocence.

When he was at home, David often played with Jessie and Emma Middleton, when her family visited—wrestling, physical games, like those he had played with his own girls. When Jessie was small they started a tradition of going out for breakfast every Sunday morning before church, if David was in the country. It was their time. 'I knew it was important for me just to listen, not to be a parent figure. I wanted to be an absorption block for her, so she could be transparent and not feel that I was going to be judgmental.' Carol had taken the same stance and was equally close to Jessie. They joked and told travel stories. Jessie had seen more of the world than most pre-teen children.

'But Dad, you're spoiling her rotten,' Tasha complained, to no avail, when he took her shopping and she came back with bags full of clothes. Grandad's own shopping style was pretty much the same, Jessica noticed. When he needed socks or some other item, he invariably stocked up with multiple items, enough to last him months, perhaps years. He and Jessie became allies. Jessie's retort when Tasha was firm with her now was, 'Well, I'll go and live with granddad.'

One morning on one of Ruth Callanta's visits to Australia, she joined David and nine-year-old Jessie for breakfast. David was to return with her to Manila for meetings the next day, and Jessie had decided that there was no way her grandfather was leaving the country without her.

'Grandad, I'm coming with you,' she announced.

'Well, Jessica, it's not going to work out this time. I won't be coming straight home,' David replied.

'But I want to come with you,' she insisted.

'I'm afraid you can't come this time,' he repeated.

'Well, then you'll just have to take me somewhere else another time. How about Disneyland?' Jessie bargained. She was half-joking, not sure if she had overstepped the mark.

'It's a deal. I'll take you when you become a teenager,' he answered, pacifying his granddaughter for now. It still seemed a long way off.

David arrived home in Sydney from that trip laden with the dozens of small gifts Carol had asked him to buy in the Philippines. She would give these to her friends and acquaintances for Christmas in a couple of weeks' time. Just as often, he carried suitcases full of small gifts the other way, for staff and friends. While he shared Carol's generosity and enjoyment of giving, receiving was hard for David. Left to his own devices he would let Christmas slip quietly by. 'I usually wince at Christmas, and I'm glad when it is over'. Christmases in Bali, a non-event where there was none of the commercialism and excessive gift-giving of the west, were the most memorable for David.

If David's ideal Christmas was quiet, Carol's was quite the opposite. This was the time when she identified most with the hurting and lonely around her. The lead-up to 25 December was a frenzy of shopping and cooking and wrapping. In the week before Christmas she fell to bed exhausted each night.

'You should take a break one year, dear, you'll wear yourself out,' Phyl cautioned. She was drawn into the event as much as Carol, and did much of the cooking and cleaning in preparation. At eighty five years old she still had the energy of someone twenty years younger. Each year Carol pulled in those around her, in her work and from the church, who were without family on Christmas Day. By now the numbers had grown to around forty, all people she knew and cared for and could not bear to see home alone on that day.

The Bussau family time was Christmas Eve and Christmas morning, when they went to church together and afterwards spent the morning as a family at home. They struggled to find David presents. If he needed clothes, he bought them overseas, and if they gave him something he did not need he would politely ask to return it in exchange for something else. As noon approached on Christmas Day it was all action, with David slicing meat and arranging fruit decoratively onto platters, a fall-back to his catering days, while Carol made the final arrangements and greeted the guests as they arrived. With the sacrifices Carol had made over the years so he could work around the world, remaining upbeat at Christmas was not too much to ask. Besides, Carol's ability to love others was one of the things he appreciated most about her. She took genuine delight in seeing her friends enjoy Christmas Day. In total contrast, the next day, Boxing Day, alternating each year between the Bussaus and the Cairncrosses, was a genuine holiday—feet up in front of the cricket on television with Garry, cat naps, and the remains of the previous day's feast.

Occasionally the crowds of people in their lives got too much for David and Carol, and they simply needed to be alone and forget their responsibilities. At these times they took to the road together, sometimes for just a few days, driving down the coast, without plans, finding places to stay as they went, taking a few carefree days to recharge before stepping back into the whirl of life.

16

New Season

David celebrated the arrival of the third millennium surrounded by his family and friends on the top floor of the church building in Bondi Junction in Sydney, looking across the rows of red tiled roofs and down to a Sydney Harbour crowded with boats. At the stroke of midnight the dull grey curve of the Harbour Bridge lit up as never before, a river of colour cascading from its underside and a headpiece of brilliant explosions soaring from its upper arch. At the end of the show the bridge was left with just the word 'Eternity' emblazoned across its side.

As usual, David's calendar was fully booked as he rounded the New Year, as it had been for many years now. In January he would be in Indonesia, Singapore, the Philippines and the US twice. The next month he would be back in Indonesia, followed by consulting work and a feasibility study in Papua New Guinea for Opportunity Australia. The four staff members in his Manila office, led by lawyer Roweena Mendoza, negotiated for David to pass through more often so they could keep up with his activities.

Though he had dates and flights booked, this could quickly change, and he never really knew where his travels might take him. In Sydney, his personal assistant, Nancy Szmandiuk, calmly adapted to his unpredictable movements. If a door opened on another continent, he might want to be there. Roweena and Nancy were David's pivot points, the only people other than Carol who knew where in the world he might be on any given day. David's constant travel was a fascination to his friend Bob Buford, who preferred to stay closer to his home state of Texas.

'Where's your luggage?' Bob asked when David arrived in Dallas on one visit, knowing David had been on the road for several weeks and wondering why he never looked tired.

'This is all I need,' David replied, holding up one small carry-on bag.

After Smokey Mountain in Tondo was dismantled in 1995, Payatas, in Quezon City, was the largest rubbish dump in Manila, home to some eighty thousand of the Philippines' poorest. Scavenger families lived in shanties nearby, making a paltry living by picking through the mountain of rotting garbage for plastic bags and other items that could be recycled.

The city of Manila often suffered from the backlash of tropical cyclones, with deluges quickly flooding parts of the city. In June it had been raining for days when a section of the mountain of rubbish came loose and crashed down, engulfing whole families before catching on fire—more than two hundred lives were lost. David was in Manila on 10 June 2000, the day the Payatas dump in collapsed.

Two Philippines partners, CCT and KMBI, had clients buried under the garbage. Some had lost children who had spent their days scampering up and down the sides of the smoking dump looking for treasures. The day after the disaster, Ruth Callanta and David visited the site. The last time they had come together, the year before, they had discussed Ruth's plans for lending programs there, whether it was a good place to work and how best to help the families. After that visit Ruth had started organising women at Payatas into groups, each with a small business. This time, they saw the bodies of children and mothers being pulled from the debris, and heard the cries of distraught parents as they recognised their own.

David had learned to work well with strong and capable professional women. Ruth had grown to trust David, and David knew Ruth's heart was fully engaged with the people she worked with. They shared a deep respect for each other.

'I'm always assured that if there is a way to help, he will give it,' she said. 'David never shows his emotions, he will just walk with you there and he will not make any promises and then the help will come. He is always low key. As much as possible he doesn't want to be recognised and identified.' This time, David connected Ruth with a foundation in the US who contributed to the Payatas work. Once one group supported a program, Ruth knew others would follow.

On 10 November 2000, David turned sixty, an event he celebrated in Sydney with a small group of twenty close friends and family over dinner in a city restaurant.

He certainly did not feel sixty years old, and he had no plans to slow down, though he occasionally talked about it. His eyes were as bright and piercingly blue as they had been as a young man. By now his hair was silver and wavy, but his back was straight and his gait was still relaxed and athletic. He could, and did, run younger men around the squash court, play tennis with Leigh whenever they were in the same city, swim laps at a club nearby, and run around Centennial Park near his home with the vigour of a forty year old. He and Carol had never even talked about retirement.

The debate over David's role within the fast-growing Opportunity International Network had been bubbling along for at least two years. By 2000, Opportunity International was making more than three hundred thousand loans each year in twenty-four countries. Over the years, almost one million new jobs had already come into existence through the programs.

Years before, in a long conversation with Em Griffin after a US board meeting, David had commented, 'There may come a time when God will stop using me in this way, in this work. I just hope I am attuned to that time, and will not try to hang on.' Considering the direction the Opportunity network was heading in, David had a growing sense that the time was fast approaching. As Opportunity went from strength to strength, he had a clear impression that he was being pushed aside. Soon after taking the helm of Opportunity International in 1997, Larry Reed had pegged the future direction of the organisation in an impassioned speech he called 'Change or Die'. He outlined a plan for large-scale lending to the poor through a series of banks in each country. The network planned to consolidate a number of smaller partners into larger, streamlined groupings, so that funding could be directed more effectively. Regional offices would be replaced by global units that would provide technical and financial support to the field workers.

David feared that some of the smaller partners might lose their cultural identity or be squeezed out in the restructure if they were too small to become financially viable. If anything would push David's button to champion a cause it was the idea that someone might be ostracised from what he saw as a family. He became a thorn in the network's side over the issue.

Yet David knew that, in some respects, Larry had no choice but to take Opportunity International in this direction. 'The primary reason for the changes, from my point of view, was stewardship. We could be leveraging much more money (savings and investment funds) and serving many more poor people at a lower cost per client if we made these changes', Larry said. The field of micro enterprise development was now sophisticated and competitive. In twenty five years it had ballooned from a few isolated business-minded people making loans from their own pockets to a global industry, with thousands of practitioners and involving billions of dollars. Opportunity International needed to grow and develop to stay abreast of the industry. In some countries, poor women, once without options when it came to raising capital, could now shop around for the best micro loan deal.

Though the expansion of sources of capital brought opportunites to the poor, it also came with potential problems. Without controls, borrowers could find themselves deep in debt to both a money lender and a non-government organisation, unable to repay either. Further, a question mark hung over the ability of non-government organisations to compete with commercial banks; the banks had noted the success of micro finance, and now pitched a range of products to the lower end of the market in the developing world.

The small loans were delivered in many forms. At one end of the spectrum was the minimalist approach—straight loans for consumer goods, mostly referred to as micro finance. At the other end were organisations like Opportunity, who concentrated on micro enterprise development, with loan staff bringing training, advice and support to clients. This brought untold value to small business people, but added to the cost of providing loans.

The first Microcredit Summit, held in Washington DC in February 1997, brought together practitioners and governments in a concerted attack on poverty. It was the first micro finance industry-wide effort to tackle the issue, and the summit set the lofty goal of reaching one million of the world's poorest families, with a focus on women, by 2005. In 2002, thousands gathered for a second summit. This time, Susy Cheston presented a paper on Opportunity International's experience of transformation within its programs, based on years of data pulled together by the US office.

By now, micro enterprise development programs had existed long enough for some introspection. Susy focused her research on changes in the lives of women borrowers, drawing upon the experiences of partners such as Sinapi Aba Trust in Ghana, and surveys of dozens of other micro finance organisations. Empowerment had always been critical to Opportunity International's view of 'holistic transformation.' Changes in self-confidence, improved family relationships, respect in the community, improved communication skills, and wider community changes were some of the aspects of empowerment—beyond financial improvements—discussed by Susy. She had also heard criticism, over the years: women were being overburdened by the responsibility of their businesses, husbands became jealous and beat their wives, micro finance on its own would not bring the structural change that would truly empower women, there should be more focus on savings, more focus on the ultra poor, more diversity of products. Some of the criticisms she could answer. Others presented the next challenge to the industry and to individual organisations. Already, the HIV epidemic in Africa loomed as the overriding challenge to those working in development on that continent. It was already emerging as a huge issue elsewhere.

Opportunity had started to examine how it might address the issue among clients, starting with education through the trust bank networks.

Twenty five years on from his first stepping-off point at the age of thirty five, when he chose to divest himself of his wealth rather than consolidate his companies into one large corporation, David was at a second major crossroad in his adult life. Opportunity International aimed to have two million clients annually within the decade, and there were disciplines and structures that needed to be put in place—this was something David had recognised years before, in his focus on governance. But he now saw that different skills would be needed. Now technical expertise at management level was prized above entrepreneurial skills.

Again, as it had many times in the past few years, the question arose: where was David's place in this more corporate environment? He had never set out to build a big organisation, though he had driven many of the new projects. Close friends knew that his creative spirit could not operate if it was contained. Personally, he had no heart for a larger organisation. His commitment had always been to people, not causes or programs. His strength was nurturing people who were committed to causes and programs. David readily admitted that he did not fit well into structures and organisations. 'I don't think of the corporate outcomes. I'm focused on where I'm putting my efforts now rather than on what the institution is trying to achieve in five years' time.'

The leadership wanted more accountability: they wanted to know where he was, what he was doing, who he was talking to. And David was being typically defiant in staking out his independence. By now he had small groups of confidants—on several continents—whom he trusted enough to keep his motives in line. He firmly believed in bringing his shortcomings into the open, and actively sought change and personal growth. He would sit within relationships that made him accountable, but he would not let an organisation have control over him, even one that he had helped give birth to.

The more the network management needed him to fit in, to play with the team, the more he bucked against it. He was still an

person in the organisation, respected and honoured in
and he used his influence to fight hard on behalf of the
pa.   in the field.

Leigh could well understand David's position. 'The up side in
his approach is very empowering. The downside is that people
feel he is not a team player. He will create a team, bringing them
on board and owning it, taking them far beyond what they would
have done as individuals. Then they look around and David is off
with five other things. I have never experienced David as not
being part of the team, once he has developed a relationship and
made a commitment.'

There was one significant difference between this stage of
David's life and his mid thirties sea change. This time it was not
about bricks and mortar, cranes and bulldozers. It was not about
dollars. His heart and identity were in Opportunity; it was an
emotional investment. For twenty five years his life had been
intertwined with this work, with the loan officers working in the
worst slums, with the management making their own sacrifices,
with the poor who worked long hours to feed and educate their
children. The people of Opportunity were the extended family he
had lacked as a child, and he had been a core part of bringing
that family together. Then there were the years of sacrifice.
Though he did not mind the travel, he was aware of the cost of
his years on the road to Carol, Tasha and Rachel and their
families.

The issue came to a head at an inopportune time. The organ-
isers of the global conference of August 2000, held at Oxford in
the UK, planned to make a special presentation on the first night
to the founders of Opportunity International. Al Whittaker, who
was now 82 years old and living in Florida, was too frail to make
the journey to England. Instead his son Donald came from
Chicago to receive the honour. Al was later moved to tears to hear
of the conference and joyfully reminisced by phone with Ross
Clemenger, who had started out in Latin America. The two mar-
velled that such small beginnings had now produced this
gathering of people from forty nations. Ross came to Oxford
without a clue that he too was to be honoured as a pioneer, alongside David Bussau and Al Whittaker.

The network board met David the day before the conference to discuss his ongoing place in the organisation so it could be announced at dinner the following night. A few weeks before, David had submitted a list of roles that would interest him, including a pastoral role, where he would continue to encourage and build the staff in the field. But their opinions were varied, and instead of developing a clear role for David, the meeting was inconclusive.

David saw their deliberations as rejection. He had come to see Opportunity as his family, yet it had grown so large that he felt there was no longer a place for him within it. He was upset and knew that something had to give. This conference was a crowning moment for Opportunity International; a time to celebrate the life-changing aspects of the work and to inspire those involved to go further. David was worried that if he stayed to collect his plaque from Princess Anne (Opportunity's UK patron), and addressed the dinner as planned, the emotional turmoil that had been brewing over the past months might bubble over into tears. The last thing he wanted was for friends to rally to his defence and divide the conference.

By dinner the next evening he had left the country. He saw it as his only option. He flew to Washington DC, where he rested and contemplated his next move. From his hotel room he phoned Carol, whose wisdom he trusted. She reassured him but inside, Carol was indignant. She knew that some had seen David's recent actions as a power play, but she understood his motives. She knew he was not a person in search of power for himself.

Some of David's deepest relationships were within Opportunity. When the time came to pull away, it was the most emotional wrench of his life. For those among the hundreds of participants at the Opportunity conference who knew him well, and there were many, there was a yawning hole after David left. Many felt robbed of the chance to thank him for his life's work. They wanted to express their love and respect for him.

As he sat in his Washington hotel room, David felt fragile, and not sure of his next move. Vinay was concerned for him, as was his good friend David Stiller. Would there be an emotional freefall? They kept in close contact.

OK BACK: THE DAVID BUSSAU STORY

d did just what he had done as a young boy. He picked himself up. Perseverance and tenacity had been carved into his character. Back home in Australia, Peter, an entrepreneur friend who had not long before had to let go of his life's work, pulled alongside David. 'We're the pioneers, not the farmers,' he reassured him. In the following months the men often walked for hours around Centennial Park, never dishing out answers to each other's struggles, just sharing their thoughts and feelings. Over the months, David was able to move towards accepting that this part of his life had been a season, a finite time, and that now Opportunity International was moving on to bigger things without him in a leadership role. He had in fact set it up to do just that when he turned down positions along the way, but had not realised how hard the separation would be.

It was a typical founder's dilemma—he had to relinquish emotional ownership. When the dust cleared he realised that the most valuable assets in everything he had ever worked on, the relationships, were still intact. He later sought to patch up any that were damaged. Forgiveness and reconciliation were tenets of his beliefs. Both Opportunity International and David would move on to other things.

David's commitment to Opportunity International Australia, which had started out as Maranatha, had not changed. He still sat on the board and was both friend and mentor to many around him. His influence could be felt even in his absence. When he returned to the office from his overseas trips, he warmly greeted and hugged each member of staff, though there were now many of them. He made time to take newcomers out for a coffee to get to know them, still sent cards and gifts for weddings and birthdays. He infused encouragement into the place as no one else could.

And now he was free to explore worlds other than Opportunity International.

Throughout his working life, David had rarely had just one business or program on the go. Back in 1998, just as he handed the day-to-day management of Opportunity International Australia over to Denis Perry, David was already working on his next project, Christian Micro Enterprise Development (CMED). He was organising a conference that would bring together specifically Christian organisations who either had plans to use micro enterprise development as a tool for helping the poor they worked with in developing countries, or were already making small loans and needed to learn how to go about it in a more professional and efficient way. There were more than twelve hundred such organisations.

Many of those working closely with struggling communities had considered micro enterprise development, a technical field, beyond their reach.

His hunch about the need was right. Some of those attempting to work in micro finance were doing it badly, and most could ill afford the training and support they needed. In 1999, David and his team pulled together three hundred participants from one hundred organisations in thirty five countries for the first CMED conference, held at the vast Ambassador Jomtien Hotel at Pattaya in Thailand. He then set up the Christian Transformation Resource Centre in Manila to act as a support to all of these organisations. He was again doing what he was best at: bringing people together and providing the resources for them to move ahead. The biggest challenge here was that the groups had such varied levels of experience. Some of the practitioners had been working with the poor for many years, others were new, and needed different resources. He would put tools in their hands and move on. The fire starter was at work again.

By now David's name was increasingly coming up in the public arena in Australia—as a conference speaker, in the media on development issues, as a social entrepreneur, and as an example of midlife career changes. It had started with an article in *Readers' Digest*, the one Rocky had seen, and continued with an appearance on a current affairs show and through magazine interviews. In 2001 he appeared on the ABC's 'Australian Story', and his story struck a chord in a society looking for role models.

One accolade, his inclusion in an article entitled 'Australia's Ten Most Creative Minds' in *The Bulletin* magazine of January 1998 carried with it a certain irony. The owner of Australian Consolidated Press, the magazine's publisher, was none other than Kerry Packer, the billionaire whose demands to fix a gun cabinet back in 1974 had intruded into David's family life, and been a catalyst in his decision to leave the business world.

His close friends wondered how he would handle the attention. He too was concerned. 'It worries me that this is just entertainment,' he once confided after speaking. 'I don't want to build my own empire.' As far as David was concerned, he could take little credit for the course of his life. 'I would say that all the significant relationships in my life are serendipitous. I have never sought to be connected, to exploit resources or people. I don't search out opportunities. God's calling has even been unexpected and surprising. I have responded, whatever it is, and taken it from there.'

A more public life brought new challenges. People loved the rags to riches story, the tale of the abandoned boy made good. When he spoke, they wanted to hear about his past. But it came at a cost. 'The more you expose the real person, the more you spill your guts, the more there is an emotional drain on you.'

People now asked him to mentor them in their business and personal lives, adding to the many other demands on his time. He had built hundreds of close relationships around the world, and just keeping up with people was now almost impossible. It was simply not possible to mark each birthday, wedding and crisis.

'Every time you enter into a mentoring relationship it costs you emotionally. There is a toll on the individual. I think maybe it is also a cost because none of us really has it together. People want me to sow into their lives what they perceive is a richness of experience or knowledge or wisdom, but there is an increasing awareness that I haven't got it all together. People are always looking for a role model.' But David's influence had worked well for Leigh Coleman, his first protégé. David and Leigh's friendship had remained strong through the years, even after Opportunity grew so quickly that they were often travelling in opposite directions. In the early days, every trip together was an adventure, and conversations revolved around the challenges of their work. Now they could just be friends.

At the age of fifty, Leigh was tired of travelling, and looked forward to the next season in his life, at home with his family. Twenty-five years' experience of enterprise development was not wasted on him. He was soon applying everything he knew on a domestic basis, helping indigenous Australians into small businesses through his local church, and surprised at his journey through life so far. 'David saw potential in me I couldn't see myself. My life was a mess, but David never saw my problems. Somehow, I got encouraged by what David was doing. He showed me a pathway to go out and get focused on other people, and in that process I could deal with my own issues.'

The Al-Qaeda terrorist attack of 11 September 2001 changed the way world citizens like David travelled their globe.

David had always had a healthy disregard for his own safety. He had travelled through wars, riots and natural disasters without concern. His family knew not to bother raising the issue of personal safety with him. Even Jessica, now twelve and a half, was old enough to know that David visited some potentially dangerous places when he left home every few weeks. He was due to leave again for the US at the end of September. It was too much for her to contemplate.

'Granddad, you can't go,' she pleaded on the phone in the following days, when news reports were filled with coverage of the attacks.

'Don't worry, Jessica, I'll be fine,' he replied casually.

She went to school in tears. Her friends rallied around her, and when she told them of her fears, they agreed: 'No, he can't go.'

Jessica found support among the younger grandchildren in her campaign to keep her grandfather at home. Then her mother weighed in—she too was concerned. There was nothing for it. David cancelled his plans and stayed home. The man who had spent so much of his life boarding planes to trouble spots as others caught buses, was stopped in his tracks, stymied by a small pleading posse of grandchildren and his daughters.

Opportunity in Australia under Denis Perry had picked up early on an important corporate trend in the mid 1990s. The big global mining and manufacturing companies had discovered that political and economic stability were essential to their operations. Companies knew that if they could improve living standards before they even started work, there would be less chance of sabotage. At the same time, governments of developing countries were making new demands—for community development—on foreign companies. Building stronger communities through job creation was one of Opportunity's strengths.

David found himself back on the ground in the consulting world, making contacts with remote communities. The island of Mindanao, at the southern tip of the Philippines archipelago, was known as a trouble spot, a breeding and training ground for rebels fighting for a separate Muslim state. An Australian mining company asked David to look at the feasibility of community development near the large city of General Santos, where they planned to mine gold.

David's job was to give an independent and objective view of community need in the area, and to explore whether micro loans could work in raising the standard of living. His contact point became the group of rebel leaders who controlled the area. They were sceptical when he explained to them how Opportunity made loans for small businesses, and mistrustful of his motives. 'You're from the government,' they accused. It took half a dozen visits before they trusted him enough to hear more about the programs in other parts of the country. When he finally established his credibility they conceded, 'If we had jobs and a decent standard of living we would put down our rifles.' While that particular project did not proceed, it gave David an insight into another aspect of poverty.

The second CMED conference, at Pattaya in Thailand on 5 June 2001, brought together five hundred micro finance practitioners from more than forty countries around the world. This would be the last of its type. After this, the groups would meet on a regional basis, where cultures and contexts were similar. David would make himself available to travel to these meetings, and for any training sessions in between. It surprised him how much newcomers valued his accumulated experience.

Priyadi Reksasiswaya from Bali also had an extraordinary depth of knowledge in the field of micro enterprise development, and was a great asset at the CMED conferences. From the earliest days, when he and David had worked on both lending and water projects across Bali, his impact had been huge. His drive to help the poor out of poverty was infectious and the demands on his staff were high. The results spoke for themselves. Under David and Priyadi, DBB had spawned sixteen new lending partners across Indonesia.

Tanaoba Lais Manekat (TLM), the partner founded in 1994 in Indonesia's poorest province, West Timor, had gone remarkably well. Eighteen thousand poor entrepreneurs had already received loans and TLM was bringing other community benefits, like discounted food supplies. Each client received a wooden safety box for their savings, a valuable item for someone accustomed to living from hand to mouth.

Across the border, the small East Timorese partner had been disbanded in the carnage following the vote for independence in 1999. Retreating Indonesian soldiers adopted a scorched earth policy as they left, destroying everything of value to the East Timorese, down to cooking implements, crops, and supplies of rice. Militiamen slaughtered thousands, and refugees flooded across the border to West Timor. The staff of TLM, who worked hard on their own programs in the area, found themselves among the few able to provide emergency aid to refugees in the first weeks. (The East Timorese partner was re-established a year later.)

After the Thailand conference finished on 9 June, Priyadi flew back to Bali. He was due to fly to West Timor two days later to meet with David Middleton and Simon Lynch, the Asian regional director. The day after arriving back from Thailand he set out to make visits to his older sister, younger brother and other relatives around the island of Bali. His life had become so busy there was little time to visit these days.

The next afternoon, a Monday, Priyadi dropped into the office of Dinari, the partner in Denpasar he had helped Alit start ten years before.

'I'm feeling so tired now,' he told Alit, who could see he was lacking the usual enthusiasm for his work. Yet Priyadi still found time and energy to make some suggestions to the cashier at Dinari, the person taking care of the loans and repayments. He then talked through Alit's work issues and encouraged him into his next step.

On Tuesday Priyadi collapsed in the bathroom at work but was not discovered for two hours. An ambulance rushed him to the intensive care unit of the Sangla Hospital in Denpasar; it was the best Bali had to offer in medical care but was lacking in the basic equipment wealthier nations take for granted. Here he was diagnosed as having had a light stroke, but the doctors failed to check his heart, for which he had been taking medication for some time.

Before losing consciousness in hospital, Priyadi had managed to write a note asking his colleague Nyoman Yulia to call David Middleton in Kupang, West Timor to say he would not be able to meet him there the next day.

'He has been stabilised and recovered some of his mobility,' she told David Middleton. 'There's no need to rush back, just come to see him on Thursday when you arrive back.'

David and Simon went straight to the hospital on their return, only to discover Priyadi had died ten minutes earlier.

It took hours for David Middleton to get hold of David Bussau in Thailand. This year he had brought all eleven members of his family to the conference. They were in the coastal region of Krabi, an hour and a half flight north of Bangkok—here Richard and Adam could rock climb on the limestone cliffs while the rest of the family lounged and swam at the unspoiled beaches. David already knew about the stroke, and like others, assumed Priyadi would come through.

'David, Priyadi's gone,' David Middleton told David in a deflated voice. There was no reaction on the end of the phone. Just a long, long silence.

David wondered if they had lost their phone connection. 'Hello?'

'We'll be there as soon as we can,' David finally responded, with barely a hint of emotion.

David and Carol felt the loss even before they stepped out of the Ngurah Rai airport in Bali the next day. For the first time in ten years Priyadi's small rounded figure was not waiting for David. It was hard for him to imagine Bali without Priyadi. For others in the Opportunity network who had learned from and worked with Priyadi, it was at once losing a cherished relative and a learned friend. And he had been only a young man. He had been one of David's first students of community development and had passed on his knowledge to many others.

Priyadi had taken care to let his wife Nani build her own friendship with David over the years. She had often come to David for advice, as he was the person who understood best the pressure Priyadi's job put on the whole family. Their girls knew David as a godfather figure who showered them with gifts and attention. Now they turned to David and Carol for support, though the Bussaus were feeling their own deep sense of loss. David was not sure of his role now, but from the time Priyadi married and had two girls, there had been an implicit understanding that he would care for them if anything happened to Priyadi.

Priyadi's farewell later in the week brought together Christian and traditional Balinese practices. In all, there were four services held in the family's home in Denpasar before the large group moved on to the crematorium near Nusa Dua, on the southern part of the island. Priyadi's daughters Mita and Yuki, sixteen and twelve years old, wailed in despair, unable to make sense of their loss. They turned to David for reassurance and he hugged them tightly.

David had kept his promise to Priyadi's father, Pak Sus, all those years ago that he would look out for his son. Now he would do the same for Priyadi's family.

At Nusa Dua there was another service with friends and family members all milling around as the cremation took place. Then the ashes were laid out on the ground and close friends each picked out a bone to place in a basket. Nani and the girls wrapped up the baskets and tied them with ribbons before moving on to Priyadi's final resting place, the ocean beyond Kuta Beach, at Dhyana Pura in Seminyak.

Here David delivered his last words about his friend Priyadi. Though he could have spoken in Indonesian, David spoke in English with Ketut Waspada translating, telling the crowd of mourners, 'Priyadi is not lost to us. His ideas and his spirit live on in the lives of the poor Indonesians he served and in those of you who have been motivated by him. His legacy will be passed on for many generations.'

David talked of Priyadi as an extraordinary entrepreneur, the architect of the national network, a man of untiring energy, someone with a strong faith and an unusual ability to reach into a community. He told them how Priyadi had earned the respect of international organisations in the US, Europe and Asia. His legacy could be found across the Indonesian archipelago, in the many thousands of poor families who lived better lives now that they had jobs to sustain them and room to think about the future—in the tofu makers, the stall holders, the farmers and mechanics who had all received small loans.

The Balinese process of saying goodbye has a beginning and an end. The checkerboard of good and bad that pervades Balinese life was played out on the beach at Seminyak. A peace fell on the crowd as Priyadi's ashes were paddled out to sea on a surfboard many hours after the first distressed gathering. A trail of petals floated behind the board, and the sight of the young girls playing in the surf and chasing each other up and down Kuta Beach eased the grief after the long farewell.

Epilogue

While still in Thailand, on Monday, 11 June 2001, David heard news from Australia that he had been included in the annual Queens Birthday Honours list, receiving the award of Member, general division, Order of Australia for service to international development. He could now carry the letters AM after his name.

An event of far greater importance to David was the 20th anniversary celebration of the TSPI Development Corporation, the first Philippines partner, in December that year. The event was marked with a service of thanksgiving and a banquet in its large head office in the Makati district of Manila. By now almost half of Opportunity outreach worldwide was in the Philippines. TSPI had been a model for others in the network and had thrived through some difficult times. Over the years there had been an impressive parade of presidents of banks and corporations, provincial governors and central bankers on its board. Its members had included the late Emmanuel Pelaez, a former vice-president of the Philippines and Philippines Ambassador to the United States. Dennis Isidro, the former Citibank vice-president who was in the first group to start TSPI's lending program, was at the 20th Anniversary celebration, though thin and weary with cancer. He passed away just weeks later, with the knowledge that he had given his best years to helping poor Filipinos.

David stood quietly among the crowd in the background as TSPI's current executive director, Ruben DeLara, proudly spelled out the achievements of two decades. From the first fifty loans given out by Leigh Coleman, there were now twenty six branches and thirty eight thousand small business clients in TSPI's portfolio. In another two years it would be seventy five thousand. Five hundred people were employed within TSPI as loan officers, technical and support staff. The people who could not have approached a bank for fear of being thrown out could now access their loans through automatic teller machines and easily make savings the same way. Poor women now had micro insurance policies to support their dependants if they died. The sights were set high: half a million clients by 2007.

In June 2002 the group of earliest IIDI people met in Washington for the first time in decades. It coincided with Vinay's 60th birthday party, an event the Bussaus could not miss. For the IIDI group, it was a time of reflection and reminiscence. There was no back-slapping over achievement, just a humble acknowledgment of the privilege of being a small part of something great. When Ross Clemenger expressed his disappointment at not having had David on stage with him at the Oxford Conference, David's comment was, 'We've had enough of man's applause, we don't need any more.'

Soon after, David and Carol returned to Bali for yet another reunion. Many of their friends from the 1970s in Blimbingsari and Dhyana Pura had fared well through the years. Ibu Wasiati, who had cared for them so lovingly in their first days in Blimbingsari, came up to them quietly. After working at Dhyana Pura as a kitchen supervisor she got a job in a big beachfront hotel at Sanur. This had allowed her to support her two children and send them to school and university. Made Wenton, the young labourer David had taken under his wing, still worked as an electrician at Dhyana Pura when the Bussaus visited that year, and his wife had a catering business. Later that year David and Carol were shocked to hear that he had died in an accident.

David and Wayan had chosen well in backing the entrepreneurs around them twenty five years earlier. Many years after buying a truck with his first AUD$2000 loan, David's foreman in

Blimbingsari, Pak Yusef, sent three hundred thousand coconuts each month to Surabaya in Java for cooking oil.

John Panca, the plucky young man who had dreamed of becoming a tourist operator, had first set himself up as a travel agent, and now owned eighteen big tourist buses, eight mini-vans and dozens of private limousines that plied the tourist trade on the busy island. Ketut Suwirya, the young economics student David and Carol knew from Blimingsari, had built and lost several businesses, including a hostel and motorcycle rental business over the years. Now he imported truckloads of raw furniture from Java, which he sanded, stained and polished before exporting around the world. He employed twenty young people in his factory and ran showrooms in Seminyak and Kuta. With long greying hair tied back in a ponytail, he looked the part of successful entrepreneur. He still owned the old Chinese-made sewing machine he bought with his first loan, but had given away numerous other sewing machines to his employees so that they could start their own businesses.

There was no hint at this happy time that only weeks later, on the night of 12 October 2002, bombs in two of Kuta Beach's most popular night time tourist spots, the Sari Club and Paddy's Bar, would rip apart the idyll of Bali. As the Indonesian terrorist group, Jemaah Islamiah, claimed responsibility for the bombings, twenty nations mourned their dead, none more than Australia, which lost eighty eight people. Two hundred and two died in total, with many more injured. Many were Indonesian.

Late in October, David walked through the site, just metres from Wayan Mastra's small hotel, where he and Carol had stayed back in 1976. He sat with construction workers hired to clear the debris and asked them in Balinese how it felt. Then he wandered along the rows of empty stalls, talking to stallholders about the bombing's impact, aware again of their fatalism. 'Perhaps we didn't make the right sacrifices,' one told him, as if it was her fault.

Opportunity clients were among those who fled the bombing that night. Christine, a mother of two, just happened to be close by, collecting plastic and glass bottles, used papers and other recyclables discarded by tourists. David came back as an act of solidarity with the Balinese and to lend support to the local

Opportunity partners, Dinari, DBB and WKP, who between them had made loans to some seven thousand micro entrepreneurs across the island. At least half of the clients, mostly women, depended on the flow of tourists to survive. The fear and uncertainty surrounding the future prospects of the women was palpable.

It took just days for the economic impact to strike. It was a cruel setback to Balinese and Javanese migrants at every strata, and a reminder of how fine is the line between survival and dire poverty. On this visit David met a Javanese widow named Nala who could no longer find rubbish to recycle now that the tourists had left the island. She had resorted to prostitution to survive. 'All I have is my body to sell,' she told David. He knew the local loan officers were already working out how they might retrain women like Nala into other businesses, where they had a better chance of survival without tourism.

For the second time that year he met with old friends. Ketut Suwirya would fare better than most. Many of his customers were in Europe and Australia, and they would still make orders for his furniture by phone and fax. But Wayan Mastra's hotel in Kuta was soon deserted, along with every other hotel on the island. David made his way out to see John Panca at his transport depot and was saddened to meet him looking despondent as his rows of buses, mini-vans and limousines sat idle.

'What am I going to do about this?' he asked, sweeping his arm in an arc towards his vehicles. 'I have eighty people relying on me for jobs.'

'Hold on to your staff, John. Look after them. People are your best asset,' David knew John would bounce back. Entrepreneurs were people with hope and optimism.

Later that same year, 2002, David visited another, very different site of death and destruction in Indonesia, this time in Manado, on the northern tip of the island of Sulawesi. During 1999, a well-trained and deadly band of Islamic extremists called the Laskar Jihad had descended upon Sulawesi and the nearby Maluku islands with the sole intention of wiping out Christian communities in the region. In two and a half years the Laskar Jihad had killed ten thousand Christians. Where Christians and

Muslims lived together harmoniously, the Laskar Jihad punished both, or incited hatred and fighting between the two groups by destroying mosques and churches. Over one million people were displaced. The result was an exodus of refugees, some eighty thousand people, to the northern extremity of the island. They arrived with few possessions, many bearing horrific injuries inflicted by the machetes of the Laskar Jihad fighters. It was not long before infection, tuberculosis, malaria and gastroenteritis, all treatable, took their toll. Over the next few months churches from around the world gave medical aid, and those who could filtered back to their homes in villages around Sulawesi and nearby islands, not sure what they were returning to. Some ten thousand could not face going home.

In Sydney, David had received a call from a pastor who had visited the refugees and seen how hopeless their lives had become. 'Do you think micro loans could work in that environment?' he asked David.

'I'm not sure, but let's take a look.' He had no idea where it would lead, but he was prepared to find a way.

The promise of a trip to Disneyland had been a standing joke between Jessica and her grandfather since she was nine. She had watched him come and go to the US four times a year since they had made the pact. She would be fourteen in January 2003. Time was running out.

In August 2002, David said to Jessica, 'I've booked the tickets, we're going.'

In December, Jessica set off from Sydney with her aunt Rachel to meet her grandfather in Los Angeles. He planned to give Jessica and Rachel the best time possible, handing them a wad of greenbacks for shopping and letting them loose in a discount store with instructions to buy whatever they wanted. There was not much they needed, but they enjoyed filling the trolley just to give him the pleasure of spoiling them. Then they spent a full four days on rides at Disneyland, with David enjoying the experience as much as his daughter and granddaughter.

In 2003, David did slow down fractionally, as he had talked about doing for years. Instead of eight weeks on the road at a time, it was two or three. Shorter trips made it easier to stay connected at home, and the workload when he returned was noticeably lighter.

He had reached a point of contentment, an acceptance that he had moved into a new season of his life. 'I've got the confidence and assurance that there is a destiny, but I don't know what it is right now. So I continue to blunder through, realising that when I mess up I am not condemned.' He was again a person in transition. 'We all build on the past, we're learning from the past about ourselves, who we are and how we interact with the rest of humanity. I would like to be seen as a person who has more understanding, more tolerance, more appreciation of the validity of other people's perspectives.'

At the end of March, the week after the US government under President George W. Bush and its allies launched its controversial attack on Saddam Hussein in Iraq, David was on a plane to Pyongyang in North Korea with a New Zealand businessman and friend, Hugh Gollan. In the weeks before the Iraq offensive, there had been vigorous sabre-rattling between the US and North Korea over the Asian nation's nuclear capability. There was talk of war on both sides.

David had a way of cutting across politics. 'The poor are not interested in the philosophical debates as to whether capitalism is good or bad or if socialism is a better system. All they really want is a better quality of life. If your kids are starving, you don't really care too much about the politics.'

The potential for war was not the biggest concern for David and Hugh. They were passing through Beijing en route to Pyongyang, and the most immediate threat to their lives was from the mysterious virus called SARS that had claimed eighty lives and infected hundreds more. Already it was crippling the airline and tourism industries in Asia—it would later affect Canada badly as well, with the spill-on reaching much further. Carol had hoped that they might suspend their plans, but David was not easily swayed. She bought boxes of face masks that he dutifully packed.

The trip was purely exploratory. There was no guarantee that a rigid communist regime would allow something as reliant on a market economy as micro enterprise development, even if it could alleviate poverty. Yet there was certainly a need. The government of North Korea (known as the Democratic People's Republic of Korea or DPKR) had tried hard to disguise the extent of hunger in the famine-ridden nation, but the world had seen glimpses of shocking human suffering, of bodies like sticks. David and Hugh would not be allowed to see this side of North Korea. They were treated as royalty, taken to an impressive circus show, chauffeured along a completely empty twelve-lane freeway to visit a monumental dam, monitored every second they spent in the country.

They had secured a meeting with a senior official from the Ministry of Finance in Pyongyang, who told them the government had established a free trade zone, not far from the demilitarised zone along the border with South Korea, following the Chinese model of a decade before. In the short time they had available to talk, the official appeared to be open to the case for enterprise development, though it would have to be development within co-operatives rather than private enterprise.

A later meeting opened another line of possibility. This time it was with the mayor of Kaesong, which was within the one thousand hectare free trade zone; one goal was that South Koreans would invest in light industry in Kaesong, while employing North Koreans. The mayor was enthusiastic about the type of enterprise development David was talking about.

'We think a business incubator might work well here,' David suggested. He went on to explain the idea. 'Say there is an order for ten thousand bicycles. We would make small loans to a number of people, and each one would make a different component of the product. We would set up a pedal maker, a handlebar maker, an assembler and so on, all in the one building. Then we'd help them diversify into something else and expand their business, help them look for markets, new products,' he said. The mayor was keen on the idea. He had an entrepreneurial bent and seemed open to bringing in something closer to free market principles.

The best test of the viability of small loans was always on the streets and in the markets and alleyways. In 2003 it seemed that the North Korean government had ever so slightly loosened its grip. Farmers in some areas were now permitted to sell their produce through a farmers' market, though David and Hugh were forbidden from visiting the market on this visit. Nor were they allowed to photograph a man fixing bikes on a street corner, as it was in theory illegal—and, philosophically, private enterprise did not exist in North Korea.

Instead they quietly conducted their market research on the streets of Pyongyang, on the lookout for signs of entrepreneurial activity as they walked around under the watchful eye of their minder. Outside the trade centre, a woman sold ice cream from a small stall. David and Hugh stopped to buy ice creams for themselves and the entourage, and grabbed the chance to ask questions. A local institution had provided her with a German-made ice cream machine and powdered mix.

'If you had the money to buy another ice cream machine, how long would it take to pay back the loan?' David asked the woman through an interpreter.

'Just three months,' she replied. If the government allowed this woman to operate, surely others could too. The next step would be a feasibility study. It was the sort of project that excited David, one that broke new ground and kick-started a process that could lead anywhere.

After all these years, David was still just responding to a call. He told Rob Harley, a New Zealand reporter who had previously travelled with him, 'The single most important factor which gives me the energy to continue doing this type of work is the recognition that I've been blessed, and that I have a responsibility to give that blessing back to others. I realise I have skills to be an entrepreneur and that those skills need to be directed to benefit others rather than continuing to just benefit myself and my family. I happen to believe that everybody is gifted, and that everybody really has the potential to make a difference in the lives of others.'

Postscript

At the time of publication, David is steaming ahead with his plans to set up micro enterprise development programs in both North Korea and Manado in Indonesia. He still roams the globe, lending his experience and knowledge to both Opportunity International and other micro enterprise programs. He plays an active board and spokesperson role within Opportunity International Australia.

In 2003, the Opportunity International Network—with David Stiller as chairman and Larry Reed as chief executive officer—loaned US$106 million, and made nearly seven hundred and fourteen thousand loans, with an average loan size of US$224. The on-time repayment rate was 97.4 per cent. More than eighty seven per cent of the loans went to poor women. The organisation now employs four thousand people. Its ability to reach out is expanding rapidly. In its first thirty years, Opportunity International made one million loans. In the past three years, it made 1.7 million. It will have made a total of three million loans by the end of 2004.

David has resumed an unofficial role as father figure and friend within the evolving network. In February 2004, he was welcomed wholeheartedly and publicly honoured at the Opportunity International global conference in Manila. Holistic transformation continues to be at the core of the work. The early participants in the first Philippines programs tell the story: at the conference dinner, Mrs Marciano, the first client, and Noel Alcaide, the first employee, sat side by side. Noel is now chief executive of the Opportunity Microfinance Bank, the first of its type in the country. Mrs Marciano is a successful caterer who donated the cash prize to the winner of the Opportunity 2003 Entrepreneur of the Year.

Carol has never stopped responding—in her own quiet way—to the needs around her. She still delivers soup and love to sick friends, finds them new homes, and feeds their pets when they go to hospital.

David Bussau, the abandoned boy left in the driveway of a Boys' Home all those years ago, was last seen boarding a plane for Monaco to represent Australia at the Ernst and Young 'World Entrepreneur of the Year' Awards.

Index

Perry, Denis
  at Thai conference 225
  heads Opportunity
    International in Australia
    245–6, 273
  trip to Sulawesi 249
philanthropists, fundraising from
  243–4
Philippines
  economic crisis 254–5
  first trip through 55–6
  local organisations in 171–2
  Maranatha Trust loans in
    131–43
  Opportunity International in
    279
  poverty in 149–50, 263–4
  revolution in 168–70
picking potatoes 15–16
pikelet machine 44–5
PIM 89, 143–4
playground in Blimbingsari 89
POSMM 245
poultry farming
  in Bali 123–4
  in Bangalore 153
  in Philippines 137–8
  Kwabena Darko gets start from
    246–7
poverty
  among women 219–20
  brick makers in Pakistan 159
  classes of 252–3
  in Bali 99–100
  in the Philippines 149–50
Prime Minister of Tonga 146–7
Priyadi, see Reksasiswaya,
  Priyadi
Pro Victimus 212
proposal to Carol 41
Puddle, Corinne 6
Punjab region, see brick makers in
  Pakistan
Pyongyang, trip to 284–6

rag pickers, aid for 153–5
Rangtay Sa Pagrang-ay Inc. 171
rape of domestic workers in
  Pakistan 190–1
Reed, Larry
  African work 197–8, 200,
    203–4
  gifts for children of 205–6
  heads OI Network 246, 264–5,
    287
  moves to Washington with IIDI
    161
  on Network Design Council
    242
Reidhead, Paris 119, 246
Reksasiswaya, Priyadi
  expands loans into Indonesia
    173–4
  illness and death 274–7
  manages MBM 121–3
  on Network Design Council
    242
  Songan work 250–1
  Sulawesi trip 249–50
  supports aid for women 225
retreats for TSPI staff 140–1
Riggs, Sherryl 37
  'adopts' Phyllis Crowder 59
  CB's bridesmaid 45–6
  encourages move to Sydney 50
Ripley, Dennis 245
Rivera, Rosa Maria 221–3
Rob (Wocky) 1, 4–5
  at Wairapa College 16, 18
  girlfriend of 26
  in Sydney 51–2
  top in maths 9
  work at Donald's 22–3
robberies, see thefts
Roby, Paul 153, 156
Rose Bay, flats in 50–1, 56
Rossum, Constance 240
RSPI 171
Runcie, Lord 163

tooth filing ceremony 124–5
tourism training school, *see*
    Dhyana Pura
TPKI 172, 213
trains, Carol's fear of 47–8
transcendental meditation 68
Tri Jata, Gusti 107
trust banks, *see* lending programs
TSKI, *see* Taytay Sa Kauswagan
    Inc.
TSPI, *see* Tulag Sa Pag-Unlad Inc.
Tulag Sa Pag-Unlad Inc. 170, 175
    Benjie Montemayor heads 185
    foundation of 133–43
    twentieth anniversary 279–80

ultralight flying 176–7
Uniting Church in Darwin 72
US, most aid coming from 243
USAID 119, 132–3, 135–6

Valenzuela 171
Vander Weele, Linda 219, 232
Village Banking 221
Vosmozhnost 233

Wairarpa College 16–17
Wasiati, Ketut 84–5, 105, 280
Waspada, Ketut 105–6, 277
water supplies in Bali 110–14
Waverley Methodist Mission 53
wedding to Carol 45–9
Wenton, Made 93, 105, 280
West Timor, aid to 275
Whittaker, Al
    approaches DB about running
        IIDI 174–5

connects with Paris Reidhead
    246
founds Opportunity
    International 129–30
meets Samuel Vinay 151
moves to IIDI 119–20
plans aid to Africa 197
Whittaker, Donald 268
Wibawa, Nyoman Irianto 254
Williams, Bruce (brother) 1–3,
    7–8
Williams, David Thomas, *see*
    Bussau, David
Williams, Lewis Edward (father) 3
Williams, Marjorie (mother) 3, 7
Wilson, Alex 45–6, 146–7
Wilson, Brooks 230
Winters, Terry 230
WKP 254
Wocky, *see* Rob (Wocky)
women
    aid for 225
    poverty among 219–20
Women's Opportunity Fund
    219–20, 222

Yulia, Ibu Nyoman 121
Yunus, Muhammad 116
Yusef, Pak Nyoman 86, 92, 94,
    281
    financial circumstances 98–9
    loan to 101–2

Zambuko Trust 199–203,
    255–7
Zimbabwe, lending programs in
    198–203